THE
WORKPLACE
SURVIVAL
GUIDE

TOOLS, TIPS AND TECHNIQUES
FOR SUCCEEDING
ON THE JOB

GEORGE FULLER

PRENTICE HALL
Englewood Cliffs, New Jersey 07632

Library of Congress Cataloging-in-Publication Data

Fuller, George T.
    The workplace survival guide : tools, tips and techniques for
succeeding on the job / George Fuller.
      p. cm.
    Includes index.
    ISBN 0-13-341660-7—ISBN 0-13-341652-6 (pbk)
    1. Vocational guidance. 2. Job hunting. 3. Managing your boss.
4. Career development. 5. Finance, Personal. I. Title.
HF5381.F795 1996   95-44179
650.1—dc20   CIP

Printed in the United States of America

10 9 8 7 6 5 4 3 2

ISBN 0-13-341660-7 ISBN 0-13-341652-6(PBK)

ATTENTION: CORPORATIONS AND SCHOOLS

Prentice Hall books are available at quantity discounts with bulk purchase for educational,
business, or sales promotional use. For information, please write to: Prentice Hall Career &
Personal Development Special Sales, 113 Sylvan Avenue, Englewood Cliffs, NJ 07632. Please
supply: title of book, ISBN number, quantity, how the book will be used, date needed.

PRENTICE HALL
Career & Personal Development
Englewood Cliffs, NJ 07632
A Simon & Schuster Company

On the World Wide Web at http://www.phdirect.com

Prentice-Hall International (UK) Limited, *London*
Prentice-Hall of Australia Pty. Limited, *Sydney*
Prentice-Hall Canada Inc., *Toronto*
Prentice-Hall Hispanoamericana, S.A., *Mexico*
Prentice-Hall of India Private Limited, *New Delhi*
Prentice-Hall of Japan, Inc., *Tokyo*
Simon & Schuster Asia Pte. Ltd., *Singapore*
Editora Prentice-Hall do Brasil, Ltda., *Rio de Janeiro*

Also by the Author

Supervisor's Portable Answer Book, 1990, Prentice Hall
The Negotiator's Handbook, 1991, Prentice Hall
The Supervisor's Big Book of Lists, 1994, Prentice Hall
The First-Time Supervisor's Survival Guide, 1995, Prentice Hall
Manager's Negotiating Answer Book, 1995, Prentice Hall

Contents

Part

I

WINNING AT WORK IN GOOD TIMES AND BAD—1

Chapter 1
COPING WITH ON-THE-JOB CAREER HAZARDS—5

Chapter 2
SURVIVAL SKILLS FOR JOB SECURITY—43

Chapter 3
HOW TO GET AHEAD—EVEN IN A DEAD-END JOB—75

Chapter 4
HOW TO SUCCEED WITH ANY KIND OF BOSS—107

Part
2

CHANGING JOBS OR SWITCHING CAREERS—137

Chapter 5
PLANNING FOR AND GETTING THE JOB YOU WANT—141

Chapter 6
CHANGING CAREERS THROUGH CHOICE OR NECESSITY—179

Part 3

THE PROS AND CONS OF RELOCATING—203

Chapter 7
EVALUATING POTENTIAL JOB LOCATIONS—207

Chapter 8
WEIGHING THE ADVANTAGES AND RISKS OF MOVING—231

Part
4

FINANCIAL MEASURES FOR AN UNCERTAIN FUTURE—259

Chapter 9
GETTING MORE BANG FOR YOUR BUCKS—263

Chapter 10
HOW TO HARNESS HAPHAZARD SPENDING—291

INDEX—323

Introduction

As you probably know, the good old days of enjoying a lifetime of work with one employer are long gone for most people. The uncertainties of the work world brought about by global competition and changing technology dictate that people will change jobs frequently, and may even be forced to seek employment in a new career field. Let's face it, this sort of insecurity isn't something you bargained for. Yet it can't be dealt with by just following the tried and true methods for career advancement, since a solid education and hard work no longer guarantee a good job for years to come.

This doesn't mean you have to sit back and be treated as a disposable worker constantly in fear of abruptly losing your job. However, to avoid this fate, you have to actively establish a game plan for job security, rather than just rely on your performance as the key to future success. This is essential if you want to guarantee your own survival, no matter what happens to your particular company or industry.

Basically, there are four major elements involved in becoming a job survivor in this uncertain work world. These include succeeding—or at least surviving cutbacks—in your present job, changing your job or career either by choice or necessity, relocating to find employment, and guarding against the financial disasters that accompany job insecurity. The purpose of *The Workplace Survival Guide* is to show you exactly what to do in each of these areas so you can successfully overcome any future career calamities that come your way.

You'll learn how to lessen the chances of being laid off in a corporate cutback or reorganization, as well as all the survival skills necessary to give yourself as much job security as possible. Beyond that, the guide will show you how to get ahead even under the worst of circumstances, such as being stuck in a dead-end job, or working for a boss who could care less about you or your career.

At some point in your work life, you will most likely have to look for another job, since the odds of having one employer for a lifetime are no longer very good. In fact, personal dissatisfaction or a decline in jobs in a particular occupation may force you to change career fields. To successfully control your destiny, you need to know how to get the job you want, or make the switch to a different line of work.

To help you manage this difficult transition in your life, *The Workplace Survival Guide* will show you how to do so without falling victim to the many pitfalls you will face. You'll find plenty of vital tips on such basics as how to find a job, succeed at job interviews, and even negotiate a higher salary than you're offered. But equally important, you'll get sound advice on what to do if you suddenly lose your job, including quick ways to reduce your expenses if you find yourself in a financial bind. And if you do decide to make a career change, you'll find valuable information on how to carefully plan your moves to minimize the risks involved.

Unfortunately, even if you have solid credentials and valuable experience, the job you seek may not be in the area where you live. As a result, you may have to consider moving to another part of the country to achieve your goals. This is always a difficult decision to make, which becomes even more troublesome if you and your spouse are both employed. You're then forced to consider the impact on two careers, along with all of the other stresses that relocation can cause.

The Workplace Survival Guide will help you cope with every aspect of relocating, whether you face the burdens of a dual career, selling a home, or uprooting the kids. There are hundreds of tips on everything from finding out where the jobs are, to seldom-considered moving costs that can break your budget. Beyond that, you'll find advice on how to decide whether or not to move, as well as how you can make it easier to settle in at a new location if you do relocate.

The final factor that everyone must deal with in an age of job uncertainty is finances. In the past, it wasn't difficult to land a secure job with a blue-chip employer that would cement your future until retirement. And when that moment arrived, you could count on a generous pension. That's history, and today both your job and financial security are essentially in your own hands. You now confront an uncertain future where you will likely switch jobs several times, and perhaps change careers once or twice during your lifetime.

Even if you're fortunate enough to have a good job today, you have to plan ahead, since it might vanish tomorrow and leave you without either a job, or the money to meet expenses while you're looking for work. And you can't ignore the very real possibility that a new job may not pay as well, or have as good a benefit package. Hopefully that won't happen, but if it does you will have to realign your spending to meet a reduction in income. To guard against any possibility, this book contains plenty of pointers on how to make better use of the money you make now, so you can breathe easier later no matter what the future brings.

To make this book easy to use whenever a job-related problem comes up, it's divided into four sections. Part 1 covers what you have to do now to improve your chances for survival and success on your present job. Part 2 deals with all aspects of changing jobs and/or careers, while Part 3 provides everything you need to consider in deciding whether or not to relocate. Part 4 furnishes the information you need to better manage the money you earn so you will have the resources available to cope with any eventuality that comes along.

This breakdown of the book's content lets you focus on the present, while still making it easy to access information you may need at a later date. For example, you may not be thinking about relocating right now, but will want to reread that section if circumstances change in the future. Likewise, you might presently be more interested in the chapters on succeeding in your present job, with no immediate thought of changing your job or career. By grouping the information in separate sections, when you want to refer to a particular subject, you can do so without having to search through the book to find what you want.

The overall thrust of this book is to give you an easy-to-use tool for coping with both job insecurity and the financial hassles of not being sure of the size of a future paycheck—or even if you'll have one. Its aim is to provide you with the facts you need to control your own destiny in the working world. Because if you don't, the corporate chieftains will dictate your fate for you. And when the choice is between profits and people, you know which one will be cut.

George Fuller

Part

1

WINNING AT WORK IN GOOD TIMES AND BAD

How successful you are at work is influenced by many factors, some of which you directly control, such as how well you do your job, along with the education and experience you now have and continue to acquire. Then, there are other ingredients for success which you can't directly influence, including corporate mergers and reorganizations which can either leave you out of a job, or hanging on hoping to survive the next wave of cutbacks. But even though you're not part of the decision-making loop in top management decisions which jeopardize your job, there are ways to improve your chances of being one of the survivors when the dust settles.

Of course, if a layoff or reorganization is being planned that will affect your job status, it's unlikely you will have any advance warning. Therefore, you have to know how to look for signs that signal future cutbacks. Beyond that, there are several things you can do that will help you retain your job, even while others around you lose theirs.

Being prepared for the worst is certainly a necessity, but you may be fortunate enough at the present time to work for a company that's growing, or at least holding its own in the marketplace. Your ultimate goal is to be as successful as you can while the good times roll. Yet even here there are impediments to success which you have to reckon with. These include being stuck in a dead-end job which makes it difficult to get ahead, or perhaps working for a difficult boss who for a number of reasons represents a real roadblock in your quest for success. So along with learning how to give yourself greater job security, you also have to learn to overcome other impediments to success at work. The chapters which follow address both these needs.

Chapter

1

COPING WITH ON-THE-JOB CAREER HAZARDS

While you're diligently working away at your job, reasonably certain that your future looks bright, events may be unfolding elsewhere that are setting you up as another addition to the unemployment rate. Something on a large scale such as a corporate merger may be in the works, or perhaps one of those periodic reorganizations is about to be announced. Whatever the cause, the inevitable outcome may be the loss of your job. You can guard against this by learning how to look for signs of change that may affect your employment status. There are also measures you can take to dodge a forthcoming layoff, or avoid being the odd person out in a pending reorganization. This chapter will explore how you can protect yourself from becoming a victim of any form of corporate reshuffling.

Beyond positioning yourself to be a survivor of any corporate juggling act, there are other on-the-job career hazards that can hinder your advancement within a company. In fact, they can even weaken your chances of being kept on the payroll if heads start to roll. These career deterrents include everything from working with incompetents to socializing with the "wrong" people.

There are other considerations that can influence your success on the job, such as knowing how to work around bottlenecks, or avoiding working long hours without having it affect your career. And there are even potential pitfalls in seemingly positive developments that may present themselves, such as being offered a work-at-home assignment. All these career impediments are covered in this chapter, but let's begin by looking at how to recognize if your job may be at risk.

SEVERAL SIGNS THAT YOUR JOB IS AT RISK

It's unfortunate, but it's often those who work the hardest who are least aware of what's going on around them. You probably know a couple of people where you work who spend most of their time engaged in office scuttlebutt. This isn't to recommend that you become a charter member of the gossip circuit. However, it can be useful to at least be aware of the latest rumors that are making the rounds at work. Of course, most of what you hear will have little validity, but on occasion you may pick something up which has a ring of truth to it. This is especially true when a rumor tends to be confirmed by other events that are taking place where you work. The source of the rumor should also be considered. So if someone in a position to have access to the information tells you layoffs are planned, the likelihood is greater than if the source is the confirmed office gossip.

There are several other details that can alert you to the possibility that your job may be in jeopardy. A decreased workload that appears to be more than temporary often signals that job cuts are coming. Usually the signs that layoffs are going to take place are evident long before they actually happen. Memos tend to circulate with directives to cut travel, training, and other areas. Overtime disappears and part-time workers are let go. Being alert to these advance warnings will allow you to move quickly to seek greener pastures if the need arises.

Of course, you have to evaluate your own situation. Even if job cuts are made, you may not be a victim. Your position in the company, salary, seniority, and your overall worth to an employer all can influence whether or not you become a casualty or a survivor of a layoff. Think about these factors carefully so you can assess your chances of being laid off, since this will determine how much emphasis you should place on looking for a job elsewhere.

On the other hand, if a good severance package is in the offing if you are laid off, it may be to your benefit to sit tight and see what happens. The important point is to be alert to the possibilities. Incidentally, no matter how secure you may feel in your current position, your resume should always be up-to-date and ready to go. All too often, people ignore this necessity until an unexpected job loss forces them to do some serious job hunting in a hurry.

Keeping your resume current has two advantages. First of all, you don't waste a lot of time preparing a resume when it should already be circulating. Equally important, by updating it as you go along, it's easier to make it as complete as possible. This isn't insignificant, since if you're preparing your first resume in several years, it won't be easy to remember the details of prior jobs, courses taken, and important projects which won you praise.

Watch for a Change in the Boss's Attitude Toward You

Although the possibility of a layoff doesn't mean it will become a reality, being aware of the potential threat to your job will allow you to take action quickly if fears become fact. A more present danger signal that your job may be threatened are subtle signals coming from your immediate boss. These warnings can take several forms. On the one hand, you may suddenly find yourself getting stuck with all the lousy assignments, or your boss may be irritable and abrupt in dealing with you. From the other extreme, you may find your formerly friendly boss avoiding you like the plague.

Of course, either situation may have nothing to do with you directly. But if a boss suddenly acts differently toward you, and this coincides with other warning signs, you may be about to get your walking papers. When you notice an attitude change taking place over a period of time, assess the circumstances from all angles. Have you been criticized about your work, or did you do something that made your boss look bad? The possibilities are endless, but the key is to be aware of any change in attitude which indicates you may be in disfavor.

It also pays to be on the alert if you suddenly acquire a new boss. This is especially true if you hold the type of position where a boss might prefer to see a familiar face. This is fairly common in top management positions where executives like to bring in their own team when they take over. Even though it doesn't receive as much attention, the same principle applies to lower-level positions. The most common example is where a boss prefers to work with a long-time secretary or administrative assistant. Even where a new boss doesn't have the authority to arbitrarily replace the incumbent in a job, a determined individual will look for justification to eventually nudge someone out of the way. So if you feel you may be vulnerable to this sort of maneuver, keep your options open if a new boss appears to be less than enthusiastic about your performance.

There are a variety of other internal situations which may put your job at risk; everything from a minor organizational change to the need to find a slot for the favorite nephew of a senior executive could put your job in harm's way. You certainly can't spend all your time worrying about this, but being aware of what is going on around you will allow you to take action to protect your own interests.

Even when all indicators presently point to your job being relatively secure, you still shouldn't blissfully neglect what might happen a year or two from now. If you're constantly reading news stories about the industry you work in facing a bleak future, these shouldn't be ignored. Naturally, you're not going to just jump ship from a great job on such skimpy evidence. But you might want to consider continuing education opportunities to acquire new skills you always wanted to learn. Alternatively, if you occupy a highly specialized position, it might be worthwhile to explore what other types of jobs your skills are transferable to.

Whether your job is at risk in the short or long term, from either external or internal causes, once you recognize this there are many steps you can take to protect your future. In fact, even if your job appears to be secure indefinitely, you can't sit idly by, since technology, world events, mergers, and other factors can quickly undermine anyone's job security. And the first tactic in protecting your own interests is knowing how to hold on to your own job, even while others are losing theirs. So let's explore how to survive a layoff.

SURE-FIRE WAYS TO AVOID THE LAYOFF AX

Of all the fates that can befall you at work, nothing can be worse than being unceremoniously told that your services are no longer required. Unless, of course, you had been contemplating leaving anyway, and a fat severance package will serve as a nice jumping-off point for you to pursue other interests. For most people, though, a layoff isn't welcome, so anything that can be done to avoid that fate is worth trying. Fortunately, there are measures you can take to protect yourself against layoffs, and some of these tactics can and should be initiated long before the possibility of a layoff looms large.

One of the simplest ways to survive a forthcoming layoff is to avoid the temptation to slack off on the job when word starts to circulate that a layoff is coming. When this happens, the rumors start to fly and people start to spend more time around the water cooler than at work. It's human nature for employees to be concerned, and you along with everyone else want to know what's going on. Nevertheless, when layoffs are coming, some people assume they will be targeted and on that basis don't put much effort into their jobs. The sentiment is simply, "Why bust my butt if I'm going to get a pink slip next week?"

Until people are actually notified they are being terminated, no one knows for certain if they will be one of the unfortunate ones. It's at this very time that your boss may have orders to prepare a list of who is to go and who is to be spared. This isn't an easy assignment, although it's hard to sympathize much with a boss when your job is at stake. But recognizing the difficulty your boss may be having in deciding who gets the pink slips is one way to hopefully keep your name off the hit list. Assuming the boss has to make choices, he or she will very likely do so on the basis of who is more valuable to keep. You can help make yourself one of these people by continuing to plug away hard at your job during this period. The boss may very well be looking around to see who is doing what. The chances are that many of your co-workers have slowed the pace down in anticipation of a layoff. If a boss notices you as being one of a few people who are continuing to work hard, this may influence who avoids the pink slip.

You might well think that since everyone is goofing off because of the potential for layoffs, there's no harm in you doing likewise. This is especially true if you have a reputation for being a good worker. Yet when a boss is faced with picking and choosing which employees to retain on short notice, the pressures of making such a decision may blur what's happened in the past. As a result, the boss may simply go with his or her views of who the best workers are at the moment. A boss may also consider who is likely to continue to work hard after the layoff is completed. Seeing you plugging away while awaiting your fate sends a signal that you perform well through thick or thin. That may end up sparing you from the ax. So, as much as you're interested in the layoff scuttlebutt, don't neglect your job at this critical time.

Be Flexible in Learning Other Jobs

Taking action to avoid being laid off from your job is an ongoing proposition. One good step you can take is to learn as many other jobs where you work as possible. Get to know the tasks your co-workers perform, and volunteer to help them out whenever you have some slack time. This not only lets you learn their job, but it has the added benefit of earning a return favor when you're busy and can use a little help.

The bottom line is that the more jobs you know how to do, the more valuable you become to your employer. As a result, when a company slims down to do more work with fewer people, it will want to retain those workers who have the flexibility to perform a number of different jobs. This approach means you have to work harder than you might otherwise do, but working hard certainly beats not working at all.

Whenever new machinery or a new procedure is introduced, be the one who learns all about it. This makes you the expert who can help co-workers who aren't as anxious to learn much at all about anything new. In the right circumstances, you may become an expert on matters that make you valuable beyond the confines of your own department. If this happens, then you have further bulletproofed yourself against a layoff.

Training is another area where opportunities exist to solidify your job security. Offers for company-sponsored and paid training are routinely turned down by workers. It's easy to shrug and say, "Why bother to learn that? I have enough to do as it is." Unfortunately, what's keeping you busy today may become a victim of new technology or some other change in the future. The people who have the best chance of surviving a layoff are those with up-to-date skills, so no matter how much experience you have, take advantage of every chance to learn new skills. After all, just because a particular type of job may be cut in a layoff, doesn't mean that other jobs will be eliminated. So even if it happened that you were targeted to lose your present job, if you have the skills to do another job, you have a leg up on surviving a cutback.

The particular job you hold may make you vulnerable to a layoff. Many staff positions that don't directly contribute to the bottom line are far more vulnerable to layoffs than sales or production positions. As a result, if your particular job is the type that is susceptible to layoffs, you may want to explore the possibilities of transferring to a more secure position. Of course that's not always feasible, but if an opportunity presents itself, you might be better off doing something that has more value in the long term.

Finally, always make sure your accomplishments are recognized. This doesn't mean you have to extol your virtues to anyone who will listen. But if you have done something above and beyond the ordinary, let your boss and others in a position of power know about it as casually as possible. In a similar fashion, if you enjoy working for your employer, display your enthusiasm. If it comes down to laying off one of two people, you can rest assured that the person who is always grumbling and groaning is on the way out the door.

HOW TO SURVIVE A REORGANIZATION

If you work in one place long enough, you're sure to experience one of the rituals of business, which is reorganization. Reorganizing departments, divisions, and even entire companies is done for a number of reasons, all of which are supposed to accomplish some valid business goal. Some realignments succeed in doing so, while others turn out to be little more than window dressing to support some executive's notion of good management.

Whatever the outcome may ultimately be for the company, it can be painful for the employees affected. It can mean lost jobs, realigned work assignments, perhaps a new boss, and even geographic relocation. About all you can do in such a situation is to do what you can to minimize the impact of the reorganization on you personally.

This isn't always possible, but many times a little bit of thought and a few shrewd moves can put you in a better position to survive than your peers who shrug and say, "There's nothing I can do, so I'll just go with the flow." Unfortunately for many people who adopt that approach, going with the flow may mean getting flushed down the ramp to unemployment, or ending up unhappy in new and unfamiliar circumstances. On the other hand, if you plot out a strategy for coping with a reorganization, you might even end up in a better position than you had before. So let's look at what your possibilities are when a reorganization looms on the horizon.

Before a reorganization actually takes place, many of the same measures you would take to survive a layoff apply equally to guarding against the ill-effects of a reorganization. In actuality, many reorganizations involve layoffs as part of the general juggling of the pieces of the corporate puzzle. Therefore, tactics discussed in the prior section on layoffs, such as learning to do as many jobs as possible, will not only help you to survive a layoff, but will benefit you when the dust settles after a reorganization.

Look for Warning Signs

Frequently when a reorganization is in the works, there are clearly visible signs before the realignment takes place. One obvious indication is when a boss and other assorted managers show increased interest in the details of how the work is performed within your group. So when a boss who typically looked for results rather than details suddenly wants to know the intricacies of everyone's job, it may mean changes are being discussed at higher levels. This is even more valid when formal studies of workload are conducted, perhaps even by outside consultants. Always remember that consultants get paid for making recommendations, and abolishing your job may be one of them. Other indicators may include managers in key departments leaving the company and not being replaced, or work previously done by a particular unit being assigned elsewhere. Actions such as these may spotlight a department that's going to be eliminated.

If you can get a handle on a forthcoming reorganization early enough, this gives you the opportunity to look for a transfer if your job appears to be in jeopardy. For example, if you're fairly certain a reorganization will take place which will abolish your group but expand another, you might want to apply for a job in the other department. Otherwise you have to take the chance that you will be one of the survivors of a cutback who gets transferred when the reorganization takes place. Even if your request is turned down, the fact that you applied for a transfer can work in your favor. When it comes time to decide who gets transferred, you may get preference since you have already indicated an interest in working in the other department. For this reason, a boss may prefer you to someone who may be unhappy with a transfer.

Be Pleasant and Prosper

When a reorganization takes effect, it can present both problems and opportunities. Among the difficulties may be a new boss and an increased workload, but whatever the hassles are, it doesn't pay to harbor ill feelings. Always strive to be pleasant about working in your new environment, since it affects how others will react toward you.

A good attitude can make you stand out in sharp contrast to others, particularly if a reorganization has eliminated jobs leaving more work for the survivors. Many people react to this by complaining about being overworked, and finding things wrong with the restructured organization. In contrast, you can stand out by digging in and accepting the change with a positive disposition. This isn't easy to do when you may be experiencing the fears and apprehension that tend to accompany reorganization, but it will make the transition a lot smoother for you.

Everyone likes dealing with someone who has a good disposition, so it's smart to try and be pleasant on your job under any circumstances. This may require some effort on your part, especially if things aren't going well, or problems on the home front have you on edge. Do what you can to maintain a pleasant demeanor, since it can only help make your workday a little bit easier.

Although reorganizations often result in more work for everyone, there are also opportunities presented amidst the initial turmoil. Before things settle down too much, you have a chance to redefine your job to eliminate what isn't essential. For example, perhaps your new boss will be willing to let you do away with routine reports which your former boss insisted upon. Whatever the specifics are, this is a good time to look for things you can eliminate from your job. Your new boss will appreciate you taking the initiative to eliminate unnecessary work, since he or she is probably wondering how to get the workload accomplished efficiently with fewer people.

WAYS TO SUCCEED WITHOUT WORKING LONG HOURS

Do you find yourself working longer hours than you want to, but not knowing how to avoid it short of getting another job? If so, you share a problem with many other hassled employees. The reasons people work longer hours than they would like differ from one situation to the next. You may be in a position where it's the unspoken rule to work long hours. Perhaps it's because the boss works late and everyone else does likewise in follow-the-leader fashion. This isn't uncommon, especially when you have a boss whose life revolves around the job. Even worse, perhaps the boss's schedule is such that working late dovetails with his or her schedule. Perhaps the boss catches a late commuter train, hangs around to avoid traffic, or has a habit of both arriving and working late. Unfortunately, you may not have the same option to set your own hours. As a result, you arrive at work on time and are then forced to wait around until the boss departs.

On the other hand, your long hours may be caused by your peers who hang around after closing as a means of impressing the boss with their dedication to the job. No one ever notices that they really aren't doing much after hours with the exception of idle chatter. This can be even more frustrating as you listen to these types continually lament about the long hours they are putting in to get their work done. Of course, there's no mandatory requirement for you to follow their example. However, as you may have experienced, if you leave work on time your apple-polishing peers might just spread the word that you aren't the hardworking and dedicated type that deserves to be promoted. Therefore, unless you have a savvy boss, you may find yourself tied to the extended paper-shuffling schedule of your peers.

In other job situations, overtime may be routinely required, and you may even be in a position to be paid for it. That's great, if you want and need the money. Unfortunately, even if the overtime pay looks good initially, extended periods of overtime can quickly turn your thoughts to things other than money. So even here, you may decide that pay or no pay, a regular workweek is what you want.

No matter what the circumstances causing your long hours, there are ways to avoid working late while still being able to do your job as well or better than those others who seemingly never want to go home. The trick is to combine doing your job more efficiently with being able to demonstrate subtly that your output is superior to your co-workers. If you can succeed at doing that, you will enjoy the luxury of more free time. You may also reap the satisfaction of having your boss wonder why others have to work late to accomplish what you get done during regular business hours.

Control Interruptions from Co-Workers

One of the best ways to give yourself more time to get things done during the business day is to cut down on the needless interruptions by others that slow you down in doing your job. In fact, until you start to think about it, you may not have noticed how many distractions occur during a typical work day. Once you start thinking about it though, you will soon see there are many culprits who consume your time. Your time is valuable, especially when interruptions can make the difference between being able to leave work on time, or having to hang around to complete unfinished business.

If you're not already aware of it, you will quickly discover that the bulk of your interruptions come from co-workers who stop by to chat about whatever meaningless topic is on their minds. This is to be expected, since these are the very people who are probably trying to stretch their work out to support their habit of working long hours. This is particularly true if people are being paid to work overtime, since to justify working extra they need something to do. As is often the case, it turns out to be work that they should have done during the day.

This doesn't say much for the degree of supervision exercised by your boss, but then again, the boss may have a different agenda. For example, your boss may be trying to prove to higher management that more help is needed in the department. What better way to do so than to show that the unit is so overburdened that long hours of overtime are needed to get the work done?

In any event, your first step in controlling interruptions is to clamp down on the pests who keep you from your work. Naturally, it's preferable to be as diplomatic as possible when doing this, since you do have to work with these people on a daily basis. Nevertheless, there may be a person or two who refuse to take a hint, and in these instances, you may have to be pretty blunt in making your point.

Beyond the out-and-out socializers, there are people who will pester you with work-related topics that consume your time needlessly. These are generally the type of people who try to stretch the simplest projects into never-ending assignments. You could care less, except for the fact that if they have to interact with you, they will go to great lengths to consume your time as well as their own in dragging things out. What you have to do in these situations is simply solve their problem as it relates to you and send them on their way. If necessary, just say, "That's all I can do for you on that, Luke; you'll have to excuse me as I have other things to do."

Learn How to Fend Off Buck-Passers

Something else to be on the alert for when dealing with co-workers are attempts to dump work on you that isn't really yours. There are people who seem to make a career out of trying to pawn their work off on someone else, and if you're the obliging type, these people will beat a path to your work location. Therefore, it may be necessary for you to learn how to say "no" to these people when they try to dump their chores in your lap. You have to be conscious of this happening, since these types are skilled at passing the buck. A common tactic is to compliment you as the person most knowledgeable about a particular subject. Naturally, you're not about to take exception to compliments, so before you know it you may be doing someone else's work because you're the designated expert. Needless to say, the choice boils down to doing other people's dirty work, or denying your expertise. Sometimes, contrary to popular opinion, it pays not to be too smart.

The more enterprising buck-passers among your peers may try to funnel work your way by using your boss as the messenger. What usually happens is the other employee is approached by your mutual boss to handle an assignment. Using some form of excuse, the buck-passer convinces the boss that good old you are the one who can best handle the assignment. This presents you with a dilemma. Even if you recognize what is being done, it looks pretty tacky to openly accuse a co-worker of dumping work on you. Furthermore, it's the boss, not the co-worker, who will give you the assignment. More than a little bit of tact is called for in avoiding these assignments.

One good way to deal with this sort of situation is to convince your boss that you are working on more important priorities. It's especially helpful if you can couch your reluctance to accept the assignment on an "either/or" basis. In other words, what you want to do is persuade the boss that what you're working on is more important, and that you won't be able to do both jobs. Say something such as, "If I handle that project, I won't be able to finish X on time." If at all possible, try to show the importance of finishing what you're working on. If you can do this successfully, then it's likely the boss will look for someone else to work on the new task.

Whatever you do, once you identify a co-worker who targets you as a candidate to pawn assignments off on, be on your guard. And needless to say, whenever the opportunity presents itself to return the favor, take advantage of it. If nothing else, that will discourage a buck-passer from using you as a scapegoat.

Eliminate Unnecessary Tasks

One of the main ways to extricate yourself from the workplace without working beyond quitting time is to look for extraneous tasks you can eliminate. At first thought, this may seem to be impossible because everything you do appears necessary. A major reason for such an assumption is that daily routines become ingrained habits. Beyond that, with the hustle and bustle of your daily workload, most likely little thought is given to what can be done quicker—or preferably not at all. Yet if you take some time to think these tasks through, you may find yourself doing a number of chores that are unnecessary, have been rendered obsolete by changes in the workplace, or that should be done by someone else.

In the area of unnecessary duties are such items as reading all the trivia that comes your way in the form of policy statements, operating procedures, and various other documents generated by others in the company. Learn to quickly scan all your reading material. If it doesn't directly impact how you do your job, just ignore it. Don't worry about missing something, since anything of importance will likely be called to your attention by someone else. This is one time you can take advantage of your unproductive peers who are more than willing to dally away the hours analyzing every piece of paper that comes their way. By their nature, they will then want to waste more time discussing anything of general interest. In this way, you can pick up any information you need regarding less than important matters without troubling to read everything.

Another potential area for lightening your workload would be to look for things you do during the day that really don't have to be done. For example, you may well be preparing one or more reports which serve no useful purpose; conditions may have changed which make the report obsolete. Yet this report may still be required for the simple reason that no one has taken the time to discover its obsolescence. If you think you're doing such unnecessary work, ask around to find out what its purpose is. You may discover that you have been wasting a lot of your valuable time. Even when something such as a report is still required, you may find that it can be shortened, or otherwise simplified, so it can be prepared in less time. You reap dual benefits when you discover practices that can be either eliminated or simplified. Not only do you save yourself time, but you also impress your boss and others as someone who is good at boosting productivity. Who knows, if you're really lucky, you may even receive an award for your productivity suggestions, which in essence would be a reward for making your own job easier to do.

The final area to think about in terms of eliminating unnecessary tasks concerns work you may do that should really be done by someone else. There are all sorts of reasons as to why this can happen. Perhaps something was assigned to your department arbitrarily on a temporary basis and then became routine rather than subsequently reassigned to where it belonged. After all, it's unlikely someone will come looking for work to do, so even when another department may be aware of this, if you're doing the work, that may be all right with them.

On a more personal level, you may have assumed duties in the past to help someone in your group out and for one reason or another never gave back the assignment. Perhaps the person left and you didn't know what to do. Maybe you weren't as busy in the past and didn't mind doing the additional work. Whatever the reason may be, when you're trying to reduce your workload, it's time to stop being shy about unloading chores that really don't belong to you.

Do Things More Efficiently to Save Time

Perhaps the greatest way to save time is to look for ways to do your day-to-day chores more efficiently. Changing how you handle any individual chore may not yield a lot of additional time, but taken cumulatively you will discover you can get a lot more done during the day if you learn how to cut corners. Although the specifics of your particular job will dictate how you can save time, a short laundry list of general areas in which time can be saved through efficiency would include:

- *Keeping your telephone calls to a minimum.* Try making calls you initiate just before lunch or at the close of the day. The other party is more likely to be cooperative in keeping the conversation to a minimum. With talkative individuals you may find it beneficial to call at times you know they won't be in their offices. That way, you can simply leave a message. If you do this, emphasize in the message that a return call isn't necessary.

- *Avoiding lengthy memos when a phone call, or a brief computer message will do the trick.*

- *Making the most of available technology.* Send a fax if it will save time. Don't churn out computer printouts just because it's easy to do. The more people you send information to, the more requests you will get for clarification or additional data.

- *Organizing your files, desk, and/or working tools so you won't waste time looking for things.*

- *Cultivating a time of the day when you're at your best.* Do the tough tasks when your energy levels are highest, and save the routine work for when you're not at your best.

- *Avoiding unnecessary meetings whenever it's possible to do so.* Frequently, you can beg off by convincing your boss of the importance of finishing your day's work.

- *Delegating as much of your work as possible if you have people working for you.*

- *Being willing to recognize that not everything can be done at once. Concentrate on getting the important things done, and don't worry about minor matters.*

Enlist the Support of Your Boss

Although many people are reluctant to approach their boss to beg off working long hours, you have little to lose by asking. An enlightened boss will be more than willing to listen to your concerns about family responsibilities which make it difficult, if not impossible, for you to work long hours. Furthermore, if you have already made adjustments to get more done during working hours, the boss may be well aware that you do more in eight hours than some of your peers do in ten or twelve. Although you're better off not doing so, if it's necessary as a last resort, suggest that you can take work home to finish if this is feasible in your particular job.

Lastly, if your workload is above and beyond the norm for someone in your position, don't be afraid to make your case for additional help. This frequently happens with employees who excel at their jobs. It's the path of least resistance for a boss to burden such people with additional work. Although this may be a recognition of your abilities, you have to learn to say "no" if you don't want to be overwhelmed.

THE PITFALLS OF ACCEPTING
A WORK-AT-HOME ASSIGNMENT

If you are fortunate enough to work in a position which offers the opportunity for work-at-home assignments, you may find this to be to your advantage. This is especially true if you have young children or elderly parents to care for. In addition, you may find that working at home will give you greater freedom and flexibility. Apart from the personal flexibility this type of assignment gives you, it's also possible to cut down on your work-related expenses. You won't have to buy lunches, may be able to cut your clothing budget, and can save on commuting costs.

All these factors may be true, and telecommuting may be right for you. On the other hand, working from home has its disadvantages, which can often get overlooked in the euphoria of what you may consider to be a dream opportunity. For this reason, it pays to weigh both the benefits and liabilities of working from home before you commit yourself to accepting such an assignment.

First of all, you have to be realistic about your ability to work on your own. Working at home requires the ability to work independently, and be disciplined enough not to let other interests interfere with your work schedule. Many people also miss the camaraderie of their co-workers along with the rumors bandied about at the water cooler. There are other disadvantages associated with working at home. It's much harder to get your work efforts noticed by anyone other than your immediate boss, and there's little opportunity to establish contacts with people in other areas of the company. This loss of visibility could hinder your chances for promotions or transfers. Of course, these considerations can be somewhat alleviated if you spend at least part of the week on-site. Working at home can also give you the feeling that your work is never done. It's easy to go to work since it's never more than a few steps away, so you may actually find yourself working longer hours than would be the case if you weren't working at home.

To be successful in a work-at-home position, a few minimum requirements must be met. At the outset, a specific area such as a vacant room or a basement office should be set aside as a work area. You should also try to discipline yourself to maintain regular work hours. Doing this will give you a set routine in terms of finishing your work. Otherwise, you may find yourself continually working evenings and weekends to finish what you didn't do during the day. Finally, if working at home was selected as an option so you could take care of your children or meet some other family responsibility, be sure this doesn't interfere with your ability to get your work done. Otherwise, you will have substituted a work problem for the child-care problem you had when you were working outside the home.

LEARNING HOW TO SIDESTEP CAREER BOTTLENECKS

Getting ahead on the job is never quite as simple as you may have been led to believe when you first started to work for your present employer. More often than not, those who initially interviewed you spoke of glowing prospects for the company in the future, as well as splendid opportunities for your own advancement. This, of course, should have been expected, since someone hiring for a position isn't about to tell job candidates that the last promotion took place three years ago, or that the company's future looks bleak. After all, that sort of shop talk isn't going to get any open position filled in a hurry.

On the other hand, perhaps the people in the personnel office may have given you a fair assessment when you took your job. Times and circumstances change for companies as well as individuals, so the bright future for the company when you were first hired may have dimmed considerably since then. In any event, you may find yourself discovering that career advancement with your employer isn't quite as simple as you thought initially. Sometimes people don't understand that working hard and doing a good job are not always the only prerequisites for getting ahead. Unfortunately, there are all sorts of career bottlenecks that have to be hurdled if you want bigger and better opportunities in your career.

The impediments to career advancement with your present employer can range from the company not experiencing much growth, to the misfortune of finding yourself in line for promotion behind several other people. Or, it may be nothing more than the fact that the more senior positions you strive for are filled with people who aren't anywhere close to retirement, and show no signs of looking for a job anywhere else. Then again, the impediments may be personal in nature, such as a lack of the necessary education or experience normally required to move to the next level.

Short of looking for a position elsewhere, whatever your career bottlenecks may be, you have to be able to work around the impediments that are holding up your progress. So let's look at some ways of dealing with career roadblocks that at first glance seem to be impossible to circumvent. The starting point for focusing your career in the right direction would be to take the time to think about your next move.

Assess Your Present Prospects

Is a promotion possible from the looks of your present job? If so, what is the likely time frame for this to occur? Give this some thought and don't just rely on past practices to establish your expectations. For instance, people one step up the career ladder from you may have been promoted from the position you now hold within a one- to two-year period. Assuming blindly that this is the same pattern you will follow can lead to disappointment when two years go by and your prospects for advancement are no better than they were when you first started. Past practices aren't an acceptable guide to follow since conditions change, and if you haven't taken the time to assess the situation, then you're setting yourself up for unnecessary disappointment.

Perhaps the company was experiencing rapid growth in the past which opened up advancement opportunities, but growth has now slowed or is nonexistent. This being the case, there will be little possibility that any kind of routine promotion will come your way with the passage of time. A slow-growth or no-growth business picture also means that the people currently occupying the positions you aspire to will be bottlenecked in getting promoted, and this means a position isn't likely to open up in the near future.

Perhaps the type of position you aspire to has diminishing prospects which makes it unlikely there will be many future promotional opportunities. This can result from a number of different causes, including technology advances which diminish the need for certain types of positions. Management policy itself can limit opportunities as many companies have reduced middle management ranks, so if you aspire to a management position, your outlook may not be as bright as in the past.

Even where these factors aren't present, the specific situation you're in may work against you. If the people occupying the next higher position are relatively young and your company experiences little turnover in these jobs, it's unlikely that the prospects of retirement or of these people leaving for jobs elsewhere will occur. These are all elements you have to consider to determine what, if any, roadblocks are in the way of advancing your career.

Another more personal impediment may be your need to acquire education or training that will qualify you for your next promotion. You may not view this as a necessity if you know other people have advanced in the past without the credentials your boss says you now need. However, you have to recognize that times change and promotion opportunities may have been greater in the past than they are now. The tougher it is to get promoted, the greater your need to excel in terms of both education and experience if you want to move ahead.

Once you have assessed the situation, your next step is to determine what you have to do to position yourself so that you improve your chances for promotion. If it's something as straightforward as obtaining additional training, then take the necessary measures to get started. Beyond this, you may still discover that you have to be creative if you want to get ahead.

Create Your Own Position

When routine advancement isn't likely, one good way to move up is to gradually create a position for yourself which can be later upgraded. This isn't easy to do, but it also isn't as hard as you might imagine. No one likes to assume additional responsibilities, particularly if there's no present payoff in the form of a pay raise or promotion. For this reason, co-workers will tend to avoid taking on any assignments that aren't linked directly to their jobs. You, on the other hand, can expand your duties by assuming these responsibilities.

How you go about this can vary. Your boss may ask you if you want to handle certain projects, while on other occasions you can volunteer to do any number of tasks. At other times, an opportunity may arise for you to assume a responsibility that everyone else ignores. This is likely to happen when a new technology or revised working procedure takes effect. By assuming these duties, whatever this entails, you will soon become the recognized expert in the area, and people will defer to your decisions regarding these matters.

You have to be careful when you do this, however, since taking on any old project won't eventually justify a promotion. You have to be selective about the additional duties you undertake. What you want to look for are projects that either require some technical expertise, require decisions to be made, or are of a complexity that goes beyond the limits of your present job. These are the factors that can eventually turn these tasks into justification for getting your job upgraded.

Once you have firmly established yourself as having assumed significant additional duties, then approach your boss about the possibility of a promotion. When you do this, be prepared to show the boss why your job now differs from—and is more complex—than that performed by your co-workers. You may not succeed at the first pass, but once your boss realizes the importance of your duties, he or she will likely have your position reviewed by the personnel office to see if it should be upgraded. The more responsibility you have assumed that makes life easier for your boss, then the greater the odds the boss will go to bat for you. After all, the alternative might be for the boss to have to take on the duties if the personnel people decide they aren't a proper part of your existing job description. And there's no greater incentive for a boss to support your cause than his or her own self-interest.

Move Sideways to Move Ahead

The hurdle you face in getting promoted may be such that the only way around it is to transfer to another position which offers better opportunities. The reason for having to do this may be nothing more complicated than the fact that you're in a dead-end job. Sometimes in these situations capable people are promoted to handle other responsibilities. If this isn't the case, then you would be wise to transfer into a position which offers greater potential for advancement.

The bottleneck working against your promotion chances may be in the form of a boss who doesn't like you and isn't about to promote you under any circumstances. At the other extreme, you may have a boss who doesn't want to lose you and in the interests of being selfish won't push you for promotion. Naturally, a boss who doesn't like you will be more than happy to see you transfer elsewhere, unless the person is sadistic enough to want you around so as to make your life miserable. However, it's quite a different circumstance when a boss doesn't want to lose your talents. In this case, the boss may be no more willing to go along with a transfer than he or she is to promote you. If this happens, assuming the boss has the power to block a transfer, try to bring pressure from the department head. Since your immediate boss won't want to appear shallow by preventing you from transferring for selfish reasons, the other manager may not have too much trouble in getting you transferred. And if the other boss is at a higher management level, you can rest assured that your transfer will be approved quickly. Finally, once you have assessed any and all roadblocks to your future career progress carefully, you may come to the conclusion that your future looks bleak with your present employer. If that's the case, then your choice is to accept that fact, and perhaps start a job search for a position with a company offering better advancement opportunities.

GUIDELINES FOR OUTLASTING INCOMPETENTS

For the most part, you won't have any trouble competing with incompetents for promotions, or retaining your job in troubled times. However, there are certain situations where less than capable individuals manage to do quite well against their harder working peers, and it's these people you have to watch out for. The reasons for their success vary with the circumstances. For example, they may be skilled at the game of office politics. Alternatively, they may excel at concealing their work deficiencies from a boss. Finally, it may be nothing more radical than having spent many years working for the same company which gives them a seniority edge in the eyes of management. Whatever the reason may be, you have to be aware of how to deal with the competition, which isn't always going to be confined to your hard working and better qualified colleagues.

Watch Out for Dirty Tricks

As you may be aware, some of your less capable colleagues can be pretty adept at enhancing their job security at your expense. To deal successfully with these types first requires an awareness of the various tactics they may use, which include:

* Throwing up roadblocks to slow your work up. This involves stalling on doing tasks which affect your work to prevent you from getting your work done in a timely manner.

* Failing to communicate work-related information to you, thereby causing you to make mistakes and being subject to criticism by your boss.

- Starting needless turf battles over work assignments and resources.

- Using you as a scapegoat for their mistakes.

- Playing politics to the hilt to curry favor with bosses.

- Consistently telling lies to avoid criticism for their subpar work.

- Claiming a lack of cooperation from others has prevented them from doing their job.

- Backstabbing any coworker who they perceive as a competitive threat.

- Unfairly pinning blame on other people.

- Taking advantage of every opportunity to belittle your work in front of others.

- Often attempting to take credit for work done by other people.

Any list of the ploys used by co-workers more interested in internal competition than in doing their jobs could go on and on, since some of those who operate this way can be pretty creative about protecting their own images while destroying everyone else's. Ironically, these people are working at cross-purposes with everyone else in an environment where teamwork and cooperation are the norm. If they succeed in their guerrilla warfare, not only do they protect their own jobs at the expense of more capable co-workers, but they seriously undermine the productive efforts of the company.

Whatever methods these co-workers use, you have to respond in some manner if they are interfering with your ability to do your job, or are seriously damaging your image as a hard-working, dedicated employee. Otherwise, in good times they will be promoted ahead of you, and in tough times you may get the pink slip while they survive to continue their dirty tricks.

How to Cope with Troublemakers

Just as your enemies at work use a variety of tactics to cause damage to your career aspirations, you should employ an assortment of measures to respond to their actions. You should always be looking for ways to negate their actions. Once they realize you're not going to be an easy target, they may cease their dirty tricks—at least as far as making you one of their targets. Some representative actions you can take include:

- *Practicing self-promotion.* Make sure your accomplishments are known to your boss and other people in a position of power within the company. That way, if someone later tries to take credit for them, the facts will already be known. People only succeed in taking credit for other people's work when the person doing the work doesn't take the credit themselves. You should, of course, do this subtly so it doesn't look like you're a flagrant braggart.

- *If someone attempts to belittle your work in your presence, don't let it go unchallenged.* Respond immediately without getting angry. Say something such as, "I'm afraid you misunderstand what happened Marsha. What I did was . . ." and then correct the misinterpretation. If the party persists in challenging you, don't get into a debate. Instead, reply with a comment such as, "I understand you have your own opinion Marsha, but everyone else involved seems to have a different interpretation."

- *If you're the target of insults, laugh them off, or respond with a bit of humor.* It takes the wind out of the sails of someone who is trying to bait you when you laugh off their remarks. It also makes them look like a jerk in front of anyone else who is listening.

- *If you have a peer who persists in being unpleasant, ignore the behavior.* It only succeeds when people become flustered and angry.

- *Turn the tables on someone by doing them a big favor if the opportunity presents itself.* This then puts them in the position of being in your debt. As a result, they may lay off, but even if they don't, they look petty by knocking someone who has done a good deed for them. Naturally, let it be known to others that you did a favor, so that if the culprit tries to make you look bad again, he or she will be seen as an ingrate.

- *If you work closely with someone who always tries to hog the credit, take steps to set the record straight.* One easy way to do this is with brief notes to your boss advising him or her of the status of work in progress—including who is doing what. Frequently, people who try to claim credit wait until a task or project is finished to grab the glory. That way, they know success is assured. However, if you have been regularly keeping the boss apprised of what's going on, the scene stealer will not only be late with the facts, but also look like the credit grabber he or she is trying to be.

- *If you have someone who continually throws up roadblocks that hinder you in doing your job, look for ways to work around them.* Perhaps you can deal with someone else, or maybe you can eliminate them from the loop. If their participation is unavoidable, pin them down with deadlines, and let your boss know the schedule. That way, if people slow things up, you can sic the boss on them.

- *Keeping the lines of communication open with your boss is the best way to prevent anyone from making you look bad unfairly, or taking credit for your achievements.*

THE PROS AND CONS OF CUTTING RED TAPE TO GET AHEAD

Every business has set practices and procedures to be followed by employees. All these rules and regulations have a well-defined purpose, or at least were created with that intent in mind. The scope, complexity, and volume of these rules will vary from business to business. The larger the business, and the longer it has been in existence, the greater the number of formal rules you may have to follow. This isn't always true of course, but it is more often than not.

For one thing, a smaller business doesn't usually have people on board who have the time to sit down and formalize practices. Plus, a smaller company won't encounter the same need for formalizing procedures, since everyone probably works under the same roof, and the number of employees is small enough for there to be individual contact by senior management. In other words, everyone pretty much knows what everyone else is doing. This sort of familiarity doesn't hold true in midsized and large companies which may operate from several locations.

Hence, rules are committed to writing to ensure that everyone is operating on the same wavelength.

Naturally, if procedures were easy to understand and follow, they wouldn't present you with much difficulty in doing your job. Unfortunately however, many of them appear to be written with the express purpose of proving that the writer is smarter than everyone else by virtue of being able to write a procedure that no one else can understand. That is an exaggeration, since most people whose job it is to commit policies and procedures to writing are working stiffs just like the rest of us. They start out with every intention of making the written rules as easy to understand as possible.

What can happen is that to be broad enough to cover all conceivable circumstances, the procedures end up being deliberately vague, which leaves them open to interpretation. That in itself doesn't always create problems. It's more often the individuals you find in every company, who for one reason or another, want to exercise their power by telling you that what you're doing doesn't comply with policy # 4.5.307 or whatever other written rule they can find to make your life difficult. The end result is that as you try to do your job, you are confronted with policies and procedures you may not understand, and even worse, bottleneck bureaucrats who insist you're not following the rules. If you're operating under these constraints, you're faced with two choices. The first is one of total frustration as everything you do is seemingly slowed down by being tied up in bureaucratic red tape. The alternative choice is to learn how to circumvent these bottlenecks without being labeled as uncooperative or insubordinate. Let's look at how you can succeed at working around this paperwork minefield.

The golden rule for dealing with red tape is to avoid it as much as possible; this isn't as hard to do as it might seem. Many procedures are written broadly enough to cover a wide array of circumstances. As a result, they often are so general that it isn't always clear whether or not they apply to a particular job. Needless to say, if you want to avoid getting bogged down in red tape, you always want to interpret any procedure as not applying to your situation.

The biggest mistake you can make here is to ask your boss if a particular procedure applies. Being busy, it's much easier for a boss to say yes rather than take the time to look over what may be a long and confusing written document. As a general rule, assume procedures don't apply to what you're working on unless you have been specifically told otherwise.

> **NOTE:** Never treat any policies or procedures relating to health or safety lightly. The same applies to any policies implementing government laws or regulations. In these areas always exercise caution in observing the rules. It's best to use shortcuts only when they apply to run-of-the-mill operating procedures that apply to your job.

Sometimes you will have to work with individuals who use written procedures as a tool to exercise power which they otherwise wouldn't possess. These individuals will tell you habitually that such and such procedure must be followed before they can give their approval to something you're working on. Naturally, if this happens to be your boss, you have little choice but to follow the directive. Many times however, the power grabber will be someone you have to go through in the approval loop. There are a couple of ways you can deal with these types successfully.

One approach is to comply with their requests when it involves work that is of low priority. Then, if you have something urgent, look for a way to avoid them. Perhaps have someone else sign off, or bypass them completely. Even if you're caught, you can plead that you tried to contact them but they weren't available at the time. State that you then moved ahead since the project was urgent. Since you have made a habit of going through channels on routine items, it's unlikely you will be suspected of deliberately trying to bypass the bottleneck. For this reason, you shouldn't get yourself in hot water.

If you have one or more complex procedures that create difficulty for you on a fairly regular basis, it may be worth your while to study the procedure in detail. If you become knowledgeable enough about it, your expertise may be accepted when you assert that the procedure doesn't apply to the particular task you're working on.

Beyond specific procedures pertaining to your work, there are often informal administrative procedures in place that are both meaningless and time consuming. If you inquired as to their origins or purpose the odds are you wouldn't be able to find anyone who could answer these questions. Most likely, you would get a shrug and a response such as this from your boss: "I don't know why we have to do that. All I know is that we've been doing it that way for years. Until someone says differently, we'll continue to do it that way."

Some of these practices are silly on the surface. For example, duplicate paper files may be kept of computerized data. Reports will be prepared for people who don't even read them and so forth. You could probably pinpoint a half-dozen useless tasks being performed around you without even giving it much thought. Some of this useless red tape exists because no one has ever weeded out the obsolete practices. Other practices result from empire building. Whatever the cause may be, the more you can successfully cut through this thicket, the faster you'll be able to get your work done. This is one of those times when you can look good by working smarter instead of harder.

HOW TO SUCCEED BY BREAKING THE RULES

Aside from the formalized policies and procedures you have to follow which were discussed in the previous section, there are all sorts of guidelines and rules prescribed by your boss and others as to what you should or shouldn't do under certain business conditions. Usually these make sense and don't cause you any great difficulty in doing your job. On occasion, though, you may find yourself faced with situations where the alternative is to follow the letter of the law laid down by your boss, or to make a decision which deviates from that edict.

For example, perhaps there's a valid reason for not following a guideline in a specific instance. Assume your boss told you to clear certain things with him before you take action. One example might be when someone outside the department comes to you asking for some work to be done. This makes sense in most cases. But what if the executive vice-president of the company appears in your presence asking for a chore to be performed right away? Do you tell him to see your boss? Not if you enjoy peace of mind and lack of controversy, not to mention a desire for a regular paycheck. Of course, you do what is asked. When you get an opportunity later, you let your boss know what happened. Unless you're working for a moron, nothing will be said. Although this is a fairly obvious example of when you should break the rules, there are other more subtle times when it's to your benefit to do so.

In order to meet deadlines it may be necessary to cut a few corners. This is particularly true if the deadline involves something important enough to have the attention of senior managers. On other occasions, it's just easier to ignore a rule rather than follow it. One of the keys to success at work is having the ability to take risks. This doesn't mean you should haphazardly go your own way and ignore directives. What you have to do is assess the risk/reward factor in choosing to bend, or ignore the standard way of doing something. In the deadline example above, there's a lot more at stake in not meeting a deadline that has top management attention than there is in bending a couple of rules to finish on schedule.

In essence, many of the rules of the workplace are easily broken or ignored without any adverse effect. The heart of the matter is knowing which ones to break and which ones to follow. Incidentally, the usefulness or practicality of the rule isn't always the criterion to go by. More important than that is whether or not your boss or someone else in power feels strongly about the subject. For instance, if there's a petty administrative procedure that is a waste of time, you don't want to ignore it if your boss considers it to be important. So if you want to improve your productivity by cutting corners here and there, make sure you know which ones to cut before you take action. Otherwise you may find yourself worse off than if you went by the book.

WHAT TO DO IF YOU SCREW UP SOMETHING IMPORTANT

Everyone makes mistakes in doing their job, and for the most part minor errors are taken in stride by both the person making the mistake, as well as the boss. Yet for a number of reasons, a perfectly understandable error can become a major hassle if it occurs on a task that has real or perceived importance. Unfortunately, when bosses have to answer for some goof that was made within the group under their supervision, in many instances the person making the mistake ends up in the hot seat.

In fact, blame is often ascribed when it isn't even justified. After all, it's a rare boss that's a strong enough leader who will take the heat for an error made by a subordinate. This is true even when the mistake may have resulted from some action or decision made by the boss. As you know, the term "rank has its privileges" is sometimes construed to mean making the employee the scapegoat for a boss's incompetence.

All this is testament to the fact that you have to know how to protect your own interests when an error is made that rightly or wrongly can be attributed to you. Otherwise, you may find yourself mumbling about being treated unfairly—to say nothing of the impact such conduct can have on your career aspirations. After all, there's nothing quite so bad as working hard to prove your ability only to be nailed for something you didn't do. For that matter, even if you make an occasional mistake, it shouldn't be held against you. So whether you're being blamed for a mistake you didn't make, or one that was justified in the performance of your duties, you had better learn how to protect your interests.

No matter how good a job you're doing, there will always be occasions when for one reason or another, the finger of blame is pointed at you. Sometimes it may be only a minor problem, while in other instances it could be serious enough to be job-threatening. In any event, when it's necessary to wiggle out of the hot seat without being burned, the following tactics may be helpful. Of course, which approach you use will depend not only upon the circumstances, but also whether you're an innocent victim, or the deliberate target of someone who is using you as a scapegoat.

Prove Your Innocence or Accept the Blame

Sometimes you may find yourself being blamed for a mistake that you didn't make. This inadvertent blame may be accidental, or it may result directly from an attempt by someone else to blame you for their goof. This type of a situation doesn't present too much of a problem if you can readily prove the mistake wasn't your doing. That isn't always easy to do, however, which is probably why the mistake was blamed on you in the first place. Clever scapegoats are always careful to pin the blame elsewhere only when it's not easy to track down where the fault really lies.

In this situation you can't openly point the finger at someone else unless you can prove your allegations. Otherwise, it will appear you're just trying to unfairly pin the blame elsewhere. Needless to say, this won't put you in the good graces of your boss. As a result, even if you're fairly certain where the fault lies, unless you have the evidence, you are better off just accepting the responsibility with a mild disavowal that you remember making such an error. Say something such as, "I'll take responsibility for doing that, but to the best of my knowledge, I didn't handle that particular matter." If you're later able to prove the error wasn't yours, you will look all the better for accepting the responsibility for someone else's goof, and at the same time, the person who tried to nail you will look like an even bigger jerk.

NOTE: If your boss was the one who made the mistake for which you're being blamed, swallow hard and accept the burden of guilt. There's nothing to be gained by going toe-to-toe with your boss over an error he or she made for which you are being blamed. Along the same line, don't pin the blame on higher-level managers if you value your job. If your boss is in the habit of blaming subordinates, everyone knows it anyway. With a boss like this, however, it's worth your while to have a few excuses handy for each and every time the boss tries to blame you for something. That way, even though you can't blame the boss, you will have some form of alibi.

Occasionally, you alone may be blamed for something for which others share responsibility. This generally happens when you are part of a team or other group working on a task. Here, of course, you have the option of saying something such as, "I apologize for my contribution toward this error, but as you know, there were several of us working on this project." Doing this can be a little tacky, especially if it's common knowledge it was a group effort. The boss, or whoever is criticizing you, may plan on doing likewise with everyone else involved. That being the case, your pointing out that the blame is to be shared will likely bring a blunt response. Therefore, for the most part, whenever there's shared responsibility for an error, it's usually preferable to take the heat and be done with it.

Sometimes there's a valid reason for an error being made. Perhaps procedures have been changed and you weren't informed. The specifics will differ, but if you're accused of doing something wrong when it was through no fault of your own, explain this to your boss. Often when an error is made, the error is highlighted and no one bothers to look for the underlying cause. By pointing out the reason, not only do you avoid the blame, but you also highlight what has to be done so there's no repetition of the error by someone else.

If you work hard, it's inevitable you will make mistakes. Most of them will be insignificant. There may, however, be a time when you make a serious error and are called on the carpet about it. If it was an honest error and there is no real justification for it, apologize and assure your boss it won't happen again. Trying to make excuses looks bad, and that sort of approach may well anger your boss. Go about your business and it won't be long before your mistake is forgotten.

THE DO'S AND DON'TS OF SOCIALIZING AT WORK

You might wonder how something as seemingly harmless as who you socialize with can have an impact upon your career. This is especially true if you don't socialize to the extent of neglecting your work. Rest assured, there are certain aspects of forming friendships at work that can have either a positive or negative influence on how you're perceived by your boss and other higher-ups. Therefore, it makes sense to know the pitfalls and practicalities associated with your interactions with co-workers.

Although a failure to think through your working relationships isn't likely to be a determining factor in your career success, in some cases the wrong moves can slow down your advancement. Of even greater impact, making the right contacts can propel you along at a faster pace. So even though you may be inclined to view your friendships at work as your own business, in certain instances you may have to decide how important particular friendships are when balanced against career considerations. The choice is and should be yours, but so are the career-related risks and rewards. Incidentally, the focus here is on socializing in general, while the office politics angle is covered in chapter three.

One of the biggest blunders you can make is becoming too friendly with an ear-bender who spends more time chatting than working. If you befriend one of these types, he or she will habitually keep you from getting your work done. Beyond that, your boss will quickly assume that you're as big a time waster as the culprit. You have to be careful with these yakkers, since even if you have no intention of befriending them they are adept at latching on to anyone who displays the slightest interest in anything they have to say. This includes simply listening politely for a moment or two before you give them the brush-off. Therefore, once you peg someone as an ear-bender, don't even make a pretense of being a polite listener when dealing with them. The best way to avoid problems with this type is not to show any interest in what they have to say from the start.

Apart from identifiable pests, being courteous and pleasant with everyone is a good guideline to follow in your relationships with people at work. This holds true even for people you may not like, since there's nothing to be gained by creating enemies. One area where this general rule can be challenged is with people who don't get along with your boss. Even here you want to be courteous, but it's good practice not to go overboard in chatting with people your boss obviously doesn't like.

Incidentally, on occasion people will express opinions of others and may even solicit your comments. Always refrain from saying anything critical about anyone, since it's only going to travel back to the person and cause unneeded animosity. You may well form friendships at work that carry over beyond the workplace. There's no particular problem here as long as it isn't a boss/subordinate relationship. It makes sense to avoid those as much as possible, especially if you're the one who is the boss. It will typically be viewed as bestowing favoritism on the friend whom you supervise.

As for romance in the office, it can cause real problems. Should it be avoided? Logically yes, but that isn't the real world. Furthermore, the workplace is one of the most likely settings for romance to blossom. Where else do you come into contact with those of the opposite sex eight hours a day for five days a week? If you spend anywhere close to that amount of time in singles bars, you better get your liver checked soon. All in all, a workplace romance doesn't pose any particular difficulty as long as you don't let it interfere with work. It is better to try and keep it low-key though, since it can be an embarrassment to co-workers who don't know how to react to the relationship.

No real difficulty arises in workplace romances while they're going strong, but when they break up, it can be a problem if the two parties work in close proximity to each other. Can you handle it? Of course, you say. That's what everyone says, but that's not what always happens. Hopefully, you won't have to deal with the problem.

WAYS TO MAKE BUSINESS TRAVEL HASSLE-FREE

If you happen to have a job where business trips are a routine part of your job, you undoubtedly know how tiring and troublesome they can be. But even if you only have to travel occasionally, business trips can still be a hassle. Nevertheless, if you plan your travel carefully, you can eliminate most of the problems associated with having to hit the road on business. To do this successfully, you have to look at eliminating both the aggravation associated with the travel itself, as well as minimizing the work that awaits your return from the road.

Naturally, the best way to eliminate travel hassles is to do as little traveling as possible, which isn't always within your control. You can, however, take some measures that may help you under certain circumstances. For instance, many bosses are cost-conscious when it comes to incurring travel costs. This is especially true if upper management is always harping about excessive travel being taken by employees. If you're fortunate enough to work in such an environment, take advantage of it to suggest alternatives to taking a planned business trip to your boss.

Perhaps you can show why the trip isn't necessary. As an alternative, maybe you can convince the party you were going to see to visit you instead. You might even want to diplomatically suggest that perhaps an associate is the best person to take the trip. This isn't hard to do, especially if you have someone in mind who hasn't yet become dissatisfied with facing yet another night in a hotel room. Then again, maybe you can't find an alternative and find yourself faced with hitting the road again. If so, some of the following tactics will help you minimize your misery.

- *Start out being well rested.* This means avoiding rushing from your office to the airport to catch a flight after a long day at the office.

- *If you have a long flight, do any necessary work early in the flight before you become fatigued.*

- *Try to plan your schedule to compensate for jet lag by having a light workload on the day of arrival at your destination.*

- *Try to avoid alcohol on flights since it will dehydrate you in the dry air of airplane cabins.*

- *Try to arrange your flights to avoid the busiest airports.*

- *If you experience downtime enroute, relax and do some recreational reading.* Stewing about delays will only aggravate you—it won't speed things up.

- *Carry anything essential aboard your flight.* That way, you can still function even if your luggage is lost.

- *Use simple organization so you know where everything is.* For example, tickets in one place, receipts in another, and so forth.

- *Ask hotels to "unfreeze" your credit.* Sometimes hotels freeze credit when you check in. Ask for it to be unfrozen when you check out. Otherwise, you may find yourself being told you have exceeded your credit limit at your next stop.

- *Check the weather forecast for your destination before you leave home.* That way, you'll have clothing suitable for the weather at your destination.

- *Make sure you have everything you need with you to avoid shopping hassles in an unfamiliar city.*

- *Secure car rentals before you leave.*

- *If you're traveling overseas, have sufficient foreign currency with you for tipping and so forth, until you can get to a bank to exchange funds.*

- *Be sure to save all your travel receipts so you can prepare your expense report when you return from your trip.* Incidentally, the sooner you prepare it, the better off you'll be. The longer you wait, the more you tend to forget incidental expenses. You will also be reimbursed more quickly.

No matter how many precautions you take to ease the pain of your next business trip, something may still go awry. If so, relax and take it in stride. After all, at least you're not paying for the trip.

One other aspect of business travel needs mentioning. One of the most irritating aspects of an extended business trip is returning to find your desk loaded with paperwork. And it's almost inevitable that the minute you sit down at your desk, the phone starts ringing and people come barging in, all looking to discuss some urgent problem that arose in your absence. It's times like this that can make you wonder why the company isn't paying you more money, if you're so indispensable?

Try to avoid this sort of panic return before you even leave for a business trip. In fact, if the trip will be more than a day or two, do a little bargaining with your boss. See if you can pawn some of your least desirable assignments off on someone else. One good way to do it is to let the boss know that something has a deadline and must be completed while you're gone. This should encourage the boss to assign someone to pick up the project in your absence.

To your dismay, you may discover upon your return that the person assigned to the project managed to get the deadline extended until your return. Your efforts have not been in vain, however. You can plead additional time is needed because X didn't finish the job while you were away. Naturally, you don't want to do this to a friend, but with a little thought you can manage this maneuver with someone who has done you a couple of bad deeds in the past.

Another useful ploy is to let people you deal with externally—such as customers—know you are going on a trip. When you do this, give them a return date which is a couple of days later than you will actually be back in the office. This will keep them off your back for a day or so until you can get your feet back on the ground.

Then there's the question of whether or not you should leave phone numbers where you can be contacted while on the road. If you supervise other people, you may want to do so, since this will prevent everything from piling up until you return. On the other hand, if you only have yourself to worry about, leaving phone numbers only encourages people to bother you while you're on the road.

So if you want to enjoy the sights and sounds of a distant city after normal business hours, don't make it easy for the home office to contact you. Otherwise, you may find yourself in your hotel room working on some hot item you were called about. If policy, or a stickler of a boss, requires you to leave a number where you can be contacted, you may want to follow the rules. Conversely, you can neglect to and if called on the carpet because someone couldn't get you, use a handy excuse. Perhaps you could say something such as, "I was busy in meetings, so I asked one of the secretaries to call and leave the numbers where I could be reached."

Chapter

2

SURVIVAL SKILLS FOR JOB SECURITY

Many people don't recognize that their job security can be enhanced by knowing how to protect their interests at work. Just doing your job and hoping for the best is the standard approach to dealing with the possibility of surviving job cutbacks if that's what the future brings. Yet by adopting some savvy techniques, you can position yourself to be a survivor if the worst should come to pass and downsizing or reorganization forces layoffs or job transfers where you work. There is, of course, no guarantee that anything you do will save your job in every eventuality. But taking the right steps will certainly give you a leg up in protecting your best interests.

One of the most effective ways to insulate yourself from adverse personnel actions is to cultivate as many supporters as you can in the ranks of those in higher-level positions. This not only helps your career on a daily basis, but it also provides opportunities for a job transfer if things start to look bleak in your current job. Beyond that, if a large-scale reorganization takes place, those managers who will be adding positions will take people whose abilities they're familiar with. Along with getting yourself recognized by other senior managers is the need to recognize who has power and who doesn't within your organization. This isn't always obvious from an organization chart, so you have to learn who is in a position to do you some good, or who may, alternatively, cause problems for you if you rub them the wrong way.

Relying on other people to protect your interests is only part of any job protection strategy. You also have to learn how to make yourself too valuable to lose. That way, your name won't be on the short list if and when cutbacks take place. Naturally, no one is indispensable, but some people are more valuable than others. In this chapter you'll find some timely tips on how to solidify your position by assuming responsibilities that others might choose to avoid. Along the same line, it's also worthwhile to take a hardheaded look at your own performance to see where and how you can improve your on-the-job abilities.

Survival skills at work go beyond just tuning up your performance and getting yourself noticed. You also have to learn how to minimize the damage when things go wrong with your work. You have to know how to counter criticism, defend against backstabbers, and protect your butt if you goof. Beyond that, you should know how to deal with the sensitive issue of discrimination, since that may be practiced subtly even in organizations where it's firmly discouraged.

PROVEN WAYS TO GAIN INFLUENTIAL ALLIES AT WORK

As much as you may wish it did, your job security doesn't rest solely on your accomplishments. How successful you are in getting ahead, as well as in retaining your job when cutbacks are in the offing, depends as much on who you know as what you know. That may be an overly dramatic assessment of the need to have supporters who recognize your hard work, but the fact remains that when companies reduce their payrolls, talent alone doesn't guarantee survival.

Who goes and who stays in a cutback may be determined at a level well above your boss. In fact, your boss may be one of the people targeted for termination. If so, no matter how highly your boss thinks of you, it's of little value if the boss isn't in a position to protect you and your job. For this reason alone, it pays to cultivate the respect of upper-level managers throughout the company. Beyond that, cutbacks and reorganizations often present opportunities for transfers. And although a transfer may not be your first preference, it can certainly beat looking for another job, especially if it means you'll be job hunting from the ranks of the unemployed.

Gaining recognition from other managers can serve you well apart from saving your skin in any work-force reduction. A senior manager who has a vacancy always wants to fill it with a familiar, well-liked worker if at all possible. Therefore, someone who thinks highly of you may offer you an attractive position that you didn't even know was opening up. And more than one manager has been skilled at creating a job to fill with a talented individual they wanted working for them. For these and other reasons, it pays to make a conscious effort to gain influential allies where you work. Internal networking can be a slow process, but when an opportunity arises to make your talents known to others, you have to be ready to seize the chance.

Your job itself presents the best possibility for making your talents known to people in higher management positions where you work. Unfortunately, not every job calls for regular contact with higher-level executives. In fact, many positions seldom provide an opportunity to make your talents known. Therefore, when a chance does come along, you have to make the most of it. Usually, your best bet is by doing an exceptional job working on something that has the interest of senior managers. For this reason, if you have the chance to volunteer for a high-visibility assignment, by all means do so. Many people try to avoid such projects since they don't want the hassle of being in the spotlight. Nevertheless, the career visibility it gives you is worth the headaches.

On other occasions, it may be a fortuitous encounter, where a higher-level manager stops by your work area unexpectedly. In any event, when you work on anything that stands a chance of gaining the attention of higher-ups, give it your best shot in terms of performance.

Fortunately, your job alone isn't the only chance you have to score points with the big shots. Every company looks for volunteers from time to time to serve on various committees. The purposes can vary, ranging from planning the company picnic to charitable fund raising. Whatever the task is, volunteer your services, since it will give you a chance to interact with senior managers. Company-sponsored recreational activities are another possibility for getting to know people who can help your career along. Needless to say, if you get the chance to be on a first-name basis with a senior manager, exchange pleasantries any time the opportunity presents itself, since this will keep your name in the person's mind.

If you can't establish a direct link with senior managers, you may be able to make yourself known through a third party. Perhaps someone you know works directly for an executive, or otherwise knows them personally. For example, it can't hurt your career if the company president stops by your work area to say hello and tells you that he was golfing on the prior Saturday with your uncle. You might be subsequently surprised to find that your immediate boss appears to be a lot friendlier with you after he or she witnesses such an encounter.

Enlist the Support of Co-Workers

Although it's desirable to be known to top management, this isn't always possible. On a daily basis, the best allies you can have are the people who can help you get your work done. They may not be able to do much to help you in terms of their influence with the power structure, but they can help you immensely with your work. In that way, they aid in increasing your performance, which speaks for itself in terms of providing you with greater job security. Naturally, gaining the cooperation of others in doing your job is a two-way street, since others have their own work to do. Therefore, the degree of cooperation you get will be in direct proportion to how you deal with co-workers. Here are some general practices to follow that will assist you in maximizing the assistance you get from others:

- *Show appreciation whenever someone helps you with something.* Expressing your thanks may not seem like much, but if people think you aren't grateful, their support may not be as enthusiastic the next time you need help.

- *Recognize other people's priorities.* You can't always expect someone to drop what they're doing to do something for you. When you see people are busy, respect the fact that you may not get what you want as fast as you would like. It also helps if you don't treat everything as an emergency. That way, when you have a priority of your own, people will be more willing to help you out.

- *Be accommodating.* Everyone has their own way of doing things, so if someone wants to do something a little differently than you would prefer, don't make an issue of it unless it's of the utmost importance.

- *Help others succeed.* Help your co-workers out whenever you can, and they will do likewise for you.

- *Cover for co-workers.* If the occasion arises where you can protect a co-worker from criticism, by all means do so. These sorts of favors will get you favors in return.

When it comes to enlisting allies, one of the best ways to get your virtues touted to your boss and others is through customers, suppliers, and other outside contacts you deal with at work. You can be sure that if you do a good job when working with these people, they are likely to let this be known to other people they deal with in your company. Furthermore, some of these outsiders may have contacts at a higher level in your company than you do. So even though treating customers well may be good for business, it can also be beneficial to your own career.

POWER: HOW TO TELL WHO HAS IT AND WHO DOESN'T

When you're dealing with people at work, one of the keys to success is knowing who has power to exercise influence over your career and who doesn't. On the surface, this appears to be obvious, with your immediate boss having the greatest capability to help or hinder your job prospects. Beyond that, anyone at higher levels of management, as well as people in staff functions such as personnel, can directly or indirectly take actions that affect your job. You don't want to alienate anyone who is in a position to cause problems for you.

Learn Who Has Derived Power

What often gets overlooked is that there are others besides the obvious holders of power who can either help your cause, or create problems for you. It's certainly beneficial to know who these people are. Some people have power out of proportion to their specific jobs for a number of reasons. Reasons can range from years of service during which time veteran employees have formed acquaintances with any number of senior managers, to something as specific as sharing a car pool with an influential manager. Others may occupy a position which in and of itself doesn't carry any direct authority, but by its nature gives the individual power beyond that associated with the position. For example, an executive's secretary may speak for the boss indirectly, even though the secretarial position itself doesn't show up as a senior slot in an organization chart. So as a starter, you can't tell who has power in a company by simply referring to the organization's management structure. Recognizing this fact is the first step in identifying those people with whom you want to work at maintaining good relationships.

Both personal observation and close attention to what's said on the office gossip circuit are essential in being able to pinpoint those who hold power beyond that dictated by their jobs. It also takes a period of time to identify the hidden power brokers in a company, since many informal power holders aren't obvious immediately. The circumstances which informally give people power out of proportion to their job titles are endless, but the key point is that their power derives from some form of association with senior managers who hold the real power. Let's look at a few of the possibilities:

- John, who works in shipping, knows the vice-president of Human Resources. The connection is their sons, who both play on the same high school football team.

- Mary, in accounting, is a cousin of the division general manager.

- Frank, a co-worker who is an avid golfer, occasionally plays with two of the company's senior managers.

- Charlie, who works in maintenance, often does weekend chores for the company president.

- Beth, who works in personnel, is having a relationship with the company president. (It's supposed to be on the sly, but Charlie knows about it and has spread the word.)

The Advantages of Knowing Who Has Power and Who Doesn't

These are typical of the many associations that exist in the work environment, but what does it mean to you? First of all, you don't want to make an enemy of someone who may be in a position to do damage to your career. It may be that you don't particularly like someone, but knowing they have inside influence will alert you to force yourself to be at least superficially pleasant with these people. It also means being careful about what you say in front of them. Complaining about senior management is typical fare in the average workplace. Needless to say, you don't want to be grumbling about the company president to someone who plays golf with him on weekends, but that can happen if you don't know who has connections with top management.

The prudent course of action, of course, is to always refrain from making derogatory comments, since that way you don't have to worry about saying the wrong thing. In reality, that may not always be possible. After all, senior managers are known to pull some real blunders that can easily inspire employees to talk about them in some choice terms. Knowing the players in the world of office politics will keep you from doing unnecessary damage to your image at work.

Information is a major source of power, so if you want to be well-informed, it pays to cultivate those individuals who have access to information that may be of value to you. For example, in terms of your job and career, anyone working in the human resources function of your company has access to a wealth of information of potential interest to you. Everything from salaries to potential layoffs can be learned from someone working there if you can succeed in developing a casual friendship. Naturally, your co-worker may not reveal confidential information, but generalities dropped during conversations often tell you all you need to know.

Aside from knowing who has derived power, either from access to individuals or information, you should also learn who doesn't have effective power even though their position or job title might indicate otherwise. Prime examples would be managers who aren't in good standing with top management. These may be people who are hanging on to their jobs waiting for the ax to fall. In other instances, they may just be indecisive and one of their subordinates may be the real source of power.

There are a couple of reasons for identifying these folks. First of all, you don't want to spin your wheels trying to get something done through these outcasts, and second, it's not sensible to be too closely associated with them—especially if they appear to be ticketed for an early departure. After all, if someone decides you're on the wrong team, you may be asked to play your game somewhere else. So along with learning who has power, or access to it, you have to identify those people who have been effectively stripped of their apparent power. If you can do this, you're a lot closer to making the power structure within your company work for you rather than against you.

SEVERAL WAYS TO BECOME INDISPENSABLE

Everyone has heard the drill about no one being indispensable, but even if you accept that argument, you have to admit that some people are more dispensable than others. You don't have to work anywhere long to recognize people who are candidates for a pink slip at the first opportunity. Conversely, every company has their share of employees who are virtually guaranteed to survive any but the most drastic of layoffs. Therefore, if you want to maximize your job security, you have to work on positioning yourself as someone the company wants to keep on the payroll through good times and bad. If you can accomplish this, you will give yourself a lot more job security than many of your peers.

The bottom line in giving yourself security against a layoff or unwanted job transfer is to make yourself too valuable for your boss to lose, as mentioned previously. In fact, this can even go beyond your immediate boss to higher-level managers. For instance, if your boss is targeted for dismissal, unless the department you work in is abolished, someone will have to run it if your boss is fired. If you play your cards right, you could be that person. The way to accomplish that is to become an irreplaceable asset to those for whom you work.

First and foremost on your agenda is to make yourself indispensable to your immediate boss. One of the best ways to do this is to volunteer for those thankless jobs that no one else will take. However, use discretion, since volunteering to do routine tasks requiring no particular expertise can mean spending your time doing jobs that get you nothing in return. Your boss may appreciate having a volunteer, but other than that, there's little to be gained.

The types of jobs you want to volunteer to do are those that are a priority for your boss. For example, projects that have tight deadlines, or anything that requires learning something new. If you establish a pattern of being the one person your boss can turn to when tough tasks come along, you increase your value in his or her eyes. This alone will set you apart as someone a boss should protect when cutbacks are called for.

It also helps if you can learn to do some of the boss's chores. This relieves the pressure on your boss, and also gives you the chance to learn your boss's job. Therefore, be willing to say, "Is there anything I can do to help you out?" whenever you see your boss overwhelmed with work. Someone who relieves a boss of burdens earns a great deal of appreciation along the way.

Always try to keep your boss updated in aspects of your job which are of particular significance. If you give it some thought, you may notice that your boss is especially interested in certain kinds of information pertaining to the work you do. Feeding this sort of need will put your boss at ease. Every boss operates differently, and if yours likes written reports, then prepare them willingly without having to be asked.

Studying your boss's likes and dislikes can also yield benefits for you. If you go about it right, you may find over a period of time that the boss starts to treat you as the second-in-command within your department. He or she may appoint you as the acting supervisor in his or her absence, and/or confide in you as to matters that your peers aren't privy to. There's a downside to this, since it means you will be doing more work. It may also mean other inconveniences, such as working when you might otherwise have taken time off, especially if the boss wants you to fill in during his or her absence. Nevertheless, this is a small price to pay for enhancing your chances of surviving a layoff, not to mention the overall benefits to your career.

The same tactics you use to be successful with your immediate boss are equally valuable in working with other managers who can potentially influence your career. Therefore, take advantage of every opportunity to make your talents known. Beyond this, always strive to be pleasant and helpful in dealing with others. Although many managers would deny that personality plays a big role in personnel decisions, the fact remains that everyone tends to do a little more for those people they like.

HOW TO ASSESS YOUR OWN PERFORMANCE

One of the best ways to determine your relative job security is to analyze your value to your employer. This isn't as hard to do as you might think if you're willing to assess your strengths and weaknesses fairly, and not just assert that since you're working hard, you're doing a good job. Evaluating your own performance in a way that can help you requires a more detailed assessment than that. Yet most employees give little or no thought to their performance until they encounter a performance review by their boss. Then, as is often the case, an employee doesn't agree with the boss's rating, yet has little or no substantive evidence to support anything different.

Identify Areas Where You Need to Improve

Taking the time and making the effort to critically evaluate how you're doing on the job has several advantages. The most obvious is that it better prepares you for your periodic formal performance evaluation. If you go through the exercise of rating yourself on the elements contained in a formal evaluation form, you will get a good handle on where you need to improve. It not only allows you to pinpoint your weak spots, but gives you the opportunity to work on improving deficiencies long before your formal review rolls around. Then, if your boss should mention you need improvement in a certain area, you may well be able to reply, "I agree with you, and for the last three months I've been working to improve in that area." You can then go on to tell your boss exactly what you have done. This sort of approach will impress any boss. After all, not only are you agreeing with the boss's assessment, but you have demonstrated your desire to show improvement. This is a far cry from the disagreements, or sullen acceptance, that many performance reviews elicit from employees. So it can only help to raise your standing with your boss.

Even if you should disagree about some rating element, having carefully assessed the area yourself, you will be better able to provide substantive evidence that may even sway the boss to revise a rating factor. Even if you're not successful, the boss will likely give some credibility to your comments—at least as long as you present them in a positive rather than argumentative fashion.

Beyond formal performance reviews, assessing your performance is valuable for other purposes as well. For example, it gives you an idea of what sort of training and experience you may need to seek a job you may be eyeing for the future. This will allow you to plan accordingly in seeking cross-training assignments, formal training, or job transfers which will put you in a better position for career advancement.

Although you may be reluctant to invest the time in going over the nitty-gritty of your job performance, it isn't something you can arbitrarily ignore. The bottom line is if you don't want to expend the effort to analyze your own achievements, you're pretty much stuck with how others view your performance. And they're far less likely to be as generous in their analysis as you are. Therefore, you had better learn how to gather the facts to blow your own horn, because no one else is going to do it for you.

Determine Your Priorities

The first step in doing a self-evaluation requires an honest assessment of what is most important to you in terms of your job. For some people, just holding on to their job to collect a regular paycheck is all they're interested in. Other people place a high priority on career advancement to the exclusion of everything else in their life. Most folks probably fall somewhere between these two extremes and look for a balance between their personal and professional lives. Establishing your personal priorities is important, since it will determine how much emphasis you want to place on improving your job performance.

For example, if you are on a career fast-track and focusing on rapid advancement to higher-level positions, then your performance should be geared toward achieving this goal. Conversely, if your personal life takes top priority, you won't want to work long hours and make the other sacrifices required to further your career. Therefore, your personal goals should be the backdrop against which you evaluate your own performance to determine where improvements can be made.

The initial step in conducting your self-evaluation is to identify your strengths. This is to some extent job-specific, but many elements of performance are common to any position. For example, are you good at determining work priorities, motivating people, working under pressure, and so forth? Are you a team player or more comfortable working on an individual basis? A factor such as this can have little or great significance depending upon the demands of your job.

How does your boss rate your performance? Have you received favorable performance evaluations in the past, been recommended for awards, or received above-average pay raises? Conversely, has your boss repeatedly criticized one or more aspects of your performance? By the way, don't overlook subtle remarks about your work, since these can indicate a boss's dissatisfaction just as well as a pointed reprimand. It's always unpleasant to criticize someone's performance and a boss may attempt to do so with a casual comment rather than be blunt about it.

If you are in a position to supervise other employees, think about how they view you as a boss. Do they frequently express unhappiness with your decisions, or attempt to go over your head to a higher-level manager? Do employees want to work for you as a supervisor, or are workers routinely transferring out of your unit? Other factors can influence these types of actions, but make sure it isn't because of your position as their supervisor. If it is, think about what you're doing wrong and how you can correct it. Many times you will find it's nothing more than a simple lack of communication.

Incidentally, if you're highly rated by your workers, yet don't do so well with your boss, think about it. Is it that you're not meeting your management responsibilities? If, on the other hand, your boss loves you and your subordinates equate you with Atilla the Hun, then perhaps you ought to think about changing your management style.

It's also useful to think about how your performance is viewed by managers other than your boss. First determine which managers are aware of your capabilities. If none are, then one of your goals may be to establish greater visibility for your efforts in the future. After all, it's of little value to your career to excel if no one in authority knows about your achievements.

In any event, consider the entire range of factors involved in your job and determine which ones you're good at and which ones might need some improvement. It's admittedly not easy to identify one's own weaknesses, but it's necessary if you want to be realistic about evaluating your performance. By identifying those areas where you may not excel, you can then determine what has to be done for improvement. In some cases, you may find it's just a matter of being more conscious of how you handle a particular aspect of your job. In other areas, you may find you need some form of training or other assistance to improve your performance.

Doing a critical self-evaluation of your job performance isn't easy, but it's a worthwhile exercise in helping you evaluate where you are and where you want to go in terms of your future. From a more pragmatic standpoint, evaluating your own performance will make your next formal evaluation session with your boss far more beneficial than it might otherwise have been.

THE PROS AND CONS OF MENTORS

There's little question that a mentor can be of invaluable assistance to you in attaining your career goals or, for that matter, simply surviving a company downsizing. It's nice to have a senior manager who offers guidance and can look out for your best interests. However, making such a connection isn't quite as easy as it seems to those who blithely advise you to "find yourself a mentor." Yet even if you're ultimately successful in doing that, having a mentor isn't the solution to all your career problems. And in some situations, a mentor can do more harm than good. So let's explore the many positives and negatives associated with having a mentor, as well as how you go about finding one in the first place.

Finding a good mentor isn't as simple as asking a senior manager to be your sounding board. After all, some senior managers may have little interest in your career progression. Others may not possess the personality or skills to best serve your interests. Beyond anything else, being too direct about looking for a mentor is just a little bit too pushy to gain much admiration, let alone a willing mentor.

The trick in getting a mentor is to position yourself so the person informally adopts you as a protégé. How you go about this can vary, but for the most part you want to take advantage of opportunities to ask a senior manager business-related questions. Don't be afraid to ask, "Can I talk to you for a moment?" but be prudent about your timing. Everyone loves to give advice, so this sort of ego-stroking is likely to fall on receptive ears. Try this on different mentoring prospects until you find one who takes a genuine interest in answering your questions. Once this happens, periodically ask for further advice until a mentoring relationship gradually develops.

Of course, you want to be choosy about whom you target as a possible mentor. For one thing, you want to evaluate potential mentors in terms of their positions in the organization. Hitching your wagon to someone on their way to the top can help your own rise up the ladder. The flip side of the coin is to avoid potential mentors who may not be connected to the power structure within the company. Even worse, don't hook yourself up with someone who is disgruntled and on the way out, since this will target you as a follower of the malcontent.

In searching for a mentor, you mustn't overlook the basic reason you want this mentor in your corner. Are you essentially looking for someone who can help move your career along, or who is in a position to give you a little added job security if tough times strike your company? Maybe those are just secondary goals and what you are really looking for is someone who can teach you the basics of doing a better job. If it's the latter, then the person's skills and teaching ability are far more important than position within the company. Here, an experienced peer may be a more valued tutor than someone higher up in the organization.

Actually, you may be better off seeking different mentors for different purposes. A senior manager who can guide your career along the way may not have the fundamental skills to teach you the tricks to succeeding on a daily basis, while someone who can do this may have little or no pull within the organization. Therefore, if it's feasible, try to find yourself different mentors to aid you in distinct aspects of your job and career.

One of the dangers in trying to emulate a mentor is that their talents and yours may not be the same. You, for example, may be detail-oriented, while your mentor may shun details and appear to you to be rather disorganized. Be careful here, since it can lead to frustration if you try to operate on the same basis as someone who isn't cut from the same mold. What works for one person doesn't always work for another. As a result, try to find mentors who more or less operate in a style in which you feel comfortable.

Finally, don't wear out your welcome. No matter how helpful someone is, they still have their own job responsibilities to handle. Therefore, they aren't always going to be available when you want to talk to them. It's also useful not to set your expectations too high in terms of what a mentor can do for you. No matter how much guidance you get, the implementation is still up to you. Mentoring relationships don't always work out, so if you can't connect with a mentor, don't despair. Most people get along just fine without having anyone in high places to look out for them.

DEFENDING AGAINST BACKSTABBERS AND OTHER TROUBLEMAKERS

You may not think your job is anything special until you find out that a co-worker is angling to take it away from you. In fact, you might not think that is even a remote possibility—at least until the layoff rumors start and everyone is scrambling for survival. But even in more stable times, there are always one or two backstabbers who may view your job as a steppingstone in their career. Unfortunately for them, you are the occupant of the position. Equally unfortunate for you, they may decide to wage a campaign to unseat you from your job.

Exactly how that is done will vary with the circumstances. It may consist of an attempt to make your performance look bad, starting rumors you're looking elsewhere for a job, a few negative comments, or any combination of these and other unsavory tactics. Whatever the culprit's methods may be, it behooves you to be on guard for these backstabbers and be prepared to defend your interests when they spring into action.

Beyond someone who is deliberately trying to undercut your job, there are any number of other troublemakers who for one reason or another can make it difficult for you at work. Coping with these people is a necessity, since if they're allowed to operate unchecked, they can undermine your credibility and hamper your job performance. Some of them may be little more than an annoyance, while others may present a real threat to your career. Whatever the case may be, knowing who they are and how to react will make your life at work a lot easier. Let's look at a few of the types of troublemakers who can cause you problems.

Battling Back Against Backstabbers

Someone who is either after your job, or competing with you for future promotions, may decide the way to win is to make you look bad. There are many forms of dirty tricks such a person can employ. It may consist of circulating rumors, blaming you for on-the-job mistakes which aren't of your doing, and criticizing your work either openly or behind your back. Whatever form this behavior takes, you can't let it go unchecked.

On the other hand, you don't want to confront the person openly in front of co-workers. If you do, the person will likely just deny your accusations leaving you looking foolish in front of your peers. Therefore, once you have definitely established that someone has been up to dirty tricks, take them aside in private and raise the issue. Control your temper and address the subject in a matter-of-fact way, as though you're making a casual inquiry. For example, say something such as, "Janet, I just wanted to let you know that several people have told me you're making disparaging remarks about my work. Do you have a problem with anything? If so, I'd like to know so we could straighten it out." More than likely, the other person will deny saying anything about you which is all right, since the important point is that you got your message across. Most of the time when this happens the negative behavior grinds to a halt.

Sometimes backstabbers play more subtle games by looking for opportunities to take advantage of you. For example, if you happen to be late one morning a nemesis may be certain to let the boss know about your late arrival. You certainly can't make an issue out of something like that and such petty actions over a period of time can work against the perpetrator. This is especially true if it's being done against several people in your department. Sooner or later the culprit will have alienated everyone and lost all credibility within the group.

Aside from letting a backstabber know you're on to his or her game, the best way to win is to go about your business and let your job performance speak for itself. These types inevitably spend more time creating trouble than they do working. As a result, their job performance suffers by comparison with others, and eventually little they say is taken at face value.

Defending Against Buck-Passers

Have you ever been brought up short by your boss saying something such as, "Mark said you were doing the reports this week. Are they done?" Of course, this is the first you have heard of it, which you quickly state. Actually, it's not unusual for people to be pinpointed as responsible for something they knew nothing about. Sometimes it's just a simple misunderstanding where the parties to a conversation weren't too clear about who was to do what. In other instances, it's a deliberate attempt to pass the buck and avoid blame for a failure to act. Whatever the case, buck-passers can cause plenty of headaches if their actions go unchecked.

Buck-passers are at their best when they are working on a joint task in conjunction with others. This makes it easier for them to sluff their responsibilities off on their co-workers. They don't carry their share of the workload and when called upon to answer for what they were supposed to be doing will claim it was someone else's responsibility. They will generally try to pin the blame on someone who isn't present at the moment so they can avoid a face-to-face challenge.

The best way to deal with confirmed buck-passers is to avoid working with them in the first place. Naturally, that's not always possible, so if you get stuck working on something in conjunction with a buck-passer be clear about who is responsible for what in terms of doing the work. If at all possible, make sure your boss knows about this partition of responsibilities right from the start. This will preclude a buck-passer from later making a false assertion about something being your responsibility.

Avoiding Being a Scapegoat

A close cousin of the buck-passer is the type of individual who uses another worker as the scapegoat when something goes wrong. This sort of finger pointing is best defended against by being able to prove you weren't responsible for the alleged transgression. Of course, someone who is good at finding someone else to blame will generally point the finger at a co-worker who may not have a good alibi. Therefore, even though a boss may accept someone's protestations of innocence, the seed of doubt may be planted in the boss's mind that the innocent individual was indeed the guilty party. Here, as with buck-passers, when you are working with this sort of troublemaker, make sure the assignments are clearly defined beforehand and made known to your mutual boss.

If something should go wrong with a work assignment when you're working alongside a suspected scapegoater, try to inform the boss of the problem before the troublemaker can say anything. Then when the jerk starts pointing the finger elsewhere, it will likely be seen as a poorly conceived excuse to avoid blame. Incidentally, if you want to painlessly avoid being the target of buck-passers and backstabbers, put yourself in the position to do them a favor. That way they will be beholden to you and less likely to use you as a target for their tactics.

Grounding Office Gossips

Office gossips and other assorted pests can cause you problems in getting your work done, but generally they are little more than an annoyance. However, if they start to get to you, then you may want to shoo them on their way—diplomatically or otherwise. For instance, listening to a constant complainer can get under your skin in a short period of time, and hearing the office gossip chirping about the latest office romance isn't much better. However, before you decide to jettison these people from your office with an admonishment never to reappear, it pays not to overlook their value as a conveyor of the latest scuttlebutt. So for the most part, it pays to tolerate these types, meanwhile keeping their intrusions to a minimum.

SUCCESSFUL WAYS TO COUNTER CRITICISM OF YOUR WORK

No matter how hard you try, mistakes are inevitable, and along with mistakes comes criticism of your work. This isn't necessarily bad, assuming the criticism is constructive and well-intended, which isn't always the case. In fact, it isn't always just your boss's criticism you may have to contend with. Other managers, peers, and outsiders such as customers and suppliers may all take aim at you if they think it is justified. Even worse, some of the criticism may be wrong, or even deliberately designed to damage your reputation. As a result, you have to be prepared to defend against criticism from a wide spectrum of sources, and for many different reasons. Let's look at how you can do this successfully.

No one enjoys hearing criticism, but responding angrily or ignoring the criticism are not helpful ways of dealing with it either. Anger just implies to the giver of the criticism that you are being defensive because of your mistake. So even when you feel the criticism isn't justified, keep your powder dry and respond with facts that prove your case. Don't overlook the fact that the person giving the criticism isn't much happier about having to do so than you are about receiving it.

One common error many people make when they are criticized is to listen to what is being said and then fail to respond. Sometimes it may be necessary to think about what is being said, and in these circumstances it's appropriate to hold off commenting other than to say something such as, "Let me think about that and get back to you." Even with that, however, there's often a failure to respond to the criticism eventually. Ultimately, whether you agree or disagree with the criticism, some form of response should be made.

If you agree with the criticism, telling the person who made the remarks that you recognize your mistake will prevent future misunderstandings. It will also mark you as someone who is willing to listen, which is especially important if the criticism comes from a source outside the company, such as a customer. It's also useful to let the person know what you are doing to prevent a repetition of the error.

If you have been criticized unfairly, not responding will signal the fact that the criticism was valid. And not replying may imply to the critic that you are choosing to ignore the criticism and not do anything to correct the mistake. Although many people don't respond to criticism for fear of arousing anger, it's far more likely a failure to respond will bring about that sort of result.

Before you respond, however, it's useful to take the time to think through what you're going to say. Evaluate what the specific action was that is being criticized, and what if anything can be done to correct it. Thinking about what you're going to say beforehand helps in a couple of ways. First of all, it lets you think about the best way to present your rebuttal. Second, it gives you the chance to evaluate the possible reaction of the other party.

Hopefully, the criticism was given in private as it should be. How-ever, even if that isn't true, you should still attempt to reply to the criticism in private. Doing so publicly will give the person an incentive to be defensive about their criticism and less likely to accept your explanation.

There are a couple of common elements important in dealing with any form of criticism. The first is not to take the criticism personally. Doing so will only lead to anger and emotional responses which won't solve anything, and in fact will just make matters worse. For this reason, look at criticism as a learning process which will allow you to improve your performance. Even if the criticism is unjustified, it still presents valuable lessons as to how the situation could have been averted. Also, always try to avoid excuses for the mistake. Excuses—even when valid—only serve to make the situation worse in most cases. Emphasize instead that corrective action will be taken.

In the work environment there are often mitigating circumstances for criticism that are given by a boss. For example, someone may be criticized for not doing something they weren't trained to do. Or, the proper equipment may not be available to avoid the kind of mistake that is being criticized. Assuming these problems have been brought to a boss's attention previously, it's pointless to simply say, "If I had received training, this wouldn't have happened" or "Until we get the new machinery these errors will continue."

This may be correct, but the boss isn't going to buy that argument. The reply will most likely be, "You still shouldn't have goofed up." Furthermore, you will have turned the boss's anger up a notch, which won't help matters any. In these situations, simply acknowledge the mistake as your responsibility, and suggest casually that training and/or new equipment (as the case may be) will help you cure the problem in the future. Either way, you're saying essentially the same thing, but how you phrase it makes the difference. The blunt approach implies the boss is at fault for not providing the necessary resources, while accepting the responsibility for the mistake avoids that tension-arousing possibility.

LEARNING HOW TO USE THE POWER OF PERSUASION

Being successful at managing your career in order to give yourself greater opportunities and job security requires the ability to compete against others in a number of different ways. Foremost is being able to do your job better than anyone else. This requires more than hard work and ability. Most of all, it means you have to be able to persuade various people with different interests and opinions to see things your way. This can take many shapes and forms.

It may mean persuading someone you're the best candidate for promotion, or it might entail convincing the boss to give you the additional resources to do your job. Perhaps it means convincing a customer to buy a product, or a supplier to speed up shipment of scheduled deliveries. The specifics will vary with both your job and the circumstances of the moment. What remains constant is that your ability to persuade people to do what you want will greatly improve your chances for career success. Not only that, but it will make your day-to-day activities a lot easier to handle.

The keys to persuading people are to build trust and credibility with the people you deal with on a daily basis. You also have to remember that some people aren't going to agree with you unless they realize it's in their best interest to do so. Sometimes this can mean exerting negative pressure on them. For example, getting co-workers to sign off on a document might mean letting them know that the boss is in favor of what's being done. Left to their own choices, the individuals might not want to agree with you, but knowing that their boss does will give them the incentive for going along with you.

Another helpful tactic in persuading people to help you out is to give them an investment in what you're doing. Solicit their suggestions and ideas on how to do things. It takes very little effort to persuade someone to go along with something once they become a contributor to the idea.

Persuading people to see things your way isn't difficult, but it does require some thought. First of all, you have to decide whom you have to convince. Then you have to think about what arguments to make to convince them to go along with you. Not to be overlooked is the need to identify anyone who might strenuously object to what you're doing. These are the people who can cause you the most difficulty and are therefore the ones you want to neutralize. Although you may not be successful in convincing ardent critics to go along with your idea, if you can at least neutralize their objections, then you will have eliminated your opposition.

Sitting down and discussing what you want to do with those most vehemently opposed to your idea accomplishes a couple of things. It allows you to present your arguments, as well as learn what the objections are. Knowing the latter gives you an opportunity to answer the objections and hopefully swing someone over to your side. Even if you can't convince someone to see it your way, the fact you are willing to sit down and discuss the pros and cons of their objections may in itself soften their opposition.

You will never succeed in convincing anyone of anything unless you display self-confidence and enthusiasm about what you're proposing. This means you may need to be persistent in weakening the opposition to your ideas. Sheer repetition of the virtues of an idea can often soften someone who was initially in opposition.

By the way, there are times when it becomes impossible to reach agreement on something you're proposing. When this happens, you may want to try to get partial or conditional approval as the circumstances warrant. For instance, obtain approval to do something on a trial basis, or settle for something less than what you wanted. Having your idea implemented is a lot easier if you can get the ball rolling initially. Later on you will find it easier to expand your goal to its original format.

A few general steps for persuading people to see things your way include:

- Thinking through what you're going to say before you sit down to try to convince anyone of anything.

- Identifying who is likely to favor your idea, oppose it, or remain neutral, if more than one person is to be convinced.

* Strategizing the arguments you can use to overcome opposition.

* Encouraging those potential supporters who will be able to help you get your idea implemented.

* Ascertaining ways to appease the self-interest of anyone who will be involved in approving what you want. Be ready to show how the idea will benefit him or her.

* Avoiding the temptation to overdo it in trying to convince people of the wisdom of your idea. Present your case without glossing it over or promising more than is true.

* Allowing yourself to quit if you're unsuccessful initially. Persistence does pay, but never become a pest.

HOW TO COVER YOUR BUTT WITHOUT GETTING CAUGHT

You work hard to do the best job you can, but have the misfortune to make a mistake that could damage your reputation for good work, or perhaps even jeopardize your job. What do you do? Confess and take the blame? Possibly, if the circumstances warrant it, and if you have a boss who is realistic about recognizing that everyone goofs up now and then. You, however, may be in a position where your boss is looking for an excuse to nail you. It might be a personality conflict, or simply a boss whose specialty is waiting around for someone to make an error so as to lower the boom.

Whatever the reason, you may find yourself in a situation where you may have to look for ways to cover your butt. This is especially true in circumstances where you may not be totally, or even partially to blame, even though outward appearances would point the finger at you. So even though this may not be an everyday occurrence, it's wise to be prepared to cover your tracks if it becomes necessary.

What's the best way to get off the hot seat? It depends mostly on what you did wrong. If it's nothing more extreme than a simple mistake made in your work, accept your boss's criticism and humbly vow never to repeat the error. Take your promise to heart, since making the same mistake once will be accepted by any reasonable boss. Repeating your error will undoubtedly convince your boss that you either don't know what you're doing, don't care, or are simply ignoring the boss's admonishments.

If the error of your ways is something that has provoked your boss, you had better do more than simply admit your mistake. Depending upon the circumstances there are a number of possibilities you can use to get off the hook. Perhaps the mistake was something totally beyond your control. If so, be prepared to prove it. Perhaps someone else contributed to the error. That being the case, although it doesn't excuse you entirely it at least gives you someone with whom to share the blame. If it happens to be another department or unit that is partially responsible, then your boss is less likely to be as irate with you. In the boss's mind, at least, the other department isn't his or her domain so it will be assumed to be the culprit.

If all else fails and there's nothing more substantive to fall back on, then you may have to resort to the good old-fashioned survival tool of the workplace: a good excuse. The key word here is "good" since every boss has heard his or her share of excuses over the years. What separates a good excuse from a bad one is mostly the element of believability. Offering proof to go along with your alibi is even better. For example, blaming a broken tool for errors is far more credible when you have the broken tool to prove your point. Unfortunately, when people are caught short by someone they often tend to blurt out the first thing that comes to mind, and it usually isn't very convincing.

Viable exuses have another hallmark, which is that your mistake was unforeseen, and therefore whatever went wrong could not have been prevented. For example, you may tell your boss you were late because your car pool driver failed to pick you up on time. That is believable and would probably be accepted a time or two. The fourth or fifth time it happens, however, it loses its credibility, especially if the boss has previously admonished you to find an alternative means of transportation. Your not having done so wrings all the credibility out of your excuse. So if you have to jump on the excuse bandwagon, keep it simple and be able to prove it if challenged.

Be Practical About Unscheduled Time Off

One of the most common uses of excuses is to take an unscheduled day off from work. No one is a robot that can perform at peak efficiency day after day at work. People get sick, are sometimes tired, and occasionally get depressed. There are also a slew of personal affairs which crop up which can't always be handled on an after-work basis. For many people this calls for taking a day off from work. Does this damage your image with the boss, and influence your future on the job? Not if you have a reasonable boss and you use some common sense.

A boss isn't generally going to make a big issue out of someone taking a day off and calling in sick. This is especially true if your department isn't operating under a sense of urgency at the moment. Some bosses are less flexible than others in accepting a day off from work as a cure for the common cold. Normally, most bosses won't challenge directly a claim you were ill, but if they suspect otherwise then it can have an adverse impact on your job. So if you have a particularly unreasonable boss, or are worried about job security, don't casually decide to take a mental health day here and there.

In taking unscheduled time off, using a little bit of practicality can also help your cause. Everyone likes long weekends, so Friday and Monday mornings are frequently prime time for employees to plead some form of ailment or an unforeseen emergency. Taking a day or two in the middle of the week instead is much less suspicious.

Better yet, schedule a day off when you actually have a cold or other minor ailment. Many people persist in going to work and spreading their germs when they're sick so they can better use the time off when they're feeling better. Your boss, along with co-workers, will appreciate someone who takes time off when ill rather than spread the flu around the office. In fact, someone who ventures into work when ill either has a misguided sense of their value to the enterprise, or is trying to substitute dedication for incompetence.

Don't Get Caught Being Cute

Everyone is late for work on occasion, and it's the rare employee who doesn't take a little longer than usual for lunch every now and then.

Some people, however, try to be cute about it, which pinpoints them as goof-offs when they're caught by the boss. When you're late for work, don't try to sneak in the back way. This, in itself, implies that you were doing something wrong. It also applies to returning late from lunch.

If you're late for work, saunter right in as if you were on time. If excuses are asked for, don't blame it on some nonsensical alibi such as your pet alligator eating your alarm clock. Simply state the reason and apologize. For instance, "Sorry I'm late. I slept right through the alarm this morning." Any reasonable boss will understand that, especially if you aren't habitually late for work. Have an unreasonable boss? Play it the same way, since he or she isn't going to believe you anyway.

PAINLESS WAYS TO FINESSE "CAN'T-WIN" ASSIGNMENTS

If you're an exceptionally hard worker you may find yourself being handed all sorts of extra assignments by your boss. For the most part, this may not bother you, especially if your boss expresses genuine appreciation for your efforts—particularly when pay raises are handed out. On the other hand, you may discover that some assignments that come your way are lost causes no matter what you do. The reasons for this will vary. Perhaps a particular assignment concerns a project which has a great deal of internal opposition. Or, maybe the assignment is such that it's impossible to complete within the time frame assigned to it. Whatever the problem may be, these "can't win" assignments can do you a lot more harm than good. For this reason, you have to be on the alert for such projects and know how to avoid working on them without arousing the hostility of your boss.

There's nothing worse to deal with—short of being fired—than getting stuck with lousy jobs no one else wants to do. These tasks can run the gamut, from projects that are doomed to failure from the start, to tasks with impossible deadlines, to jobs that are just thankless and boring. For example, perhaps your department has been assigned a job by top management which is impossible to complete as required. If your boss isn't the stand-up type, then the odds are the assignment will be accepted. Your boss then will go about looking for one or more employees to work on the project.

From your standpoint, these projects can do nothing but cause headaches; you will waste time spinning your wheels on something that is doomed to fail. To complicate matters, you may also be expected to complete your regularly assigned work, and an even greater danger is that you may ultimately be blamed when it's discovered that the project isn't working out. After all, your boss isn't likely to take the rap. For these reasons, it pays to be ready to duck these types of "can't-win" assignments.

Show You're Too Busy to Work on the Task

A common precursor of trouble ahead is when your boss asks you whether you're busy, or what you're working on at the moment. More often than not, this is the opening remark in a conversation that may leave you muttering, "How did I get stuck with this mess?" Your primary weapon in avoiding this fate should always be a ready response which indicates you're working on a high priority task. This tactic will encourage your boss to seek out someone else.

You will not always be working on a top priority job when your boss confronts you in these situations, however. As a result, you will have to learn how to attach importance to whatever it is that you are doing. Even routine work can be used for this purpose if you attach a presumed priority to it. For example, every job has one or more routine tasks that no one likes to do and as a result this sort of work tends to get backlogged. This can be used to get you off the hook if necessary.

Accumulate this work as a safety valve and when your boss inquires as to whether or not you're busy, you will be in a position to say, "Are you kidding? Look at this pile of work! I'm still trying to catch up." Your boss may press you further as to whether or not this catch-up work can wait until a later time, but it's just as likely your assertion will be accepted. After all, your boss isn't about to say that what you're working on isn't important, since that will be seen as encouraging you to let it sit there forever.

Assuming your boss doesn't fall for your ploy and says something such as, "Drop that until later. This is more important . . ." then this is your chance to put one of your lazy co-workers to work. Suggest to your boss that someone else is more familiar with what he or she wants done. If it's possible, give a specific example of how this person handled something similar in the past. Assuming you can be convincing, you will be off the hook.

If you're still unsuccessful, use the "I can't do this and my other work" plea. At least if you have to do the dirty job, you may be able to farm out some of your work to others. If this doesn't succeed, it at least gives you a defense at some later date if a short-memoried boss wants to know why you're behind in your work.

Assuming that pleading and logic both fail and you end up working on the can-of-worms project, make sure you're not left out there alone to hang when things don't work out. Get as many people as possible involved in working on the project, and keep your boss posted regularly. Incidentally, even if you hate writing memos, this is a good time to lose that aversion. A few strategic memos will provide a paper trail, which at a later date may be useful if everyone involved has occasion to plead ignorance about any mistakes that have been made.

Recommend Someone Else for the Job

There are other tactics you can try to ward off these unwelcome assignments. If the assignment involves some degree of complexity, perhaps you can plead you don't know how to do what is required. This, of course, reflects upon your capabilities. Nevertheless, if the risk of failure on the assigned project is worse than the impact of admitting your insufficient experience in handling the job, this may be the preferred course of action.

Furthermore, you only want to use this excuse in situations where it's reasonably believable, such as not knowing how to operate a certain machine, or being unfamiliar with certain procedures. Your chances of success in avoiding the assignment in this manner are improved substantially if you are able to refer your boss to a co-worker who is familiar with what has to be done. After all, your boss isn't so much interested in who does the job as in getting it done. So if you can make a good case for someone else being more qualified to do the job your boss may move happily along. This is not the kind of task you will want to pawn off on your best friend.

It's reasonable to expect that the person you recommend for the assignment may find out about your referral and raise the issue with you. If so, defend your actions by saying, "I thought you had done this sort of assignment before, Marsha, or I wouldn't have mentioned you." If it's brought up, deny any knowledge that you consider the assignment to be in any way a bad one. In fact, if it's feasible, you might want to imply you thought you were doing the person a favor. For instance, say something such as, "What are you complaining about? That assignment gives you a chance to interact with the big shots. That certainly can't hurt your future prospects." Don't overdo it on this angle to the extent that your reasoning becomes transparent.

WHAT TO DO IF YOUR EMPLOYMENT RIGHTS ARE VIOLATED

One of the most serious experiences you can encounter at work is to find that your employment rights have been violated due to the actions of one or more managers or co-workers. A company may have all the policies and procedures in place to provide equal employment opportunities, yet these can be easily undermined by the deliberate or inadvertent actions of one or more individuals. If you are the victim of such actions, then it's incumbent upon you to challenge this behavior head-on.

Avoid Being the Victim of Subtle Discrimination

You may find yourself working in an environment where you feel you're being treated in an underhanded fashion that amounts to subtle discrimination. It may be that you don't feel there is any evidence to prove this, but you may have a genuine concern that you're not being treated fairly. This type of conduct can be a form of discrimination which is illegal— such as ageism, racism, or sexism, or may be in the form of favoritism practiced by a boss toward those who are less deserving in terms of job performance.

Anything illegal should be challenged and the proper steps taken to remedy the situation. Some subtle discrimination may not be legally actionable or prohibited by law. Nevertheless, it still presents a roadblock to you in the pursuit of your career. So it behooves you to make a conscious effort to protect your interests to the best of your ability. How you go about doing this will vary with the details of your situation, but there are several measures you can take to counteract this sort of behavior.

One of the most common forms of subtle discrimination takes place against women in the workplace. Their male counterparts may follow the letter of the law in terms of actionable discrimination, yet ignore the spirit of the law by some of their actions. For example, a female worker in a predominantly male environment may find her recommendations being ignored or belittled. She may also find herself being socially ostracized by not being invited to lunch and other business-related functions. This is difficult to deal with by virtue of its very subtlety, but if you are in such a situation you have to recognize it or face being relegated to second-class status.

Unfortunately, it isn't that easy to confront, since sometimes it can leave you wondering if the actions are deliberate or merely a figment of your imagination. Rest assured that if it happens on more than one isolated occasion, it's a real problem. Awareness is the first step in combating this form of discrimination. If you're on your guard for this sort of behavior you will eventually notice that one or two males in your work group tend to be the major perpetrators of these actions. Knowing this will give you the basis for working on the problem.

There are two approaches that can prove to be helpful. First, make every effort to establish good working relationships with those members of the opposite sex who aren't sexually biased. Aligning yourself with these people will, over a period of time, isolate the one or two practitioners of subtle discrimination. Once they see they have no audience for their actions, it will most likely be curtailed.

The second approach to take is to make every effort possible to be assertive in presenting your viewpoints. Invite yourself along to lunch and make your position known in meetings and other business gatherings. Remember, the objective of those practicing the subtle discrimination is to alienate you. If you don't assert yourself, you will be aiding them in accomplishing their goal. The same form of subtle discrimination can be practiced against any group whether it's based on age, minority status, or sex. Needless to say, you can accept it or combat it. Accept it, and those that discriminate win, while standing your ground will defeat the perpetrators.

In terms of protecting your rights when they are violated legally it is in your best interest to be aware of actions that appear to affect you adversely and may be in violation of one or more laws protecting your employment rights. If the action is taken by an individual, then you may want to follow the formal procedure set up within your company to rectify the action. Then again, if you feel your employment rights are being violated and you can't get satisfaction from within the company, you are well advised to consult an attorney experienced in these matters.

THE SENIORITY TRAP: IT ISN'T THE SAFEGUARD IT USED TO BE

You may be in a position where you have spent a number of years in a job, and for that reason feel that your job is secure. This may have been true in the past, and for a fortunate few today it may still have some validity, particularly if you are in a union job protected by a labor agreement, or a profession where the more experience you have the more valuable you are.

For the most part, however, beyond the experience required to become fully productive in a job, additional experience doesn't translate into additional gains in productivity. Seniority brings with it higher pay levels, and many cost-conscious employers no longer have a paternal attitude about retaining high-priced help as a reward for long years of service. As a result, if you are counting on your length of service for job security, you may one day discover to your dismay that it's more of a handicap than a help.

Employers aren't going to pay more for older experienced workers if they can get the same level of expertise a lot cheaper by employing someone who is younger and less expensive in terms of a paycheck. There are, of course, laws against age discrimination, but when money is involved there is no shortage of high-priced hired guns who look for loopholes in even the most airtight legislation. Therefore, as you go about your job feeling secure that your age and seniority protect you from a pink slip, there may be a consultant's report circulating in top management recommending ways to reduce payroll costs. One of those ways may be to substitute less expensive labor to do your job. If so, you may become reorganized, merged, or downsized out of a job.

For everyone in this situation, this isn't necessarily all bad, especially if early retirement suits you fine, and a generous severance package solves your financial concerns. On the other hand, if you want to keep working, or can't afford early retirement, then even if you have a great deal of seniority, you have to think about career alternatives. The bottom line is that no matter how much time you have had on a job, you should always be taking courses to keep your job skills current. That alone can make your position more secure if cutbacks become reality. In addition, it's prudent to explore other job alternatives that you can pursue if you are targeted for a layoff.

If it's early in your career, even though you are in a position that has historically provided secure employment through to retirement, don't take this for granted. Otherwise, you will be ill-prepared to adjust if the situation should change and your job becomes vulnerable. There will always be some people who spend a lifetime with the same employer, but they will be few in number, so it's not wise to try and play the odds. Instead, always be looking for ways to improve your range of skills so you maximize your job possibilities no matter what might happen. That way, your future will be under your control, and not the control of a single employer, industry, or the economy in general.

On the other hand, if you like what you're doing, and the immediate outlook with your employer is reasonably secure, don't arbitrarily job hop. Those who move up the career ladder fastest are often those who spend the better part of their working life with one employer. After all, whenever you start a new job you're beginning again as an unknown quantity. Therefore, you have to prove yourself all over again. So if you're fortunate enough to have a good job with stability, don't jump the gun. Prepare yourself for any eventuality, and that way you can guarantee your future security.

Chapter

3

HOW TO GET AHEAD— EVEN IN A DEAD-END JOB

There will always be a lot of competition for promotions, but with companies tending to operate in a slimmed-down mode, it's even tougher to get ahead. This problem is compounded if your particular job isn't one that offers solid opportunities for advancement. Nevertheless, no matter how poor the promotion prospects are where you work, there are a number of measures you can take to improve your promotion opportunities.

First, you will need to learn how to get your talents recognized by those with the power to promote you, either within your present department, or somewhere else within the company. This means learning some simple tactics such as how to sell your ideas to superiors, and otherwise practice a little bit of self-promotion. After all, if you don't toot your own horn, no one else is going to do it for you. Of course, the trick is to do so unobtrusively, since obvious boasting can hurt rather than help your cause.

There are a number of ways to get yourself recognized. One is by being able to solve the tough tasks that come your way. Most people are quite competent at handling their routine work, but many tend to buckle under and beg off when problems come their way. Therefore, if you can gain recognition as a problem solver, you're well on your way to the first rung on the promotion ladder. Another useful tactic is to impress people outside your immediate department with your capabilities. Recognition comes a lot faster when a boss hears about your abilities from elsewhere within the company. This, incidentally, tends to make your boss look good too, and that alone can get you preferential treatment the next time a promotional opportunity rolls around.

Beyond these strategies, there is the routine need to practice a little bit of office politics. It's something some people tend to neglect, but even if you don't find it to be a particularly pleasurable task, it's a factor that can't be ignored if you want to get ahead. Unfortunately, the biggest obstacle you may face is the job itself. You may have the misfortune to be working in a job with no apparent likelihood for any type of promotion. Even in that case everything isn't lost, and you should avail yourself of opportunities to learn new skills which will help you to move up elsewhere. This chapter explores all these topics, as well as others that focus on how to advance your career even when the odds may be stacked against you.

SOME SHREWD WAYS TO GET PROMOTED

If you are willing to sit patiently by waiting for your turn to be promoted, then you had better have plenty of patience. Everyone wants to get ahead and some people are pretty aggressive about pursuing this goal. So anyone who plugs away with the expectation that his or her efforts will be recognized automatically won't be seeing a fatter paycheck in the near future. The simple fact is that you have to know how to manage your career to position yourself for a promotion. Otherwise, you will watch your peers who are skilled at doing this moving ahead of you on the career ladder.

Have you ever seen a promotion take place where someone wasn't griping because they didn't get the job? Actually, it's good to have the self-confidence to think that you can do a job better than someone else. Sometimes though, these subjective conclusions are reached without delving too deeply into the facts of the situation. If you think back to the last time someone was promoted where you work, you can probably pinpoint quite accurately why the losing candidates were unsuccessful.

Generally, promotion selections revolve around the dual factors of competency and cooperation. Which of these two factors receives the greatest weight depends primarily upon the judgment of the manager making the selection for promotion. Competency is simply the accumulation of factors that represent a person's ability to do a job better than someone else. It encompasses education, work experience, and so forth. Cooperation is the selecting individual's mainly subjective evaluation of how well a candidate gets along with the person doing the promoting, and to a lesser degree how well they interact with other people. If the candidate being considered for promotion doesn't work for the manager doing the promoting, this judgment is based upon interviews and recommendations. Therefore, except for the rare promotion that is given primarily on the basis of favoritism, the promotion selection process isn't as complicated as it sometimes seems to be.

This being the case, why the constant carping by those who don't get promoted? One source of dissatisfaction are employees who base their gripes on being on the job longer than anyone else. They feel that seniority alone deserves recognition in the form of promotions, even though they may not have the education and/or technical skills of the successful candidate. Rather than face this reality and pursue the necessary education and training they lean instead on the seniority crutch. Therefore, no matter how long you have worked at a job, step number one in positioning yourself for promotion is to get the necessary training to be current in your field.

The other major trait that unsuccessful candidates for promotion exhibit is an inability to get along well with those people who hold power positions within the organization. First and foremost is their immediate boss, but this also includes others who are in a position to influence promotional decisions. Someone who is perceived as not getting along well with others isn't considered to be a team player. Cooperation with others, however, is the element over which you can exercise the most control to influence your career progress at work. This means demonstrating a "can-do" willingness in working with others and avoiding conflict with your boss over the nitty-gritty annoyances of the work-place.

Aside from the two general considerations of competence and cooperation, there are a number of specific measures you can take to gain an edge in the competition for promotion.

1. *Don't be afraid to accept horizontal moves to gain additional experience.* The more skills you have in as many areas as possible, the greater your value to the company.

2. *Be highly visible.* Make sure your accomplishments are known to others. You may be the hardest worker in the world but if no one knows about it you may be laboring in vain. Do this subtly by such tactics as writing briefing memos and progress reports, and if it's at all justified, send copies to people who are in a position to further your career.

3. *Give credit to others.* Sharing the credit for your accomplishments will build you a base of allies who will not only tout your skills, but will assist you in pressure situations when you're trying to get a tough task finished.

4. *Be willing to take on tough tasks that can further your career.* Just be careful to avoid those projects that are "can't-win" assignments.

5. *Be positive in your outlook on a daily basis.* This is especially effective during pressure situations, when many of your peers may be exhibiting pessimism.

6. *Be flexible in your thinking.* With constantly evolving technology and corporate upheaval, being flexible about adapting to changes sets you apart from those who are resisting change.

7. *Discuss your career goals with your boss.* Ask for guidance and advice. Letting your boss know of your goals enlists him or her as a coach in terms of spelling out what you have to do to be successful. Don't be afraid to let your future expectations be known. The alternative may be to hear a boss say, "I would have put you in for that promotion, but I didn't know you were even interested."

8. *Keep records of your accomplishments and don't overlook what at the time may seem to be trivial.* If the time comes to plead your case for a promotion you want all the ammunition you can muster readily available.

9. *Know your boss in terms of what pleases and displeases him or her.* Inadvertently alienating your boss can undo all of your other efforts at working toward a promotion.

10. *Position yourself to be where the action is within your company.* Look at where the company is focusing its resources, since the growth areas of the business are where the promotional opportunities will be.

TACTICS FOR PROVING YOUR WORTH AT PERFORMANCE APPRAISAL TIME

Formal performance evaluations are something that is dreaded equally by the person doing the evaluation and the person being evaluated. There are several reasons this is so. One of the more prevalent causes of poor evaluations is the form used itself, because it is often poorly designed to cover the components of the job being evaluated. Another problem is that many managers just aren't very good at evaluating people. This isn't entirely their fault, since it requires a fair amount of preparation to do a good job, and most managers don't have the time to do this properly.

A lesser known reason for less than satisfactory evaluations is a failure on the part of employees to be prepared to prove their value when they sit down to be evaluated. All too often, employees say little or nothing, sign off on an evaluation, and then grumble about it to family and friends. Much of this failure lies in not taking the time to periodically assess your own performance, as discussed in chapter two. But even when this has been accomplished, there still remains the need to present your position properly when you sit down with your boss to be evaluated. So let's look at some of the do's and don'ts that can make your next performance evaluation session more productive.

Be Prepared with Documentation

To be successful when you sit down with your supervisor for your next performance evaluation, you have to be prepared to demonstrate what you have accomplished since the last rating period. You can't expect your boss to have kept detailed records of your performance. It's too time-consuming, especially when you consider that there are a number of people being supervised by the same individual. Also, you may have had compliments and achievements of which your boss isn't aware. These incidentally don't have to be of any earth-shaking significance. The important factor is that they indicate a steady performer who excels at doing his or her job.

Putting together a record of your achievements is an ongoing task. If you wait until just prior to your evaluation to start thinking about what you have accomplished since the last rating period, you may discover that your memory isn't quite as good as you had thought. Furthermore, a lot of what has transpired may seem relevant when it happens, but won't be remembered very long after the fact.

For example, you may frequently volunteer to do difficult jobs, but unless you keep some form of record then all that either you or your boss can go by are generalities. As a result, a block for cooperation on a performance evaluation form may be filled in by your boss with a remark such as, "employee is very cooperative." That's fine as far as it goes, but if you have readily available evidence of volunteering for twenty difficult assignments during the past year you can point this out to your boss. This could lead to a more specific comment on the form such as, "Employee is very cooperative, as evidenced by volunteering for twenty priority projects during the past year." This type of definitive record of your accomplishments is much more convincing when people review your evaluations.

This sort of specific information is seldom contained in the formal record of performance evaluations. The reason is simple. Neither the boss nor the employee have a record of what the employee has done in the preceding period. In fact, if a boss remembers anything it may well be any negative aspect of your performance. It isn't that the boss is being vindictive, but merely that any action requiring the boss to criticize some aspect of your performance will be remembered and documented, while your ongoing performance—no matter how good it is—is likely to be taken for granted. For this reason, if you can provide documentation at review time to assist your boss in making specific comments about your performance, you will end up with a better performance evaluation.

Incidentally, you don't have to be too detailed about collecting and keeping track of performance-related information between review periods. A simple folder into which you can throw notes where you jotted something down about your performance is sufficient. You can also retain any written memos or other documentation you may receive from others which praises your performance.

As for the type of information to collect, don't overlook anything that may add gloss to your record. It's easy to do this, since most of the praise you receive will be in passing and not of particular significance in and of itself. Its importance comes from cumulative impact over the performance period. For example, another department head commenting that you did a nice job on something is relatively uneventful. However, many of these comments over the course of six months or a year are direct evidence of your superior performance over an extended period of time.

Along with keeping notes of your positive accomplishments, it's also worthwhile to keep a record of anything that went wrong during the evaluation period. This sort of information can come in handy if your boss should raise some negative issue concerning your performance. It may well be that there were extenuating circumstances beyond your control that contributed to the mistake. Having this information available to refresh a boss's memory can prevent a heated disagreement over what has happened in the past.

Incidentally, don't just treat the evaluation as a summary record of past performance. Take this opportunity to discuss with your boss what steps you can take to become a more valued employee. This is a great time to get a commitment for future training which might ordinarily be shuttled aside with a "see me later" during the normal course of business. This is one of the few opportunities during the year—if not the only one—in which you and your boss have time to discuss your future, so take advantage of it. Hopefully, you will agree jointly on goals for the forthcoming year, but often these are so generalized as to be useless.

Therefore, avail yourself of the opportunity to agree on goals that are as specific as possible.

No matter what happens, always avoid getting involved in a heated disagreement with your boss. This can happen, since your boss will undoubtedly bring up areas where improvement on your part is sought during the coming year. This is almost a "knee-jerk" reaction to the desire of a boss to motivate employees to improve their performance. Therefore, unless the areas where improvement is sought are unrealistic, don't get involved in a nit-picking disagreement. Instead, agree with the boss that you too feel improvement can be made in such and such an area. Doing this gives you rapport with your boss, who probably isn't any happier about giving criticism than you are at receiving it.

Being realistic and recognizing that you do have areas where improvement is called for helps make the evaluation session go a lot smoother for both you and the boss. If that's not incentive enough, keep in mind that in most cases a pay raise recommendation will be forthcoming sometime shortly after the evaluation is concluded. So it's to your advantage not to have an unhappy boss when the evaluation concludes.

HOW TO TURN PROBLEMS INTO OPPORTUNITY

At work, as in life in general, things don't always go as smoothly as one would like. Problems arise, and have to be dealt with. Although you may view on-the-job problems as one more hassle to be dealt with, they shouldn't be dismissed simply as just another burden with which to contend.

No one likes job-related problems, but if you learn how to become a good problem solver it will substantially increase your visibility with your boss and other senior managers. After all, coming up with the solution to a perplexing problem at work can make life easier for your boss, and that isn't likely to go unappreciated. Naturally, every problem won't present an opportunity for you to shine, but when the occasion arises it pays to know how to proceed.

As you know, anyone who goes looking for problems is generally viewed as being young and reckless, or on the verge of senility, depending upon the age bracket in which they fall. These aren't unreasonable thoughts, since opening up a can of worms isn't the sort of golden opportunity people seek out. Yet problems at work arise on a regular basis and someone has to solve them. For many of your peers, the appearance of a problem sends them scurrying to the boss on the assumption that solving problems is what the boss gets paid to do.

On the other hand, if you look at it from the boss's perspective, people bringing problems to the door are about as welcome as a cold shower in the morning. For this reason, a boss can quickly develop a soft spot in his or her heart for any employee who goes about solving problems, or at least presents them with recommended solutions. Therefore, although you don't want to go hunting for problems to solve at work, your ability to resolve those that come your way can do much to further your value in the eyes of your boss.

How do you go about solving problems? The nature of the problem will dictate what specific actions you take, but in terms of general problem-solving techniques there are certain steps to be followed. These include:

1. *Decide if you have a problem in the first place.* Something isn't a problem just because someone says it is. Everything from routine complaints to one-time mistakes are a daily given in the business world. Unless something is preventing you from doing your work effectively, or is otherwise affecting your working environment, it's probably not anything you have to worry about. As a general guideline, unless something requires some action to be taken to resolve it, it isn't a problem you have to worry about.

2. *Pinpointing the problem.* Problems aren't always what they appear to be and jumping to conclusions in identifying a problem can only make matters worse. For example, let's assume you have been making too many errors in some aspect of your work. Your boss may jump the gun and chew you out on the assumption you're screwing up. In actuality, the errors may result from your having to rush to meet deadlines because you are not receiving the input you need on time. Here, the problem isn't that you're goofing off, but that information you need isn't being furnished on a timely basis. Before this particular problem can be resolved, it's necessary to find out why the input is late. Only after identifying the reason for the tardy

information and taking action to cure the situation will this problem be resolved.

Naturally, a good manager will make inquiries before jumping the gun and pinning the blame on someone erroneously. Yet the underlying causes of some problems aren't always obvious unless you take the time to identify them.

3. *Look for alternative solutions to the problem.* Many problems can be solved through a variety of solutions. Always try to consider the alternatives and identify the pros and cons of using each solution.

For the most part, many of the problems you have at work won't require a lot of digging to determine either the problem or the solution. It's the occasional problem that requires a little bit of thought about how it can be resolved that will give you the chance to stand out as a problem solver in the eyes of your boss. Why is this so? Let's think about the reality of what happens when someone runs up against a problem. Most people head for the boss's office and drop the problem in the boss's lap. If it's something that concerns them, and it usually is or they wouldn't be dealing with it in the first place, they may badger the boss to resolve the problem. Since the boss isn't a magician, he or she will obviously have to go through the exercise of getting the facts before deciding what to do.

Let's suppose that you nail down the problem, its cause or causes, and come up with one or more possible solutions before you go to the boss. Not only have you saved the boss a lot of legwork, but you've also showed you know how to think on your feet by pinpointing the problem and coming up with solutions. The end result is that you turn a problem into an opportunity to showcase your problem-solving skills to your boss. Even if you're a cynic who feels your boss couldn't care less about your problem-solving abilities, look at it another way. He or she will sure appreciate you doing the work they normally have to do when your peers play dump and run with their problems. So even though some of your work-related problems can be headaches, at least you can use them to your advantage.

FOOLPROOF WAYS TO PRACTICE SELF-PROMOTION

Your nature may be such that you have little or no interest or inclination to do any self-promotion, in terms of touting your good work to those in a position to do you some good. You may, in fact, be someone who gets upset when you see a co-worker who is always trying to convince anyone who will listen as to how he or she—to hear them tell it—is the glue that holds the company together. Naturally, someone who practices such overt self-promotion isn't taken very seriously by anyone. There are, however, others who are skilled at practicing more subtle forms of polishing their image with the people who matter. Although you may find this to be distasteful, it is in your best interest to practice a minimum of self-promotion if you want to get ahead.

If there's one secret to successful self-promotion, it's being able to do it without being obvious about it. Frankly, the basic element in promoting your image is to go about doing your job as efficiently as possible. Unfortunately, that in itself doesn't always suffice, since you have to compete with peers who continually seek to sell themselves as the best and the brightest. Therefore, you can plod away in obscurity without ever getting the recognition you deserve, while less conscientious and competent peers are rewarded based on little more than their public relations efforts. So if you happen to be someone who is reticent about touting your abilities, you had better strive to overcome this trait. Otherwise, you may find yourself seething with frustration as less competent peers get the acclaim, pay raises, and promotions that follow.

Use Memos to Promote Your Cause

Fortunately, you don't have to act like a circus ringmaster to publicize your achievements. All you really have to do is invest a little time and thought into how to get yourself some recognition without seeming to do so. The first step in your strategy is to learn the knack of writing timely and effective memos to your boss and other senior managers. If you're like most people you probably don't write any memo you don't have to. Nevertheless, sending brief updates on your work in progress gives you a chance to show how you are solving problems and otherwise doing an all around bang-up job.

You don't just want to pepper your boss with paper, so you have to think about what to send and when to send it. The trick is to send a memo anytime you have succeeded in solving a problem involving some project on which you're working. By letting the boss know about it, you're keeping him posted on the job which you should be doing anyway, and also promoting your own cause.

Certainly, there are bosses who don't like to receive memos, preferring instead to be briefed in person. If your boss is this type, then use your meetings to demonstrate subtly how competent you are. However, it's still good to get things committed to writing since this provides a permanent record. One way to do this is to brief the boss and at the same time state that you worked up a memo containing further details if he or she wants more information. Chances are the boss may not even read it under these circumstances, but other people on the distribution list will.

In deciding which people to put on the distribution list for your memos, make sure to include any senior manager you can possibly justify as a recipient. Making yourself known to these people is crucial to your long-term success. A word of caution though. If you are working on something which has the potential to become a disaster, you may not want to be sending out memos until the task is far enough along to be certain of its success. Otherwise, you may find yourself being remembered as the one who worked on the project that got all screwed up.

NOTE: By the way, even more important than practicing self-promotion is avoiding self-destruction. This can happen if you're working on something that isn't going the way it should, but you neglect to keep your boss posted until a crisis occurs. The last thing any boss wants is surprises, so when things aren't going as planned, don't keep your boss in the dark. You may not earn any points for letting a boss know about potential trouble, but it's preferable to do this rather than to let your boss look bad because he was not informed of problems beforehand.

Cater to Your Boss's Whims

Since your objective is to practice self-promotion, what could be better than having the very person you are trying to convince do some promoting for you? That person is, of course, your boss, but can you get your boss to sing your praises or is this just pie-in-the-sky wishful thinking? Actually, it's not that hard to do, but is easily overlooked.

What you have to do is cater to the likes and dislikes of your boss in terms of operating procedures. Everyone's personality is different and every boss has his or her own little quirks about how they want things done. Many of these idiosyncrasies are often ridiculed by subordinates out of earshot of the boss. Some employees even make a practice of trying to slip something by the boss without conforming to the boss's way of doing things. This usually doesn't succeed in achieving anything other than the boss telling the person to do it the way the boss wants it to be done.

You, on the other hand, can play this game for all it's worth by catering to the boss's pet peeves. If the boss likes memos to be written in a certain format, then do it that way. If the boss wants lengthy reports, or conversely, no reports at all, then follow his or her wishes. Bucking a boss's desires, no matter how silly they may seem to be, only serves to tick the boss off. So whether it's inefficient, ineffective, or reinventing the wheel, giving the boss what he or she wants without quibbling about it puts you a step ahead of your peers in the boss's eyes.

Where does the promotional aspect come up? A boss who is continually frustrated by employees who don't do things the "right way"— which is the boss's way—will often single out the one subordinate who always follows directions. At staff meetings, a comment may be made such as, "Phyllis is the only one who always uses blue buck slips on everything I have to sign. I hate to keep reminding you people, but this is how I know what needs to be signed and what doesn't."

Whatever the specifics may be, your own boss is touting your abilities. Naturally, your peers may not think highly of your bureaucratic achievement, but the boss will, and that's the person who counts. It's also not uncommon for a boss to make comments to other managers about such and such being the only one who knows how to follow directions. This may seem to be a pretty minor matter in the broad scheme of things;

it isn't though, for one simple reason that a lot of people tend to over-look: Despite all the rhetoric about experience, credentials, and hard work, whom the boss does favors for is, in large part, a subjective judg-ment based upon whom the boss likes. Everybody likes those people best who do things the way you want them to be done. For this reason, cater-ing to the boss's personality is a self-promotion device that shouldn't be overlooked.

There are several other aspects to self-promotion that are worth men-tioning. The first is personal appearance. Although you don't have to march in lock-step with the fashions of the moment in terms of how you dress, you do want to try and not stand out like a sore thumb. After all, the objec-tive is to call attention to your talents, not your mode of dress. The second factor is to always avail yourself of opportunities to do favors for people on the job. They will usually reciprocate when you most need a favor which helps you with your work. Beyond that, it puts people in a frame of mind to want to help you out, and you never know who may be the recipient of a nice word about your willingness as a team player. Finally, you should always take advantage of opportunities to do charity work and get your name mentioned in internal newsletters or trade publications.

HOW TO GET OTHERS TO PRAISE YOUR WORK

As discussed in the prior section, you have to take the initiative in get-ting your performance noticed by people who are in a position to give your career a boost. One successful strategy results in having others sing your praises to the boss. The major benefit of this approach is that it doesn't have the self-serving undertone that can taint the message when you're doing your own self-promoting. There are two distinct avenues to pursue in getting other people to tout your achievements. One is to gar-ner praise from people within your own company. The second approach is to have customers and suppliers commend your work if your job requires you to deal with outsiders. Since satisfied customers are one of the fundamental concepts stressed by many companies, an employee praised by a customer will earn instant recognition. Therefore, learning how to get outsiders to tout your talents will go a long way in nudging your career forward.

You may be familiar with the term *rainmakers,* which refers to lawyers, consultants, and other professionals whose strength is attracting business to their firms. In effect, you want to become a rainmaker in terms of bringing in favorable comments from outsiders. How do you go about harvesting this praise? For the most part, it consists of doing a good job in dealing with customers or suppliers. Customers who are pleased with the treatment they receive from you may well mention this to your boss or other people they deal with within the company. In fact, some customers may go to the extreme of not wanting to deal with anyone but you in transacting business. If this happens, your value to your employer is increased immeasurably.

There's no particular secret in garnering customer satisfaction with your work. It simply requires you to always remain calm and courteous and attempt to satisfy the customer even under trying circumstances. This isn't always easy to do, since if your job does require you to deal with customers, you know some of them can be downright demanding and testy.

Keeping a calm demeanor when dealing with an irate customer will go a long way toward calming the person down. Although an angry customer may not sing your praises to others, if you try to resolve the problem in a reasonable way, he or she isn't likely to make a complaint. Although this doesn't score any points from the favorable side of the ledger, at least it prevents negative comments from reaching your boss and others. That in itself works in your favor, since if your peers have customers complaining to the boss and you don't, this alone is a feather in your cap. After all, if there's one thing a boss doesn't like, it's having to deal with angry customers.

Perhaps your job requires you to deal with suppliers rather than customers. Here, too, diplomacy can work wonders. Although with suppliers you may have to be hard-nosed in getting on-time deliveries, as well as bargaining on price, doing so reasonably can work in your favor. For example, if you develop a reputation for treating suppliers fairly, then they will be more willing to come through for you in a pinch when you may need an expedited delivery to meet urgent needs. Developing a reputation as someone who can get the goods delivered will have you held in high esteem by those within the company who depend on timely supplier response in order to do their jobs.

Perhaps the nature of your job doesn't involve any outside contact with customers, suppliers, or the general public. That doesn't mean you won't have people who depend upon your performance to do their own jobs. No matter what someone's job is, to some extent they deal with people who are in effect customers for their work output. This may be other departments or groups within your company, or perhaps just your peers within your own department. No matter, if you are efficient and cooperative in meeting their needs, then they will be appreciative. Beyond that, in an informal way, they will make their satisfaction with your efforts known to your boss. It certainly doesn't hurt your cause if your boss is having coffee with other managers and is told about what a crackerjack employee he has.

All in all, always striving to do your best work can get you the recognition you deserve. It may not be as often as you would like, so when someone makes favorable comments be prepared to take advantage of them. For example, sometimes someone you deal with either inside or outside the company will send you a letter or memo thanking you for your efforts. Don't just file it away. Instead, send a copy along to your boss, since this serves two purposes: It will get you the recognition you deserve, and your boss will welcome this since it reflects upon the performance of his unit. As a result, the boss may well show these memos to his boss, since it's a good second-hand way for the boss to tout his managerial skills in the guise of praising an employee's performance. In this way, your efforts are made known not only to your immediate boss, but also to higher-level managers.

TEN POSITIVE WAYS TO IMPRESS PEOPLE

You may know people at work who are very good at their jobs, but find their skills to be overlooked due to a less than satisfactory attitude in their relationships with other people. The particular deficiency in people skills that is lacking can vary. Some people are short-tempered, while others exhibit an obvious attitude of superiority. Either of these traits, or any other form of bad attitude, will only serve as an obstacle to career success. Although being liked isn't linked with career success directly, being disliked is a real roadblock.

You may wonder about this statement, especially if you know senior managers who by any standards aren't very likable. That may be true, but you can rest assured that they didn't exhibit any unpleasant traits with their superiors back when they were intent on climbing the corporate ladder to success. These people were probably the same miserable jerks they are today, but they undoubtedly kept their unpleasant side subdued until they achieved a position of power.

Naturally, you can't be expected to wage a popularity campaign to curry favors from people. On the other hand, if you always act professionally, treat people fairly, and preserve your sense of humor, it will serve to create a favorable impression on the people with whom you work. Whether it's a co-worker, someone in another department, or your boss, people respond better to people they like. So let's look at some ways you can impress people on a daily basis.

1. *Be sincere when you talk to people.* Giving phony compliments fools no one, including the recipient of the compliment. If you don't mean something, don't say it.

2. *Apologize to people whenever there's a need to.* Everyone tends to lose their cool now and again at work. By apologizing, you show the other person that you recognize the error of your ways.

3. *Be nice to everyone.* People respect others who treat everyone with dignity, and not just those who can do something for them.

4. *Strive to do every task equally well, not just those in which your boss or someone higher up expresses interest.*

5. *Be willing to do favors for others.*

6. *Don't make excuses.* Be willing to do what needs to be done to get every task completed.

7. *Be cooperative.* Don't beg off when called upon to help others, or they'll do the same in return.

8. *Meet your obligations.* Don't leave people dangling because you procrastinate and don't meet deadlines.

9. *Maintain your sense of humor in pressure situations.* People respect those who don't buckle under when the going get tough.

10. *Be a team player.* If you practice teamwork, you will have a team supporting you when you need it. If you go it alone, you will sink or swim alone.

BUILDING A POWER BASE YOU CAN COUNT ON

No matter what your job is, your degree of success is dependent upon factors other than your own hard work. If you lack the proper resources, performing your duties can be severely impaired. Naturally, if you lack resources which your boss knows you need, but budget constraints or other factors prevent you from obtaining them, then this is a factor beyond your control. The quantity and scope of the assignments you receive can also influence your output. This, too, is to a large degree something you can't influence directly.

However, there is one area that can significantly impact one's capacity to do his or her job, which is often overlooked. This involves the ability to gain the cooperation and respect of others in general, but in particular those in a position to help you perform your duties more efficiently. In effect, what you want to do is build a power base of support, which you can call upon for assistance when needed.

For example, if you have a good working relationship with the manager of another department, you can probably use this to your advantage if you need some priority assistance from that department in completing a rush assignment. Establishing this sort of rapport isn't something that can be accomplished overnight. It requires nurturing on your part, and many times involves you helping others out so they will be willing to reciprocate when you call upon them to do so.

In order to succeed, it's frequently necessary to secure the cooperation of people who don't work in your department. This isn't always easy to do for several reasons. First of all, there's probably little self-interest involved in someone from another department helping you out. It may be part of their job, but they may have other work which they consider to be more important. In addition, their workload may not coincide with yours. In other words, when you want something right away, they may be busily engaged doing something else. Finally, there's the matter of differences in personalities. Some people are easier to work with than others, but most of the time you don't have the luxury of picking and choosing which ones you want to work with.

To make matters worse, your priorities may not coincide with your co-worker's responsibilities. For example, a project which you consider to be of top priority may be of little importance to someone whose assistance you need to get the job done. As a result, you may at times have to use everything from humor to pleading to get the cooperation you need.

The most obvious way to motivate people to cooperate is to develop good working relationships. The simple fact is that people are more willing to help those they like. Therefore, always try to be pleasant even when you have to deal with unpleasant people. In addition, show respect for the other person's viewpoint. Avoid offending anyone, including employees you don't usually interact with in business, since you never know when you might need their assistance. Furthermore, people get reassigned due to promotions, job transfers, and reorganizations, so you never know when in the future someone will be in a position to help you out.

It's also useful if you learn to recognize the idiosyncrasies of people you deal with on a regular basis. Some individuals can't handle pressure, while others will rant and rave and then cooperate. Then again, you may have the misfortune to deal with someone who always promises to help, but never comes through for you when needed. Recognizing these personality traits will help you to learn ways to work around them.

Assess Your Priorities

One good rule to follow is to respect a co-worker's priorities just as you would expect him or her to respect yours. Whenever possible, try to fit your work requirements into the less demanding parts of your co-worker's schedule. This not only improves the chances that the assistance you want will be forthcoming, but it also earns the gratitude of everyone with whom you work.

Always make a conscious effort not to overstate the urgency of your requirements when you're seeking assistance. If you make a habit of labeling everything as a priority project, those you deal with will soon start to treat everything you bring them as routine. You can also try to bargain with people whose cooperation you need on a fairly regular basis. For example, perhaps on occasion you can modify the requirements of what you need, or alter the deadline for completion. Doing this will make it easier to secure assistance when you most need it.

Another useful technique would be to have some flexibility as to when you will need a co-worker's help. This will enable you to work around people who claim they are too busy to assist you at the moment. The person will then offer to do the work sometime in the future. Whenever you have a priority project, though, make your completion requirements earlier than is actually the case. For instance, if you need something within a week, give the person you're dealing with a deadline of three or four days. This will give you some leeway, not only with people who instinctively object to deadline dates, but also in the event of a possible glitch.

It's even wise to learn how to overcome routine objections. No one likes to see more work arrive when they are already busy. So when you ask someone to do even a simple task, try to develop as many individual approaches as you can to counter this reluctance.

For example, giving someone plenty of advance notice doesn't put you in the position of being the person coming in the door with unexpected and unwelcome requirements. You may also want to look for ways to help people out in unrelated areas that will tend to make them feel indebted to you. The specifics of how this is done will vary, but the important point is to always be on the lookout for creative ways to gain the cooperation you need from others.

HOW TO INCREASE YOUR INFLUENCE WITH HIGHER-UPS

Whether you're looking for a future promotion, or simply hoping to survive the next round of cutbacks, nothing can help your cause more than being respected by upper-level managers. If you're known and liked at the top, your chances of success are enhanced substantially. After all, it's top management that has the final say in everything, so if you're in management's good graces, even your immediate boss may treat you differently.

The obvious question is how to garner such influence, especially if you're not fortunate enough to be the next-door neighbor of the company president. It admittedly isn't easy to do, and it does take time, but if you're successful the effort will have been worthwhile. It should be mentioned that the size of the organization you work for also has a direct bearing on your chances for success. In large corporations, it's next to impossible for anyone at a lower level to get to know senior managers. The nature of your job has an impact as well. For instance, if you're located in a small regional office and the top brass are located at headquarters hundreds of miles away, then there's little you can do.

Nevertheless, if you have at least a passing shot of gaining some recognition from the top, it behooves you to avail yourself of the opportunities. In fact, sometimes it may not be as hard as you might imagine, so long as you become aware of how to go about making yourself known. Let's explore how that can be done.

An all-hands meeting can be a rare opportunity to impress the company leadership. When one of these group meetings takes place, it's practically standard procedure for the speaker to ask if there are any questions. Human nature being what it is, a few extroverts usually ask either the wrong questions, or the right questions in the wrong way.

For example, suppose the company hasn't been doing well, layoffs are about to take place, and a salary freeze has been imposed. Top management obviously wants to pitch the "Let's work harder and everything will work out all right" theme, which any high-school cheerleader knows as, "Go team go!" Naturally, the company president isn't going to say, "The company's going down the drain, so bail out quick or goof off until the lights go out."

These morale-building speeches are predictable, and it's equally predictable that you and everyone else want real-world answers such as, "How long will I have a job?" or "When will the salary freeze be lifted?" Unfortunately, these are not the kinds of questions the top brass wants to hear. Consequently, you can really look good by asking a question that plays to top management's tune, such as "What are the long-range prospects for the company?"

This is the type of soft question that will be loved. It's general enough to be answered without difficulty, and it gives the executive room enough to roam when giving an answer. It also indicates that you're interested in the future of the company, while questions about layoffs and salary freezes evidence self-interest. Sure, that's what you really care about, but other employees will ask those questions anyway—and get evasive answers. In the meantime, you can strike a blow for your own self-interest by not appearing to do so.

There are a variety of other possibilities for getting yourself known in the executive suite. Any work project that requires briefing senior executives is an obvious possibility which may present itself if you work in a position for which such presentations are viable. As mentioned before, serving on corporate-wide committees for charitable or other purposes may bring you into contact with top executives as well. Also, having your name in the company newsletter is another way to gain indirect exposure. Then there's always the possibility of earning recognition by virtue of being a participant in an awards ceremony. Being realistic though, the likelihood of a senior executive remembering you by virtue of any short-lived encounter is slim to none.

As a last resort, you may want to introduce yourself at some company social function. This can be a risky venture since you don't want to appear to be pushy, and the chances of anything being said that's noteworthy enough to cause the executive to remember you is pretty remote. For most people, the opportunity to be known by top management is unlikely if it's a large company, unless you happen to work in a position that calls for contact. Nevertheless, if the rare opportunity does come along, try to make the most of it.

SELLING YOUR GREAT IDEAS TO GAIN RECOGNITION

Employees often grumble that their boss is never willing to listen to their suggestions about the best way to perform their work. Sometimes this is true, while on other occasions it's simply a matter of employees not adequately justifying why their idea should be adopted. On the other hand, even when a boss encourages workers to participate in determining how best to do things, employees don't always present their ideas in a practical way.

Having someone willing to give a fair hearing to an idea is only one side of the coin. It's equally important for the person offering the idea to adequately make a case supporting the wisdom of adopting the suggestion. It's in this latter area that your success ratio in getting your ideas adopted will be based. In short, you can have the best ideas in the world, but if you don't do a good selling job, there's little likelihood they will be adopted. Fortunately, learning how to pitch your ideas isn't complicated, but does involve taking some simple measures to give your idea a better shot at being approved.

To start with, you should consider what your suggestion will achieve. If it's something that promises cost savings, for example, it has a better chance of getting a fair hearing from your boss. On the other hand, if it's something to make your job easier to do, but will cost money, it's not as likely to receive a favorable reaction. If your idea will present significant savings to the company, or alternatively increase profits, you want to show in detail the facts and figures that support your claim. This is the sort of documentation that will propel your idea forward toward approval. Incidentally, the figures you use will be estimates, but everyone knows that anyway, so don't worry about it. Just don't overdo it with outlandish claims, and support your rationale logically.

It's also important to think about the scope of the idea, since this will determine the amount of resistance you encounter in getting your idea approved. If the suggestion only has an impact on your own job, then there's little reason for anyone else to object. Conversely, if you're suggesting something that will change the way many people do their work, then it's virtually guaranteed that a lot of people will want to have their say as to whether or not the idea is implemented.

Before you even begin to pitch your idea to your boss, you should first pick it apart by yourself. By raising every possible objection you can think of, you will be able to come up with answers to explain away the potential pitfalls. This is by no means a useless exercise, since the very objections you bring up will be raised by others. Having worked up the answers beforehand, you will be able to overcome any reluctance. Of course, if you find you can't answer your own objections satisfactorily, it's better to put the idea on the back burner rather than expend your energy in a losing cause.

Assuming your idea is of sufficient magnitude that several people will have a say in its approval, you should first think about who these people are. What interest do they have in the idea? Are they likely to be for it, against it, or neutral? If you think certain people will oppose your idea, it might be worthwhile to try and enlist their support ahead of time. Perhaps there's some way you could incorporate their suggestions into your idea. If so, this will convert them from an opponent to a supporter.

Once you have collected any informal feedback, you are ready to go forward with your idea. Whenever practical, try to present your idea in person, since you will be able to counter any objections on the spot. It also makes it harder for people to raise objections to an idea when you're there in person. In addition, written requests for approval take longer and written comments of a negative nature are harder to overcome.

Incidentally, it's easy to overlook steps in the approval process if you don't learn what that process entails before you begin your quest for approval. Frequently, people unknown to you may play a pivotal role in the approval process, and an idea can be shot down by those whom you didn't realize had a say in the matter. This is especially true if you work for a larger company with a more formal and involved approval process. So if you don't know the path that your suggestion will follow to garner approval, learn it before you begin. That way, you will avoid unwelcome surprises, such as your dreaded nemesis sitting on the review board.

HOW TO ACQUIRE NEW SKILLS WHILE WORKING IN A DEAD-END JOB

You may find yourself becoming frustrated by virtue of working in a position where there is little or no hope for advancement. Admittedly, this can be discouraging, and if you don't fight the urge, it can lead to resignation on your part toward making the effort to better yourself. It's important not to give in to despair, since with enough effort you can acquire the necessary skills to work your way out of career oblivion.

There are a couple of approaches you can take in achieving success through a dead-end job. One is to expand the duties of the job itself to create another more rewarding position, while the other consists of taking measures to work your way out of the job into a position in another part of the company. Let's explore how you can go from oblivion to being recognized as a candidate for bigger and better things.

Take On the Tough Tasks

Becoming a stand-out at work can be a speedy process if you're willing to volunteer for projects that others shun. The only caution would be to make sure that these are not "can't-win" assignments. There is always some risk involved if you botch up an important task, yet it's possible that no one will remember that you volunteered for the job after everyone else turned it down. In short, there's both upside risk and downside loss if you take on a tough assignment that isn't your responsibility. In any event, if you're in a dead-end job there's little to lose and much to be gained.

Tough tasks, incidentally, don't have to be complex chores. Every department has jobs that are just plain drudgery, and these are avoided like the plague by most employees. They may be boring and/or repetitive tasks, such as filing droves of documents, an endless inputting of data into a computer, or preparing detailed reports. However, distasteful assignments can cover any range of things, from serving on senseless committees, to organizing a large meeting or company social activity.

While on the surface many of these projects have little appeal, some of them can give your career a big boost. The catch is in sorting the wheat from the chaff, because if you volunteer for the wrong assignment you may find yourself saddled with an extra chore on a more or less permanent basis.

Planning or volunteering for dirty jobs depends to a great extent on the specifics of where you work and the nature of your job; nevertheless, there are a few guidelines which are universal. One thing to consider is the visibility you can gain from taking on any unwanted task. The most obvious benefit is the gratitude of your boss for your cooperation. Any advantage this confers will depend upon 1) how badly the boss needs the job done, and 2) whether your boss is the type who demonstrates appreciation visibly when pay review time rolls around.

Some otherwise thankless tasks are beneficial if they give you a chance to broaden your contacts within the company. This type of project will allow you to meet and work with people from other departments. If they get to like you, this could eventually lead to a future position in another area of the company. The higher the position held by the people you work with, the better your chances in this regard. Committee assignments of one form or another are one good way to meet the movers and shakers within your company. In fact, there's no better opportunity for someone buried in the bureaucracy of a large corporation to get to know senior executives.

Even if that's not possible, any assignment that provides for interaction with other departments can be beneficial. By the way, if your immediate boss is a bottleneck to your advancement, then you should welcome any chance to work for someone else. It's a good start if securing a transfer is uppermost in your mind.

Remember, the more jobs you become familiar with throughout the company, the more valuable you become. Gaining experience in several areas not only gives you a wider range of career opportunities, but can also save your job if layoffs take place. Without question, people who can fill in anywhere are more likely to be kept on the payroll than are employees with less versatility.

Expand Your Duties

You can even increase your value to the company within your own department. Simply pick up the slack that exists all around you by expanding the duties of your job. There are a number of ways to do this. The simplest is for other employees to cede some of their work to you, which shouldn't be a problem. This approach does have certain pitfalls, since people tend to farm out their grunt work. Another handicap is that your diligence may go unnoticed by your boss. This is especially true since the self-defense theory of job security is far more popular than giving credit for a helping hand. Therefore, co-workers aren't likely to advertise that you're helping them out, and if your boss isn't aware of what's going on, your efforts will go unnoticed and unrewarded.

In fact, you'll just be making a co-worker look to be more efficient than he or she is. Always keep in mind that at work there's a fine line between lending a helping hand and becoming a dumpster for someone else's drudgery. For these reasons, proceed with caution if you try to expand your duties by absorbing other people's work.

If you try this approach, you might be better off approaching your boss with a well thought-out suggestion. That way, the boss will be in the loop and you will also be able to choose the work you want to pick up. All you have to do is convince the boss that so-and-so is overworked and you would be glad to take over. If you pull it off right, the boss will make the decision and the other employee won't be able to pawn less desirable tasks off on you.

Another effective means of expanding the powers of your position is by filling the gap when new procedures or equipment are introduced at work. People resist change and it's frequently the employees who complain constantly about boring jobs that resist the most when changes are made to alleviate the boredom. This creates an opportunity for you to become the resident expert on new equipment and procedures. It really doesn't matter whether it's a new computer system in the office, a revised reporting procedure for salespeople on the road, or a different technique for controlling inventory in a factory. If you dig in and familiarize yourself with the change, you'll probably become the unchallenged authority on the subject.

This will put you in a very favorable position, since if your boss relies on your expertise, you increase the power of your position, not only versus your peers, but also your boss. This can then be translated into future monetary gain. At the least, you should be rewarded when your next pay review rolls around. Beyond that, if your new-found expertise is significant to the operation of your department, a revised job description, job title, and salary may result. On a longer-term basis, you have improved your prospects for future promotion, either to your boss's job when he or she moves on, or elsewhere within the company.

REAPING BENEFITS FROM THE RUMOR MILL

You may wisely have chosen long ago not to place much faith in the constant stream of rumors that swirls around the workplace. Whether the gossip is basically scandalous, or purports to convey valuable information about some aspect of the company, it usually has little substance. In fact, even what starts out as a nugget of truth is generally so distorted after it starts to make the rounds that it might as well have been fiction from the start.

Despite the unreliability of rumors, they do serve some useful purposes. For example, it's certainly of value to you to know beforehand that your department is being eliminated in three months. Most rumors you hear, however, aren't of such earthshaking significance, but some can be useful. Knowing that the company president is making an unannounced tour of the work area one day will enable you to be shipshape and prepared. Therefore, if up until now you have been ignoring the rumor mill, you may want to reassess that strategy in the future. The fact is that there are times when you can learn a lot from the rumor mill, assuming you know how to filter fact from fiction and verify what you hear.

Assessing the credibility of rumors starts with gauging the reliability of the person giving you the information. You doubtless know one or more individuals where you work who are always spreading some form of scuttlebutt, most of which usually proves to be false. Anything you hear from such a source shouldn't be given much credibility. Despite the rare occasion when a rumor spreader proves to be correct, it isn't worth the effort to try to separate fact from fiction based on this individual's predisposition.

On the other hand, if you're told something by someone who isn't in the habit of spreading rumors, it may have some credence. But you shouldn't jump to conclusions. Instead, think about the reasons as to why what you're hearing may or may not be true. To do this, start by thinking about the person who is giving you the information. For beginners, you will want to know the source of the rumor. If he or she has access to the alleged source of information, then there's a stronger possibility the information is accurate. Nevertheless, you should still think about the personality traits of the individual giving you the news. If he or she is not prone to spreading rumors, there's a stronger likelihood that you have been fed some valid inside information. On the other hand, if he or she is gossipy and known to distort things, you should take this information with a grain of salt.

If this individual maintains the source is confidential, then you have a validity problem. Assuming he or she does verify the source, you should then assess the source's trustworthiness. You should also think about whether the individual confiding in you has an ax to grind or some other self-interest in promoting the rumor. If so, this also weighs against the possibility that what you're hearing is factual.

Whatever the source of the rumor, you should always try to check its validity with that of other sources. This is especially true if you decide to take some form of action based upon the assumption the rumor is correct. For the most part, the rumors you hear at work will tend to be of general interest and not really impact you personally. Yet it's still nice to be "in the know" on the scuttlebutt, so there's little harm in listening to the latest rumors, just so long as you don't act upon them in haste.

THE PRACTICAL APPROACH TO OFFICE POLITICS

You may have no interest whatsoever in getting involved in office politics. Some people have nothing but scorn for their co-workers who seemingly spend more time playing politics than in doing their jobs. It can be even more frustrating if one or more of these individuals is successful enough at the political game to receive preferential treatment. But whether you like it or not, politics is as much a part of the work routine as it is in the hallways of Congress. In fact, those skilled at office politics may be more successful at achieving their goals than their Congressional counterparts. So to best protect your own interests, it may pay to overlook your reservations about playing politics, and learn how to promote your own cause.

You Can't Ignore Office Politics

To begin with, how well you play the game of office politics can have a significant impact on your career. Although it may not be your nature to practice back-slapping and flattering your boss and other managers, a failure to observe the basics of office politics will work against you. For this reason, no matter how reluctant you may be to play politics you have to participate minimally to act in your own best interest.

There are several basic practices that you should follow. First off, if you hold a supervisory position, you should discourage workers who try to get on your good side through flattery instead of job performance. If they succeed, you will have a real morale problem, since other workers will perceive you as playing favorites even though you don't. So always keep the apple polishers at arm's length, but do so with enough diplomacy to avoid alienating them. Otherwise, your efforts will only succeed in getting you pegged by subordinates as being antisocial. The judicious use of excuses will work well in most situations. For example, you can turn down invitations to socialize by giving some excuse, such as being busy and so forth. You also want to be careful not to confuse someone being friendly with someone who is just playing politics. It's not always easy to separate the two, so it's important to always be pleasant with people even though you turn down their overtures to socialize.

Always be aware of the reality of your work relationships in the office politics game. It's wise never to criticize people behind their backs, since the office gossips will soon see to it that the word gets back to the individual. Once this happens, you have made an unnecessary enemy—which is the last thing you need at work. Furthermore, a few vindictive office politicians won't bypass an opportunity to knock anyone who resists their efforts to weasel their way into favor. Consequently, always be pleasant and use as much tact as possible whenever you choose to ignore the overtures of office politicians.

Don't Avoid Company Functions

If your inclination is to go to work and do your job and limit your friendships to outside the scope of work, it's unwise to avoid all the social aspects surrounding your job. For example, most companies sponsor various employee outings in the form of holiday parties, summer picnics, and the like. If you don't attend these events, you will be conspicuous in your absence. It's then only a small step from there to classify you as standoffish. The comments tend to follow the form of "What, does Carolyn think she's too good to socialize with us?" Carried to the extreme, it can lead to a conclusion that you're not a team player, which is a factor that can hinder your career. Therefore, even though you may have valid reasons for refraining from attending company-sponsored events, try to make an effort to go. Make an appearance, and bow out early.

Avoid Cliques at Work

It's natural enough that you will tend to socialize at work with those people who best share your interests. There's nothing wrong with that in and of itself; however, sometimes cliques are formed which can sometimes create the wrong impression with a boss. For example, if you consistently have lunch or coffee breaks with a certain group, then you will be known by the characteristics of that group. If it happens to be a hard-drinking, partying group known for long liquid lunches, then you are likely to be pegged as that type of individual. It doesn't matter if you don't drink and go out of your way to avoid overstaying your lunch break. In effect, you assume the group identity which supersedes the real you in the eyes of your boss. When this happens, you become the inadvertent victim of the company you keep. Therefore, since managers tend to view cliques at work as detrimental to teamwork, it pays to exercise caution in being identified as the member of a clique. In addition, managers frequently believe that cliques undermine their authority, which means that hanging around with a clique at work better bring you pleasure, because it's not likely to yield any dividends in the form of pay raises and promotions.

Develop Rapport with Your Boss

People who are well-liked do better than people who aren't. There's nothing surprising about this, but it does contain a message for you in terms of your relationship with the boss. The better you're able to establish a good relationship with your boss, the better your chances of getting ahead. Simply put, take advantage of every opportunity to get to know your boss better. If you are fortunate enough to have mutual interests apart from work to discuss, all the better. If not, at least take advantage of opportunities to praise your boss to others. There's nothing a boss likes better than hearing that one of his or her employees was singing the boss's praises to another manager. Little courtesies such as thanking the boss for doing something for you also helps. The important point is not to be a phony about it. Praising the boss about something inconsequential or otherwise brown-nosing to the extent that is obvious won't work. A good manager will recognize it and be scornful, and your peers will resent it and cut you off from the office scuttlebutt.

Don't Overlook the Little Things

Other aspects of office politics include with whom you choose to eat lunch. It can never hurt to eat lunch with your boss, so if the invitation is forthcoming, don't pass it up. On another level, eating lunch with your peers will give you an opportunity to stay tuned to the latest scuttlebutt at work. Aside from the politics involved, even though you may enjoy eating lunch alone at your workplace, getting away from your work for a while in this social setting will do you good.

You may think you're in a position where it's unnecessary for you to cultivate contacts beyond your immediate boss. This may be because you're well-liked by the boss and are a top performer on the job. This can give you assurance that your career is on the right track. Things change rapidly in the business world, however, and reorganization, or your boss leaving for another job can change things overnight. Therefore, it's important to have as many contacts as possible for the long term, which makes it worthwhile to cultivate good relationships throughout the company.

Chapter

4

HOW TO SUCCEED WITH ANY KIND OF BOSS

A lot of people like to grumble about their bosses, but rare is the individual who takes the time to think about the best way to cope with a boss. The ability to manage your boss is equally as important as the ability to do your job if you want to get ahead, and it's a lot harder to succeed at this if you have a less than ideal boss. However, there are ways to make the best of even the worst of bosses.

There are any number of ways that a boss can cause difficulty for you, some of which you can control and others which you will have to learn to accept. This chapter explores a wide range of issues surrounding the employee/boss relationship. You'll learn how to work around an indecisive boss, succeed even though your boss has no influence, and cope when your boss delegates anything and everything to you.

You will also discover some tactics for dealing with a new boss, as well as how to compete when the boss plays favorites. Beyond this, you will learn how to win when your boss rejects your requests, and when to recognize whether it's time to complain or remain quiet. Let's start by looking at what to do if you work for a boss who has a tendency to make you look bad for his or her own benefit.

WHAT TO DO WHEN YOUR BOSS MAKES YOU LOOK BAD

Your success on the job is contingent upon many factors, not the least of which is what kind of boss you have. If you're fortunate enough to have a boss who recognizes and rewards performance, you're in good shape. The flip side of the coin is that you may have the misfortune to work for someone who survives by pinning the blame on subordinates when mistakes are made. In extreme cases, you may even have a boss who is so insecure that he or she looks for ways to downgrade your efforts even when nothing goes wrong. Simply put, you may have a boss who goes out of the way to find fault with your work. If so, you may rightly feel that you're basically in a "no-win" situation, where you're assessed blame no matter what you do.

If you have a boss who consistently uses subordinates as scapegoats, then you are left with three basic alternatives: Find another job, resign yourself to constant criticism for problems you didn't create, or learn how to cope with these finger-pointing tactics. Since jobs aren't easy to come by, and accepting blame for someone else's errors will do little for either your ego or your career, learning how to counter scapegoating tactics makes sense.

Learn How to Manage Your Boss

A favorite topic of everyone is to complain about some real or perceived fault of their boss. Usually, these are inconsequential complaints, and most people will acknowledge they could do a lot worse in terms of an immediate supervisor. Of course, an unlucky few face the daily drudgery of dealing with a boss who seemingly doubles as a dictator, an office politician, or is otherwise incompetent—at least in the hearts and minds of employees.

What most people tend to overlook in dealing with a boss is that good or bad, every boss has likes and dislikes, as well as good and bad days. Bosses may also have prejudices, play favorites, and have a boss of their own with which to contend. In fact, it doesn't much matter whether you're a trainee on your first job, or an executive in a large corporation. You're still answering to someone, and many of the problems in dealing with bosses are similar.

This means to win at work, you have to learn how to manage your boss. But learning how to successfully manage a boss requires some thought, since dealing with a boss's individual personality is critical to your future. Furthermore, getting a boss to appreciate you isn't something that can be accomplished overnight. It's a slow process to build a boss's confidence in your abilities.

One basic step in earning the respect of a superior is to be open and honest in answering questions. Admittedly, it's often easier to avoid calling attention to potential problems in projects. This is especially true if a boss isn't aware of the details and is therefore unlikely to discover the inadequacies.

However, if you don't level with your boss, and the pitfalls in a project are later picked up, certain conclusions may be drawn—none of which are favorable to you. These include the impression that you either don't know what you're doing, or even worse, were trying to cover up your mistakes. And since no one likes a subordinate whose work is loaded with hidden land mines, leveling with your boss is a good way to build the trust that is needed.

Another confidence builder is to avoid the gossip circuit at work. As the saying goes, you're judged by the company you keep, and if you associate with office gossips, you will be assumed to be one yourself. Generally, managers view office cliques and gossips as detrimental to teamwork in the work place. An office clique may also be viewed as undermining the boss's authority.

One of the easiest methods for maintaining good relations with a boss is to do things the way your boss wants them to be done. This seems simple enough, but the trap is that everyone operates according to their personality traits. Where one person may be a stickler for details, someone else may not care about anything but results. A problem can arise if you have one particular tendency and your boss has a different method of operating. As a result, always strive to do things the way the boss prefers rather than the way you tend to favor. Quibbling over different means to the same end is a form of meaningless bickering which can hamper your career advancement.

Have Your Talents Recognized By Others

Of course, you may be one of the unfortunate few who have a boss less than skilled in the art of leadership. The most practical route to success at work if you have an ineffective boss is to get your talents noticed by others within the company. Although this is a fairly obvious approach, it's difficult to accomplish, since discretion is necessary when working around the person who has the greatest power over your success or failure on the job.

The best excuse for bypassing a boss is an urgent task that needs immediate resolution. Take maximum advantage of these opportunities when your boss is occupied elsewhere. It's also helpful to work well with other managers who are on the same level as your boss. Hopefully, they will let others know about their respect for your work. This approach comes in handy if you ever decide that you want to transfer elsewhere within the company.

Although it requires some degree of effort to master the art of managing your boss, it's a skill that is equally as important as managing subordinates in terms of career success. Actually, most of the issues surrounding a manager/subordinate relationship are resolved readily if you are willing to think about a boss's potential reaction to your actions. Above all else, always think about problems from your boss's perspective. This will not only improve the immediate relationship, but also serve you well in achieving your long-term career goals.

Working for a Know-It-All

If it's your misfortune to work for a boss who assumes he or she is the sole source of wisdom in the world, then you may have real problems to cope with. These people have an opinion on everything, and nothing you do will be right as far as they are concerned. A know-it-all is never wrong in his or her own eyes and can't be convinced otherwise. If you provide facts to prove a point, he or she is likely to shrug it off by saying something such as, "That wasn't what I said." To make things even more difficult for you, this individual will take the credit for anything you do that's right, and blame you for everything that goes wrong.

Know-it-all bosses can present a good appearance to those who don't have the misfortune of having to work for them. They come across as intelligent, in charge, decision-making individuals—which are typical characteristics of success in the business world. Unfortunately, they can't distinguish between what they know and what they don't know. Even on those rare occasions when what passes for praise crosses their lips, it's usually condescending enough to masquerade as an insult. For example, "You know, Kate, you can really do good work when you put your mind to it."

How do you deal with a know-it-all? The simplest way is to agree with everything they say. If it contradicts reality then go ahead and do it your way. You may even avoid criticism, since know-it-alls are so caught up in their own self-importance that they generally forget what they said thirty minutes ago. If you are caught not following their directions, act humble and profess forgetfulness. Anyone with a know-it-all's ego is likely to place more importance on your deference than on anything else.

NOTE: If you have reason to be unhappy with your boss, have a short temper, and enjoy a drink or two now and then, you may want to refrain from attending the annual company picnic, holiday party, or any other company-sponsored social event. Many an unhappy employee will attend such an affair, have a couple of drinks, and then decide it's time to level with the boss. This is disaster waiting to happen, so be honest with yourself. If you face this possibility, avoid these events, at least until things improve. The last thing you need to do is to make a bad situation worse.

HOW TO HANDLE A CUTTHROAT BOSS

While a boss who uses employees as scapegoats when things go wrong is a career hazard, a cutthroat boss is simply vicious. This sort of individual specializes in yelling at employees, embarrassing them in public, using profanity, and belittling people at every opportunity. If this sounds like the boss from hell, it is. Unfortunately for you, he or she may be in residence as your boss, which means your workdays are probably less than pleasant.

You may wonder how such a boss can survive. The reality is that if the work gets done, there's little likelihood that upper management will even take notice. Furthermore, most employees are inclined to suffer in silence when they work for a tyrant. After all, their livelihood is dependent upon this individual and any complaints registered are likely to find the employee targeted as a troublemaker. For this reason, an employee is likely to think that it's better to be berated as part of a group, rather than be singled out for individual abuse from a boss they have challenged.

There are ways to cope with an abusive boss, and in the interests of your mental health it pays to know what they are. Otherwise, you will go on suffering until you finally find a job that gets you out from under your tormentor. The measures you take to counteract a cutthroat boss will vary somewhat in any given situation. A few general guidelines for survival include the following:

- *Assess the pros and cons of working for such a boss.* Some bosses who are pretty brutal to work for have compensating qualities such as being very good about rewarding achievers. Therefore, if you are pretty tough-skinned, you can move your career along by sticking it out with a tyrant.

- *Don't exaggerate the negative qualities of a boss.* Some people have short fuses and tend to fly off the handle rather easily. However, they recognize this trait and apologize when they think they've gone too far.

- *Evaluate the basis of the negative behavior.* Does it only happen at certain times such as under pressure situations? Is it just work-related or is your boss hostile habitually? If you can identify certain types of incidents that provoke anger, you may be able to minimize your exposure to the boss's wrath.

- *Is your boss miserable with everyone or just you?* It could be that you and your boss have a personality clash.

- *What is the nature of the behavior that bothers you?* Many bosses get pegged as being generally miserable, although their behavior is confined to one unacceptable trait. For example, a boss who is otherwise quite acceptable may earn a reputation based on an excessive use of profanity. This isn't to condone the use of such language, but the pluses and minuses of a boss have to be weighed.

- *If you suffer from a boss who is an intolerable bully, you may want to make your position known.* Tell the boss in private that you show respect and you expect the same in return. Genuine bullies often pull in their horns when they're confronted. Just be careful not to lose your temper during the discussion. This won't cure the problem for everyone else, but you may find the boss easing up on you.

- *If you have the confidence of other managers, discuss your thoughts with them.* If morale and productivity in your department are low, it may well be that top management is looking for an excuse to shunt your boss to the sidelines. Proceed with caution though, since the last thing you need is for your boss to hear you're trying to undercut him or her.

If you find the situation to be unbearable, then you may want to look for a job elsewhere. If you like your present employer, then try to transfer internally. Don't, however, say that you are unable to get along with your boss. Other managers may not be aware of your boss's behavior, and if your boss has the support of top management, there's nothing to be gained by complaining.

WAYS TO WORK AROUND AN INDECISIVE SUPERIOR

Your boss may be someone you really like and respect, which is a bonus in itself, if you've had the misfortune to have a miserable boss or two in the past. Despite this, you may discover he or she has an inability to make a decision. This, of course, isn't confined to bosses who happen to be pleasant, since indecisiveness can afflict mean-spirited bosses just as easily. The only difference is that you may want to be more diplomatic about working around a pleasant boss to get your job done. But nice or cruel, if you have an indecisive boss, you have to learn how to work around him or her or you'll never get your work finished on schedule.

Dealing with the Survival Instincts of an Insecure Boss

Indecisive bosses are masters of survival and will go to any extreme to conceal their inadequacies. They learn to survive by living off the talent of others. Your decisions are adopted as their decisions. They know the likes and dislikes of their own boss and cater to these whims. As a result, anything you do will be adopted as their achievement, unless it has the remotest possibility for controversy. Indecisive bosses are also prone to nit-pick as a means of justifying their role as the boss. They will change a word here and a sentence there in anything you write, and make other inconsequential changes in minor details of your work. The substance of what you do will likely be unaffected, since to make changes in that aspect of your work would require them to make decisions.

One of the problems with indecisive bosses is that they are hesitant about signing off on anything they think has the potential for controversy. As a result, they like to cover themselves with concurrences from others as a security blanket. The end result is you will get projects handed back with comments such as, "Have the marketing department sign off on this." If you have a really jittery boss, you may find yourself getting a whole string of concurrences until your boss is satisfied enough people are involved to share the blame should anything go wrong.

This "cover all the bases" approach causes other difficulties. Sometimes the people you ask to sign off on something haven't the remotest involvement in the project. If they're cooperative, it doesn't present a problem, and sometimes these unwitting accomplices give their approval routinely. On other occasions, you'll have to deal with people who are either on to your boss's game, or refuse to sign off since they have no responsibility for any aspect of the work. As a result, they give you—the messenger—a hard time. If there's any saving grace in this, it's that you get to develop your interpersonal skills by convincing others to help you over hurdles you didn't create.

Incidentally, before you sit down for a performance evaluation with an indecisive boss, rest assured that your performance evaluation will be mediocre. This is because an indecisive boss will be reluctant to lose a good worker by way of a promotion. Beyond your evaluation, such a boss will downplay your contributions in public. After all, since you're a good worker, it makes the boss's life easier to keep you right where you are.

Coping Tactics

You will have to use a little bit of ingenuity to counteract your misfortune in working for this type of a boss. Aside from a transfer or employment somewhere else, the alternative is to learn how to maneuver around the boss. The obvious route to your long-term success would be to get your talents recognized by other managers. Although it's easy to recognize this necessity, it's not quite that simple to accomplish, because you have to promote your cause without your boss recognizing what you're doing.

The first thing to remember is not to underestimate the self-protection skills of an indecisive boss. They'll go to any extreme to protect their position. In the same vein, the same weak-kneed traits that keep such a boss from making decisions will also prevent him or her from criticizing you—constructively or otherwise. This isn't good because you will never know when you're being criticized behind your back. Therefore, discretion is the better part of valor when you're trying to earn recognition by circumventing an indecisive boss.

The best opportunity to showcase your talents is when your boss isn't in. Since these bosses like to practice decision avoidance, an indecisive boss may well schedule time off around controversial projects. A typical scenario would include having a priority project dumped in your lap, accompanied by an announcement that the boss is going on vacation.

Fortunately for you this isn't as bad as it seems, since it gives you an opportunity to show what you can do. You may very well be busy with your own chores, but if necessary put them on the back burner, and wrap up every assignment the boss gave you before he or she returns. This will give you the chance to present the results of your work to the boss's boss and comparisons of performance shouldn't be hard to make.

Unfortunately, these opportunities don't present themselves very often. Consequently, you will have to learn how to outmaneuver your boss on a regular basis. Being insecure as well as indecisive, your boss may insist that everything go through him for review. Such people worry when they see a subordinate talking to their own boss, so as a practical tactic see the next tier manager when your boss is off somewhere at a meeting or hovering over someone else.

Since you're going over your boss's head, it's prudent to have an alibi, such as an urgent task that needs immediate approval. Incidentally, avail yourself of the chance to engage in social banter if it's initiated by the manager you're seeing. You may hit it lucky by discovering you have a mutual interest such as gourmet cooking or golf. If so, you may be able to develop a relationship around this angle. It's admittedly a stroke of luck if this happens, but in your position you need to try and make a little bit of luck happen.

> **NOTE:** Circumventing your boss isn't recommended as standard practice, but only in situations where it's essential to get your job done. Some companies encourage open lines of communication and don't operate in a rigid chain-of-command format. In these situations, dealing with an upper-level manager isn't as likely to be frowned upon. Yet, it's always a matter of courtesy and respect to keep your immediate boss posted as to what you're doing.

CRAMPING THE STYLE OF BOSS'S PETS

One of the most irritating practices you may have to contend with is a boss who plays favorites. Some bosses do so fairly openly, while others go to some lengths to avoid the appearance of favoritism. Nevertheless, it's a natural tendency to like some people better than others, and in this regard a boss isn't any different from anyone else. This is to be expected. What can cause problems, though, is when some employees go to great lengths to curry favor with a boss, and to the misfortune of other employees, find their efforts being rewarded.

This can cause serious morale problems when a boss regularly gives the best assignments to certain workers, even though they may not be either the hardest working or best qualified individuals within the group. If you have the misfortune to have to compete with these individuals, your hard work can be overlooked easily in favor of someone who is better liked by the boss. For this reason alone, it's well worth the effort to do what you can to overcome this handicap.

Getting along with your boss can result either from doing your job well, or doing a little bit of ego stroking. The surest way to a good working relationship is a combination of the two. It's easy enough to rationalize that you shouldn't have to cozy up to the boss to get ahead. It helps, however, to look at this from a different angle. If there's relatively little to differentiate the job performance of two people, what separates the two in the minds of a boss? Common sense dictates that the person the boss likes best will be favored in any situation that requires the boss to make an either/or choice between two or more employees. This is the logical way anyone would react, so it's unfair to expect a boss to do otherwise. Of course, if a boss practices overt favoritism, that's something else again.

Some bosses are susceptible to the overtures of duck walkers who waddle along mimicking the boss's every move. Other managers, confident in their own abilities, are keen enough to recognize flattery when they see it. Observation alone will soon tell you which camp your own boss falls into. In any event, to compete with people who toady up to the boss, you have to practice some personal public relations aimed at your boss. If you find it distasteful to join the panderers, there are several job-focused factors you can concentrate on to impress your boss.

Good Work Practices Will Win the Boss's Loyalty

First of all, always practice loyalty toward your boss. Surprisingly enough, this can frequently give you an edge over the biggest butt kissers in your department. That's because some of them may be so interested in furthering their own ambitions that they aren't particularly interested in being loyal to a single manager. As a result, they may seek to ingratiate themselves with other managers, even if it's to the detriment of their own boss. Naturally, they do so on the assumption word won't get back, but it invariably does. As a result, all their efforts to pander to the boss are undermined by their overzealous efforts to succeed.

You can build a trusting relationship with your boss by keeping him or her informed as to anything that might become a potential problem. This protects your boss and prevents him or her from having to answer to superiors for something that goes wrong, of which he or she was unaware. Along these same lines, always strive to protect your boss from criticism. There may be occasions when you have an opportunity to criticize your boss to other managers for something that goes wrong. Refrain from doing so, and if necessary accept the responsibility yourself. Falling on your sword for a boss in this manner will win his or her confidence.

Leave your personal problems at home instead of dropping them in your boss's lap. There may be occasions when you need time off to attend to personal problems, which is to be expected. Some employees, however, consistently use personal difficulties as a crutch to cover their inability to do their jobs properly. Needless to say, even the most understanding boss doesn't want to enact the role of guidance counselor. So as much as possible, keep your personal adversities to yourself.

Be cooperative with both your peers and your boss. Adopt a positive "can-do" attitude instead of a negative "can't-do" disposition. A boss isn't likely to appreciate any worker who tries to justify not doing something by complaining that, "It's not my job."

Work at avoiding the little things that can arouse a boss's ire. Everyone has their pet peeves, so learn what your boss's are and avoid creating unnecessary animosity. For example, some bosses seethe if someone is two minutes late for work, while others go ballistic over some petty aspect of the way something is done at work. Knowing these tendencies will allow you to avoid these offenses.

You may think—with some justification—that your boss doesn't appear to like you as well as some of your peers. If you feel this way, try to determine what it is that your well-liked peers do that you can imitate. Also, think about what you may be doing that irritates your boss. Sometimes even minor adjustments in how you deal with a boss can make a big difference. For instance, you could be unknowingly aggravating your boss by approaching him early in the morning when he's not at his best. This may lead you to believe you're not liked because you receive a gruff reception. Once you realize the cause and correct it, you can eliminate the problem.

Even though you may decide not to bend over backwards to curry favor with your boss, you should still practice some measure of diplomacy. If you don't, your boss may sense that you don't like him. If this happens, then there's no reason for the boss to go out of his way to do you favors. As a minimum, always be pleasant and at least engage in a little bit of idle chitchat with the boss. In fact, through such conversation you should look for some common interest which you both share. No matter what extent you go to in developing a working relationship with your boss, always keep in mind that this relationship, like any other, requires consistent attention. There will be ups and downs and occasional disagreements, but if you're doing your job and are basically friendly you can hold your own against any of your peers.

COPING WHEN YOUR BOSS DELEGATES EVERYTHING

Perfecting your skills and being efficient at your job go a long way toward making both your immediate job and your long-term career more secure. However, in spite of this, there can be a downside to these positive attributes if you have the bad luck to have a boss who delegates anything and everything. In this situation, since you are one of the better workers, you can expect more than your fair share of extra work to do.

At first blush, this may aggravate you to no end, but over the long isn't all bad, since some of the assignments you are given may give you a golden opportunity to show off your skills to senior managers who may be in a position to do your career some good. Then again, your boss may be clever enough to do the delegating in such a way that everything is funneled back through him or her. In effect, you will be doing all the work and your boss wil be getting all the credit.

At first blush, this may aggravate you to no end, but over the long haul there's little to worry about. Over a period of time, everyone will get to know who really does the work, irrespective of who is getting the credit for it. So a boss who plays this game won't fool people for too long. Therefore, your immediate problem is to take advantage of the opportunities that come your way to expand your ability to handle as many of the boss's duties as he or she is willing to pawn off on you. Look at it this way: The more of the boss's job you can do, the better your chances of being the one selected to replace your boss. Nevertheless, you can't do everything and there are several pitfalls to avoid when a boss delegates assignments willy-nilly. These include:

1. *Your boss doesn't explain what is expected of you.* In these situations, a boss may dump an assignment on you with no instructions as to what is required to be done and within what timeframe. As a result,

you're left to set your own parameters for completing the work, which may vary from your boss's expectations. In these cases, always ask enough questions to be fully satisfied that you know what has to be accomplished to meet your boss's objectives.

2. *You don't have the time to do the job the boss is delegating.* This problem will arise inevitably when you work for a boss who delegates everything. This type of manager usually dumps the work on the best workers in the department, which means you will sooner or later have more work than you can handle. If you can't complete an assignment on time because of workload constraints, let the boss know when the task is assigned. This forces the boss to assign it elsewhere, or say something such as, "Just do the best you can."

If you have a boss who is likely to criticize you later for not finishing the job on time, make sure you have some form of written record showing the time constraints you were under. Be careful to do this without incurring your boss's wrath. One good way is to send a briefing memo to the boss outlining the tasks you have to do and the priority you will give them. Be sure to include the completion dates you can meet based on your workload. This way, if the boss later starts to berate you for being tardy in finishing an assignment, you can casually pull out the memo and say, "Gee, boss, I told you about this before I started the assignment." This should put the problem to rest.

3. *You aren't given sufficient resources to do the job.* A similar problem is the failure of your boss to provide the resources necessary to do the job. This can consist of people, equipment, or some combination of the two. Whatever it is that you need, let the boss know right away and protect yourself with a memo outlining what you need and when you need it. If the resources aren't furnished, then you're off the hook for not completing the task.

4. *The boss delegates a task which is political poison.* You may have the misfortune to be delegated a task which has garnered serious opposition within the company, or is otherwise going to make you unpopular with managers whom you don't want to alienate. Whenever possible, try to avoid these assignments by pleading you have too many other things to do. If you do get stuck with the job,

quietly let it be known that this was delegated to you against your wishes. Otherwise, you may end up making enemies without ever intending to do so.

5. *The boss always delegates the lousy jobs to you.* You may find that there's no advantage to be gained by working on jobs the boss delegates, since all you ever get is grunt work. If this is happening, mention to the boss that you would like to receive more challenging assignments. Sometimes grunt work is farmed out to a particular person because they are obliging and don't complain about doing it. This may be the situation you face. The unpleasant alternative, of course, is that your boss doesn't like you very much, and if that's true, then you already know why you're getting a raw deal.

6. *Your boss is always unhappy with the results.* No matter how hard you try, you may find your boss complaining that the task wasn't done the way it should have been done. Although you might want to say, "Do it yourself the next time," suppress the urge. You probably work for a perfectionist, but not an ambitious one, otherwise the work wouldn't have been delegated in the first place. Although it is frustrating to be criticized consistently, since it is a frequent occurence you can learn to accept it as part and parcel of the boss's personality. With some people, nothing is ever right, so don't lose any sleep over it if you have this type of boss.

7. *Your boss takes credit for the successes, but blames you for the failures.* This isn't something you should worry about, since when a boss delegates everything to those who work for him, everyone soon knows where the work is being done. Therefore, although you may not be getting credit for your good work from the boss, everyone else, including other managers, knows where the credit belongs.

PLAYING THE GAME WHEN YOU WORK FOR A POLITICIAN

The way your boss operates, you may sometimes wonder whether you're working in the business world or in the political arena. Having a boss who is an overt politician can at times be frustrating. It's nothing you can't cope with as long as you are aware of the games your boss plays. If you're not, then you can find yourself in disfavor without ever knowing what you did to wind up in the woodshed.

Protecting your butt when you work for a boss who plays politics to the hilt requires you to carefully observe the boss's relationships at work. Whom does the boss pander to, and who is virtually ignored? Knowing this will give you a good idea as to who is important to the boss, and who is considered to be an adversary. With this knowledge you can act accordingly in your dealings with these people. It also pays to be alert for any changes in the boss's relationships, since expert office politicians shift their alliances even more frequently than their elected counterparts.

Watching whom your boss plays up to within the management structure can give you a pretty good idea as to who the real power figures are within the organization. If you have to do work for any of these people, give it your priority attention for two reasons. First of all, this gives you an opportunity to show what you can do to those with influence. Second, it keeps your boss happy, since the last thing an office politician type of boss wants is someone not doing their best for senior managers the boss is trying to impress.

Many bosses who overtly practice office politics have mentors they tend to follow from employer to employer. How does this affect you? If your boss likes you and follows his or her mentor to another employer, then you have a viable contact for the future with another company. On the other hand, you risk alienating other managers if you align yourself too closely with the boss and those to whom he or she panders. This is a potential problem if either your boss leaves for employment elsewhere, or his sponsors—along with your boss—fall into disfavor with top management. This can be damaging to you if you are seen as a card-carrying member of the boss's clique.

For this reason, even though you want to treat everyone the boss cozies up to with deference, don't neglect your relationships with other managers. Try to walk a fine line whereby you are equally helpful with everyone. This will prevent you from being perceived as an office politician who is following in the footsteps of your boss.

In terms of your duties, you have to be careful to give priority to any tasks that your boss considers to be important, because they're being done for someone with whom the boss is trying to curry favor. In the actual scheme of things, the tasks may not require such treatment, but they get blue-ribbon care because of the parties for whom they are being done. Usually, there won't be any problem in your having to decide on job priorities, since your boss will be sure to tell you where to concentrate your efforts. All you have to be careful of is to avoid any argument with the boss over which job is more important. In your boss's eyes, it's the one that has political overtones, and as long as you're aware of the boss's tendencies in this regard, you shouldn't have any problem.

You may find it distasteful to have to factor your boss's politicking into your work routine. It shouldn't be that difficult, since the times when it will have any direct impact on you will be rare. For the most part, your boss's political games won't be of your concern. Looking at it from another angle, your boss's connections may directly or indirectly do you some good. If your boss has the right connections at higher levels within the company, it gives him or her access which other managers don't have. It also places your boss in a favorable position to request and receive resources for your department that won't be available to other groups. So the next time you need new equipment, or some other resource to do a job, your success in getting it may be linked to your boss's abilities as an office politician.

THE RIGHT TACTICS FOR DEALING WITH A NEW BOSS

If you work at the same job for any length of time, you may find yourself outlasting a boss or two. This can be either good or bad, depending upon how much you liked working for the boss who is being replaced. Whatever the situation may have been with your prior boss, a new boss presents a new set of problems for you. First and foremost is how you should react to the new boss. Should you operate on a "business as usual" basis, or seek guidance from your new boss as to how things should be handled? This is just the starting point for a number of adjustments you will have to make in learning to work with a new boss who may operate quite differently from your prior boss.

The old chestnut about "first impressions" applies to getting started with a new boss as well as in other situations. Therefore, your first consideration is what to do immediately after the new boss's arrival on the scene. At the first opportunity to have a private conversation, offer to be of any assistance you can to the new boss. Perhaps your offer will be accepted and perhaps not. Many a new boss will wisely not gravitate toward individual employees for assistance until they have a better feel for who knows what within the unit.

At the same time, ask if you should just keep doing your work as before, or whether or not the boss would like you to do anything differently. Naturally, having just come on board, the boss isn't going to change anything right away. This isn't the real basis for your comment. By making such a statement, the new boss will view you as someone who isn't going to cause a lot of resistance about adapting to his or her operating methods. This will serve you well in the weeks and months ahead, as several of your peers will likely take exception to every change that comes along.

With a new boss on the scene, you also have to be careful about what you do or say until you are able to assess how your new supervisor reacts to certain situations. For starters, this means observing the fundamentals such as being on time for work, and not taking extended coffee or lunch breaks. The prior boss may have been lenient in this regard, while the new manager might have a different viewpoint. Until you can get a handle on the operating practices of your group leader, it pays to err on the side of caution. It won't take long to find out what adjustments you will have to make to meet the requirements of your new boss.

If your new boss is unfamiliar with the work practices of the unit, be sure to explain thoroughly what you're doing if you are asked questions about your work. This will not only be appreciated, but it will also give your supervisor an appreciation for the work you do. Be patient about explaining anything, since this will give the boss confidence in being able to ask you questions and get answers. This will encourage the boss to see you as the "go to" person for information. Some of your peers may get off on the wrong foot by being abrupt, or showing disdain for the manager's lack of knowledge. This will not endear them to the new supervisor.

Initially, you don't want to confront your superior with complaints, or issues that need resolution, unless it's absolutely necessary to do so. The last thing a new boss needs is to have to deal with all sorts of petty problems that may have been sidetracked for months by the prior boss. Naturally, you should bring relevant issues that can't wait to the boss's attention, and try to offer proposed solutions as well. A few of your peers may get off to a bad start by seeing this new boss as an opportunity to raise petty complaints; as a result, the initial impressions they will leave will be those of constant complainers. These first-time impressions take a while to overcome, so there's no point in making your adjustment to a new boss more difficult than it has to be.

Be considerate of the novice status of your boss by not upstaging the boss in front of others. Always try to keep the boss briefed before meetings that will require him or her to relay information to others. Along the same line, don't do any end runs around your boss by going over his or her head. There may be a temptation to do this for expediency, but your boss may not view it in the same light. In fact, a sensitive boss may see it as an attempt to undermine his or her authority.

For better or worse, with a new boss you start all over again to prove your worth. This is great if your relations with the prior boss had been less than ideal. Conversely, you may feel frustrated at having to adjust to the management style of the new boss. Don't let this bother you, since if you were recognized as a top performer by the prior boss, the chances are your new boss has heard about your good reputation. Furthermore, other managers will undoubtedly be cluing the boss in as to the capabilities of everyone in the unit. Incidentally, this is one more reason why it pays to work well with other managers on a regular basis. When occasions such as this arise, those managers can serve as unofficial goodwill ambassadors in touting your talents.

After your new boss gets acclimated, you may find changes being made that aren't to your liking. Do your best to go along with these revisions as long as they don't severely impact your ability to do your job. If a particular change is a problem, sit down and discuss it with the boss. The odds are if you point out the difficulties in making the change, the boss will see things your way. This is especially true if you haven't made a habit of badgering the boss about every minor detail. All in all, the impact of a new boss is never quite as serious as initially imagined when they first take over. The final outcome will undoubtedly be that you and the new boss will both survive nicely.

LEARNING TO SUCCEED BY MAKING YOUR BOSS LOOK GOOD

The quickest and best way to get along with a boss is to make your boss look good. Obviously, you do this by doing your job to the best of your ability. There are steps beyond this, however, which can earn the appreciation of your immediate superior. For example, you don't want to say anything in front of other managers which could reflect upon your boss unfavorably. For that matter, never openly criticize the boss to anyone, including your closest co-workers. You never know who will carry what you said right back to the boss. So, careless comments leave nothing to gain and much to be lost.

Cover for Your Boss

Other opportunities will arise for you to offer support to your boss, and these can include the need to cover for your boss on occasion. The boss, just like you and others, may either be late once in a while, or slip out a little early. Some subordinates, looking for revenge, would like nothing better than to have a chance to get the boss in trouble for this. Therefore, if a senior manager or staff person comes looking for a missing boss, the cutthroat will announce happily that the boss isn't in yet, or has left for the day.

Other than personal satisfaction, an employee who does this isn't going to gain anything by it. In fact, it's likely to cast the person in an unfavorable light, not only with the boss, but also in the eyes of the person making the inquiry. After all, no one is enamored of informants, with the possible exception of law enforcement personnel. Furthermore, it's likely to get back to the boss, perhaps with a comment such as, "One of your loyal employees told me you ducked out early yesterday afternoon." Needless to say, this individual would be well advised to adhere to time and attendance policies in the future.

Covering for your boss in such a situation doesn't require you to lie. In fact, that can make you look foolish if the person looking for the boss finds out you made up a story. For example, you tell a senior manager who is looking for your boss that she's in a meeting in another building, even though you know the boss left fifteen minutes early to pick her daughter up from softball practice. As luck would have it, your boss may have already told this person she was leaving early, only the person forgot about it. Alternatively, the boss will say where she was the next day, since your boss puts in sixty-hour weeks and no one questions her leaving early on occasion.

The best approach is to simply be evasive in such a situation. For example, if asked where your boss is, instead of saying she left, you could say, "I don't know." After all, it's not your responsibility to keep track of your boss's whereabouts, so you can't be criticized for not knowing where the boss is. However, you can cause problems for yourself by knowing where the boss is when you're not supposed to know.

Another aspect of covering for a boss concerns work-related problems. You may be in a meeting where someone at a higher level, or from another department, is trying to pin a mistake on your boss who isn't in attendance. Loyalty to both your boss, and your department, dictates that you should defend your boss in this situation. This is a typical scapegoat situation, where the person not in attendance gets the blame for what went wrong. Even if you're not aware of the facts, say something such as, "That doesn't sound like what M. J. would do. Why don't I go get him right now?" The chances are your offer will be refused, but it will probably be the last time your boss will be criticized in your presence. You can also rest assured that someone in that meeting will tell your boss about how firmly you defended him. That sort of loyalty to a boss isn't forgotten quickly.

Complement Your Boss's Abilities

Everyone has their strengths and weaknesses, so there will be areas of work where your boss has weak spots. It might be in doing detail work, or perhaps preparing reports. The key is to discover what your boss likes to do least, and volunteer to do work in these areas. Just make sure it's in areas where your strengths are, since it's of little value to either you or the boss for you to assume duties at which you're not proficient.

You will want to be subtle in how you approach the boss on this, but you shouldn't have much difficulty in having the boss relinquish some of his or her most burdensome tasks. You may get an opportunity if the boss complains to you about having to do such and such reports, or whatever else it is that is a headache. If this happens, simply say, "I'd be glad to help you out with that." Another approach would be to sit down with your boss and ask what you can do to be more supportive. Helping your boss out in this way not only earns the appreciation of the boss, but also trains you in some of the boss's duties, which is good experience for the future. Beyond that, it puts you in a position to establish a strong working relationship with your boss, which is always something from which you can benefit.

Keep Your Boss Informed

Always communicate openly with your boss so that he or she isn't blindsided by not being informed about something. Incidentally, this doesn't just apply to potential problems. It's also useful to let the boss know about something that is praiseworthy, such as completing projects ahead of deadlines, and so forth. This gives the boss ammunition for touting the department's performance at staff meetings and with higher-level managers. In the ordinary course of events the boss will learn most of these things, but sometimes too late to use effectively. Therefore, those people doing the work are in a better position to let the boss know right away about what's happening—good and bad. So don't be shy about letting your boss know what's going on. Making your boss look good also means not making him or her look bad.

WHAT TO DO WHEN YOUR BOSS HAS NO INFLUENCE

One of the hardest positions to be in when you're trying to earn career recognition is to work for a boss who wields no influence within a company. No matter how nice your boss is, if that person doesn't have the respect of those higher up in management, it can create all kinds of problems for you. You may not get the resources you need to do your job, since your boss can't convince upper management to furnish the resources. This same reasoning may result in you being overworked because your group is understaffed. Most significantly, a boss without influence doesn't have the power to push employees for promotion, which means you may be in a dead-end job for no better reason than having an ineffectual boss.

Obviously, you have to take steps to combat this sort of dilemma; otherwise you will be laboring in obscurity, with the reward being your share of the lousy jobs which are dumped in the boss's lap. Without a boss who can get anything done within the organization, you're forced to use your wits to obtain any resources you need, and to keep your career on track. In terms of getting resources, you can try to scrounge to the best of your ability, but this won't always suffice. After all, when it comes to supplies and equipment, every department competes for limited resources. Therefore, if your boss isn't pushing for a fair share necessary to operate the department, then you may be out of luck.

What you can do when you need something is to try and get it without going through the formal approval process. Establishing good contacts with those people who operate in the supply, maintenance, and purchasing areas can help you out to some extent. In fact, you may be surprised how much red tape can be cut when you know the right people to contact when you need something.

Another good approach is to walk your own requisitions through the approval cycle. This is especially helpful if one reason your boss doesn't have influence is that he or she isn't liked by people in other areas. This dislike shouldn't carry over to you, so if you walk your requests for resources through the approval chain, you may be successful in getting what you need.

A boss without influence in the company often becomes the dumping ground for undesirable assignments that no one else wants to do. As a consequence, if you're not careful you may find yourself with the misfortune of working on a lot of dirty jobs that get assigned to your department. If you're in this situation, unlike normal circumstances where you want to pitch in and help your boss as much as possible, in this case you have to learn to avoid as much of the grunt work as possible. Do your best to justify to your boss that you're busy when the more undesirable tasks come along. Unfortunately, with your boss wielding no power, almost all the work the group gets may be undesirable. There may be no way to get around doing your share of no-brainer work.

When you work for a boss without power, your own chances for career success are impeded. All you can do is work at making your talents known to other managers within the organization. Along the same lines, getting other managers to praise your work, particularly in writing, can be very helpful. After all, no matter how much your boss may tout your talents, it isn't likely to carry much weight. It's also worthwhile to try to get a transfer to work for a manager for whom you will have a chance both to utilize your talents, and gain recognition.

HOW TO DISTANCE YOURSELF WHEN YOUR BOSS IS ON THE WAY OUT

If it isn't bad enough that you work for a boss who has no influence within the company, it's even worse to work for a boss who is apparently in line to be dismissed. The only redeeming feature in this scenario is if the dismissal comes sooner rather than later. Then again, if you're particularly unlucky, such a boss may hang on for an extended period of time, leaving you working for someone who is powerless to accomplish anything.

This sort of situation can have other ramifications, especially if you have had good relations with your boss. This could lead to you becoming unpopular with management, by virtue of your close association with this person. It may not be fair, but very little ever is when it comes to the political intrigue that takes place in the business world. To guard against this, you have to distance yourself from such a boss discreetly without being noticeable about it. This in itself is a tricky undertaking. Nevertheless, you have to be careful when you have a boss targeted for a pink slip, or you may find yourself on the same slippery slope to the unemployment office.

For one thing, you don't want to be too closely tied to any work projects your boss may be heading up. Higher-ups may be setting your boss up to be fired by giving him a project doomed to fail from the start. You don't want to be caught in the net when it's lowered by virtue of working on the project. Consequently, you have to be alert for new assignments you receive that are out of the ordinary. Even though you may have to do some work on an assignment if it is given to you, don't associate yourself too closely with your boss in working on it. If others in the group are also working on the task, there's no real problem, but try to avoid getting stuck working solo with the boss.

From another perspective, your boss probably knows his job is on the line and may put his own self-interest before anything else. If this happens, the boss may try to make you the scapegoat with regard to anything for which the boss may be criticized. You can guard against this by being careful to document what you do with memos which keep the boss and others apprised of the status of everything on which you're working. It's certainly not necessary to be paranoid about everything that transpires, but it is wise to be on the alert when you work for a boss who is not in favor with top management.

Aside from working for a manager who is targeted to be fired, you might find yourself in a position of working for a boss who is close to retirement. In and of itself, this usually shouldn't present problems for you. In fact, if you play your cards right, you may be selected to take over the position. Nevertheless, if your boss is coasting along toward retirement there may be a reluctance to do anything even vaguely controversial, such as backing you up if something goes wrong. Furthermore, if the boss is no longer concerned particularly with productivity, the group's performance may suffer. That isn't your responsibility, but you don't want to be painted as a goof-off inadvertently. If you face this sort of situation, don't slack off, since you'll still be there to face the music long after your boss has moved on to retirement.

WHEN TO COMPLAIN—AND WHEN TO KEEP QUIET

As you are well aware, everything doesn't always go smoothly at work, which can lead you to wage a complaint with your boss. From past experience, you may have found complaining isn't always the smartest move in the world, especially if you receive a less than pleasant reaction from your boss. An occasion like this may leave you scratching your head wondering why the boss becomes so mad. Complaints probably seem quite logical and the proper course of action. But just because complaining to the boss appears to be the right move, doesn't always mean it's the smartest move, for a number of reasons.

For example, you may find yourself complaining about a new procedure that isn't working out. Unbeknownst to you, the ineffective measure may be the dreamchild of your boss. So by knocking the procedure, you're in effect criticizing your boss, and we all know how people just love to be criticized.

Another possibility for arousing the ire of a boss by complaining may just represent frustration on the boss's part. Perhaps the boss has complained to higher management time and time again about the very issue you're raising. As a consequence, the subject has become one the boss just doesn't want to hear about. Accordingly, when you raise the issue, you trigger the boss's wrath. Admittedly, one could argue that the boss could have explained this to you calmly without biting your head off. But bosses have the same human frailties as the rest of us, and don't always think before they act. These are just a couple of examples of knowing when you should and shouldn't register a complaint with your boss.

Use Tact When You Complain

No matter how cautious you are, you may still raise the boss's hackles. On some occasions, the nature of the complaint will be such that the boss's reaction shouldn't even be a consideration. But for the most part, if you learn the nuances of complaining to the boss, you will find yourself meeting with far more success and a lot less wrath when you bring the boss your latest gripe.

In order to achieve success when you approach your boss with a problem, you should first evaluate how your boss reacts to complaints. Otherwise, you will just be spinning your wheels. Decide at the outset whether or not your boss is a good listener. If he or she isn't, then you're just going to be wasting your time. If the gripe can be construed as criticism of your boss, think about his or her potential reaction. Some bosses welcome criticism as a means of knowing how employees feel, so they can make any necessary adjustments to correct problems; others will react angrily at the slightest suggestion that they are a contributing factor to any problem.

If your boss is the defensive type, you have to be particularly careful as to how you phrase your complaint. Avoid using language such as, "You did this," or "You didn't do that." Instead, focus on the issue itself. Here are a couple of examples:

Wrong Way: "You're always giving me the dirty jobs to do."

Right Way: "I'd be interested in doing something more challenging."

| *Wrong Way:* | "You always find something wrong with my work." |
| *Right Way:* | "I'd be interested in discussing with you what measures I can take to improve my performance." |

Your goal is to generalize the problem without pinning any blame on your boss. By doing this, you prevent the boss from becoming defensive, not to mention preventing the possibility of the discussion degenerating into an argument. By framing the issue in terms that suggest you want to do something to improve your performance, you put the boss in a frame of mind to be helpful. As the discussion ensues, you will still be able to get your point across. All complaints won't be able to be couched in these terms, since they may involve something or someone other than yourself. Yet phrase the issue in general terms, so you don't come across as being critical of your boss. In essence, it's not what you say but how you say it that will spell the difference between success and disaster.

Learn to be particularly tactful with subjects or situations that your boss may be sensitive about. For example, belittling a procedure that has been developed by your boss isn't going to get you anywhere. Also, a young boss may resent any comment that implies he or she is lacking in experience. Whatever the ticklish topics are that can provoke your boss, either avoid them entirely, or if you still want to register a complaint, use as much tact as you can muster.

When you complain about something, listen carefully to what your boss has to say. Sometimes, what isn't said is as important as what is. For example, suppose someone we'll call Judy complains about a new operating procedure and her boss says, "That was written at the request of Alex P.," without saying anything in defense of the procedure. Alex P. happens to be a senior vice-president, and Judy's boss is letting her know the procedure won't be changed. By not even trying to justify the procedure, the boss is probably indicating he doesn't like it any more than Judy does. The boss, however, is also wise enough not to openly criticize a senior manager. If Judy reads between the lines she will drop her opposition to the procedure, since it's not about to be changed, at least not until someone at higher levels decides to revise it.

Finally, if you're going to register a complaint with the boss, and you're apprehensive about doing so, think about the best approach to take. Decide what you're going to say beforehand, and try to anticipate the boss's responses. Above all, weigh your chances of getting any satis-faction from your complaint. If, after doing this, you think it unlikely that anything will change, then you might as well keep the complaint to your-self and avoid making a bad situation worse.

HOW TO WIN EVEN WHEN YOUR BOSS SAYS "NO"

If someone wanted to conduct a survey to determine who was the best-liked boss where you work, they could probably accomplish it by sim-ply determining which boss was most likely to say "yes" to any and every form of employee request. Even though that may be a quick and dirty way to determine a well-liked boss, it doesn't follow that this is the best boss, either from a company or employee standpoint.

A boss who isn't doing his or her job isn't the best boss to work for, and a boss who agrees with every employee request isn't likely to be around too long. So if you don't have what may seem like an ideal situ-ation, don't despair. You shouldn't expect a boss to agree with your every request, since your supervisor has to make decisions based on what's best for the group and the company—not what's necessarily best for any individual worker.

Nevertheless, if you plan your moves accordingly, you may ulti-mately get what you want even after your boss turns you down. It does, however, require some thought in planning how best to approach your boss on any given issue. There are several ways to turn a negative request around. One approach is to get a future commitment. This works very well in situations that involve spending money, such as making equipment purchases, off-site training, and even pay raises.

What you have to do is be ready to shift gears when you get your initial rejection, and then raise the prospect of approval being granted in the future. Usually this isn't hard to do for one simple reason, which is that a boss generally won't just give you a flat-out "No." Instead, you will be given some rationale as to why your request can't be approved. For example, "I can't get you a new computer because it's not in this year's budget," or "I can't approve your vacation request until I see how much backlog we'll have in July."

Many times people hear this sort of a statement and that's the end of it, but it shouldn't be. What you have is a ready-made opening by which to get some form of future commitment. In the examples above you could come back with a response such as, "Can we put the computer in next year's budget?" or "When will you know about my vacation?" If you do this, the chances are your boss will give you some form of future commitment. All you have to do is be certain to follow up when the time comes. This method may not be as good as getting what you want right now, but it sure beats walking away empty-handed without any hope for the future.

Another useful tactic in some circumstances is to settle for less than what you wanted as a form of compromise. Most bosses want to be obliging, assuming an employee isn't making an unreasonable request. Unfortunately, a boss has to look at things from a different perspective than the employee. The boss's desire to accommodate someone practically assures some form of compromise. For example, if a two-week vacation can't be granted, perhaps the boss will go along with one week. This sort of technique can be used in a variety of situations. You just have to be alert to the possibilities and be ready to make the suggestion if your original request is turned down.

Sometimes people get a "no" answer from a boss when they could just as easily have received a positive reply. Therefore, if you want to limit the negative responses you get, there are a couple of simple rules you can follow. First, try to catch your boss at a time when the response is more likely to be favorable. If you are able to gauge your boss's mood, this won't be hard to do.

Second, don't ask your question in such a way that makes it easy to say "no." For example, "Boss, can I have the first two weeks in June off?" This requires a one-word answer which is most likely going to be "no." However, if you say, "Boss, I have hotel reservations booked for the first two weeks in June. There shouldn't be any problem in my taking a vacation then since it's always a slow business month." Phrased this way, you have indicated you have a financial commitment for the hotel, and you have implied that there shouldn't be any reason to turn your request down. If the boss wants to refuse your request, he or she is then forced to think about it and have a good reason to turn you down—unless you work for a jerk, who may turn you down without a solid reason. However, the odds are much more favorable that you will get a positive response.

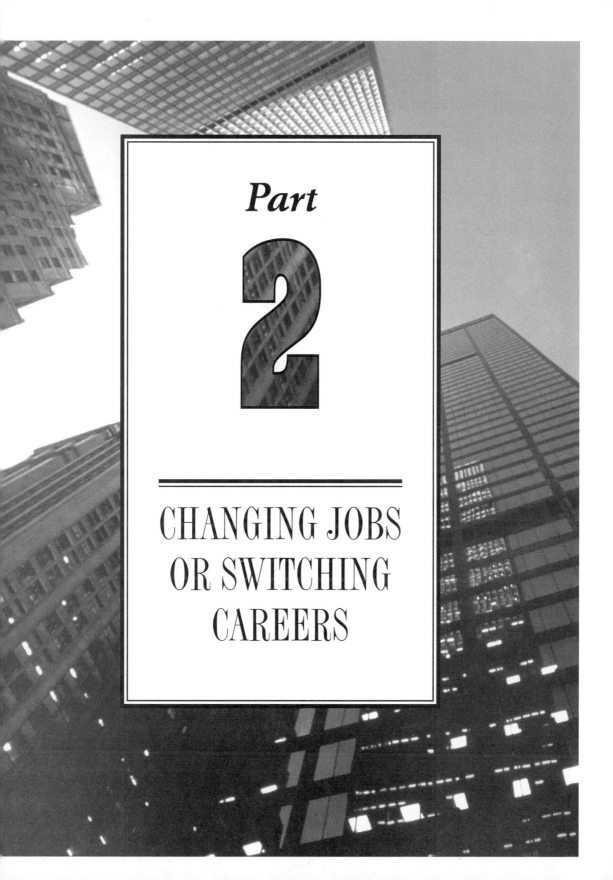

Part

2

CHANGING JOBS OR SWITCHING CAREERS

Most people work for a number of different employers during their lifetimes, and many also decide to switch career fields one or more times. These trends can be expected to accelerate in the future as competitive forces and technology combine to create new opportunities, while simultaneously eliminating jobs in other areas. These shifts in the job market mean lifetime job security with a single employer will be rare, and by choice or necessity, you may be looking for a new job in the not too distant future. Of even greater significance, by personal desire or economic necessity, you may decide to try your hand at a different career.

The competition for good jobs has always been tough, and switching jobs for career advancement or other personal reasons isn't new. In the future, with people changing employers more frequently, the competition should be even tougher. A demand for people with up-to-date skills no longer allows someone to fall back on years of experience as their ticket to another job. Looking for—and landing—a better job requires careful planning and a properly executed job search.

Although you may be relatively content in your present position, you should be prepared to market your talents at any time. That way, you won't be scurrying around willing to take the first job that comes along if you lose your job unexpectedly. Furthermore, with employers becoming increasingly picky in their hiring practices, it pays to know how to both develop and market your credentials to prospective employers.

Although changing jobs is a challenge, switching careers is a step that many people avoid simply because of the risks involved. Yet for many individuals, a new career can mean excitement and challenge. For some people who work in fields where the future isn't bright, a career change is a necessity that has to be confronted sooner or later. Savvy planning can make both of these transitions a lot smoother. Chapter five addresses the many aspects of successfully changing jobs, while chapter six explores the issues related to switching careers.

Chapter

5

PLANNING FOR AND GETTING THE JOB YOU WANT

There comes a time in life when most people decide it's time to move on and look for a job somewhere else. If that doesn't happen, perhaps you may be in the unfortunate position, because of cutbacks, of finding yourself forced to look for a new job. In either event, searching for a new job isn't a task to be undertaken lightly. It requires careful preparation and a good deal of persistence if you want to land a position in which you feel comfortable. On the other hand, job hunting doesn't have to be an anxiety-filled search for the first opening that comes along if you have prepared yourself properly beforehand.

This chapter explores the steps necessary to secure a new position that meets your needs. It also covers several factors you should consider before you even start looking for a job, including the signs to watch for that indicate it's time for you to look elsewhere. These may be due to your own dissatisfaction, or warning signals that your job isn't on firm ground.

141

In this chapter, you will learn how to create your own job opportunities with your present employer, as well as master how to market yourself to others. You will also find plenty of tips on resume preparation, interviewing, and how to negotiate salaries. In addition, there are a number of factors covered which you should consider before accepting any job offer. And of course, if you lose your job unexpectedly, your financial pressures can force you to accept a job other than what you really want. Therefore, you will find tips on how to quickly reduce your expenses while you're between jobs, so as to lessen the urgency to accept the first position that comes along. So let's start by exploring some indications it's time for you to look elsewhere for employment.

TEN TELLTALE SIGNS THAT IT'S TIME TO MOVE ON

You may recall that the first topic in chapter one discussed how to recognize signs that your job may be at risk because of a pending layoff. Besides this factor, which is essentially beyond your control, there are a number of other reasons why you may have to decide that it's time to look for a job elsewhere. Let's look at some of these possibilities so you will be in a position to make your move at the moment that's right for you—not when you're forced to make a job move because of factors beyond your control.

1. *Your prospects for promotion are bleak because there are a number of other candidates ahead of you.* Sometimes circumstances such as this which are beyond your control will lead you to decide it's time for a change. Yet it's wise not to jump ship from a position you're reasonably satisfied with until you have given the decision some careful thought.

2. *You're bored stiff with your job and can't wait for the weekend.* Very few people have an ideal job, but if your situation is so bad that you're bored out of your skull, perhaps a job or career change is in the cards. Before making a move, however, look for ways to relieve the boredom of your present job. Perhaps you could ask your boss for more responsibility, transfer to a more challenging position, and so forth.

3. *You find a continual overload of work or other factors are stressing you out.* If you find yourself locked into a position where you are essentially overworked and underpaid, then if there's little likelihood of things changing, you might want to move on.

4. *There's been an organizational change which relegates your department to second-class status.* As a result, your future prospects aren't bright.

5. *Your working hours are changed and it's impossible to work out a reasonable compromise.* This is just one of a number of different personal situations which may have you considering looking for another job. Your job could be moved to another building several miles away which makes your commute more difficult, or perhaps you recently bought a house in an area which makes your commute much longer. Whatever the reason might be, always look for ways to make adjustments before you decide to look for another job arbitrarily.

6. *Despite your best efforts you find it nearly impossible to get along with your boss.* There are times when personality conflicts are best resolved by one or both parties going separate ways. So if you're in this fix and you can't persuade your boss to find another job, then maybe you should start looking for another job.

7. *Your responsibilities keep increasing, but your salary doesn't.* Sometimes a competent worker is given all the work he or she can handle, but not the pay to go along with it. If you find yourself in this predicament, talk to your boss about your pay. After that, if there's little likelihood of proper compensation, you may want to find a job where you will be paid for your efforts. Incidentally, be certain that you are truly underpaid in accordance with the going market rate for your type of position in the area where you live.

8. *You took a new job recently, but it turns out that the job wasn't what you expected.* Assuming you give yourself sufficient time to adapt, it may turn out that the job you took wasn't the job you expected. It may even be that the job was misrepresented. In any event, if you find yourself in a position you know you can't cope with, you might as well start your search over. It doesn't do you or your employer much good for you to hang on where you are unhappy.

9. *You were in line for a promotion but were passed over in favor of someone else.* When this happens, you have to think long and hard about your future with your present employer. Some people try to rationalize that they will get the next promotion, while others feel quite the opposite. If from any objective basis you were the logical candidate to be promoted and you lost out, then it's probable that you aren't going to go anywhere fast with this employer. As a result, if you want to move up the ladder you had better find another job where someone will let you start to climb it.

10. *You don't have a logical reason, but your gut feelings have been telling you for some time to get yourself another job.* It's your job and it's your life and you can do what you want with it. How true, and if you just feel you want to try something else for a change, then do it. The bottom line is that it's your own contentment that matters, so there's no point in being miserable wondering what it would be like doing something else. Give it a try and find out for yourself.

HOW TO CREATE JOB OPPORTUNITIES ON YOUR OWN

If you're unhappy in your present position, or else just want to expand your opportunities and fatten your paycheck, one of the least thought of ways to go about it is to create your own job opening with your present employer. Perhaps your company is expanding, or maybe new technology presents an opportunity for a new position. It could even be that a particular job function has grown in importance and no one has yet seen fit to create a position to handle the duties on a full-time basis. Once you recognize such a possibility, the trick is to convince management to create the position and fill it with the right candidate—namely you.

There are several ways to go about this. In fact, sometimes you don't have to do much more than assume some new-found duty and become the resident expert. You can then expand the responsibilities gradually until the bulk of your time is consumed with your new duties and it's time to lobby for a new position for yourself. This isn't always as hard to do as you might think. Often when some new element is introduced into the workplace, people are reluctant to accept the change. This leaves an excellent opening for someone with an open mind to learn everything they can about the change, whether it's a new piece of equipment, or a new and complicated procedure which no one wants to learn. If you avail yourself of the chance to become the resident guru, you will soon find people coming to you for answers. You have now gained a measure of power by being the most knowledgeable person on that particular subject. You have accomplished the first step in creating your own job.

Naturally, there are pitfalls in taking this approach. For one thing, you have to assess carefully whether the change has the potential to occupy someone full-time in the future, or is just a temporary measure with no job-creating possibilities. Otherwise, you will find yourself doing a lot of extra work for nothing. Another pitfall to avoid is finding yourself creating a position with a nice title to go with it, but nothing in the way of additional pay. If you're one of those rare people who prefers prestige to pay, so be it. If not, once you create a position for yourself, make sure you get the money to go along with the work. However, if circumstances are such that a substantive pay raise won't go along with the additional responsibility, the job can still be of value if the experience will enhance your career prospects.

Give Luck a Helping Hand

Luck is something that's often mentioned in discussions of people who are successful. It's hard to argue that being in the right place at the right time is indeed good fortune. What gets overlooked is that it's possible to give luck a helping hand. For example, take two employees who work together. The boss asks the first to figure out how to use some new computer software. The employee doesn't want to get stuck with an extra assignment and tells the boss he is too busy.

The boss then asks the second employee, who says she would be glad to do it. She then goes on to learn the program and become the resident expert, not only for her group, but for other departments. Since she is spending the bulk of her time training others, a position is created for her as a training consultant. As the company grows and training needs increase, she quickly becomes a department head making substantially more money than she would have made in her old position. Someone might say she was lucky, but she made her own luck by taking the risk of accepting an extra assignment, while the employee who refused the assignment lost out on the opportunity. The point is that it doesn't hurt to get a few breaks along the line, but more often than not you have to be ready and willing to take advantage of these opportunities.

Redesign Your Job

One way to get yourself a better job is to use a bit of creativity in reconfiguring your present job to meet your needs. How you do this will depend somewhat upon what it is you want to accomplish. For example, if you are seeking more responsibility, then you will look for ways to acquire tasks that will accomplish this. Something as simple as asking your boss may be sufficient, or you may casually assume some of the burdens of your peers. Lots of folks are more than willing to give up some of their responsibility, especially when they can find a ready and willing volunteer to take on their chores. This may have to be cleared with the boss, but it isn't likely to present a problem, because the boss's interest isn't so much in who is doing the work as in making sure that the work will be done.

Maybe your goal is to cut down on the detail work you have to do. In this case, the problem is one of looking for ways to eliminate some of your chores. This may not be as hard to do as it appears, once you start to explore the possibilities. For instance, you may find that one or more of the reports you spend hours working on won't really be used by anyone. It may have long since ceased to have any value, but no one has ever bothered to question its validity so it is still prepared. Once you start looking at these angles, you will uncover lots of detail work that is a waste of time. By eliminating it, you will not only make your job more interesting, but you should receive some credit for increasing productivity by getting rid of unnecessary work.

Other approaches to making your present job more attractive include revising your work hours, telecommuting so you can work from home, working part-time, or perhaps just redoing the layout of your office or work area. Naturally, not all these options will be available to you, but whatever it is that you want to do to revamp your job, if you explore the possibilities you may be surprised at what can be accomplished.

THE KEYS TO MARKETING YOURSELF TO OTHERS

Once you have decided to look for a job elsewhere, you then have to embark on a campaign to market your talents. In fact, this is a task you should undertake on an ongoing basis in a low-key way. The better the job you do of making your talents known far and wide, the greater the possibilities for landing a good job once you start a search in earnest.

Although in most instances searching for a new job involves looking beyond your present employer, that isn't always the case. If you work for a fairly large company, there may well be job opportunities within the company that appeal to you. So, your first stab at job hunting can be internally. This will offer advantages, but it can also have its liabilities.

For example, your boss may be reluctant to lose you and may throw roadblocks in your path if you attempt a transfer. As an offshoot of this, other managers may be reluctant to hire someone if the potential transfer's boss isn't happy about losing the person. This won't be a problem if you have a supportive boss who encourages and supports employees in furthering their careers. As a matter of fact, a good manager will learn of promotional opportunities elsewhere within the company, and aggressively market his or her subordinates for these positions.

Are You a Generalist or Specialist?

With rapid technological change, global competition, and service sector jobs supplanting those in manufacturing, successfully marketing yourself consists of far more than sending out a resume with solid credentials. One factor which is consistently debated is whether you should be a generalist or specialist in terms of experience.

One argument goes that companies want generalists who are flexible enough to switch from one field to another, while the opposing view holds that employers will favor people with specific in-depth skills in one area of expertise. To win either way, the trick is to be viewed as both a generalist and a specialist. For example, someone with several years of general management experience may also have developed specialist skills in one or more areas. Unfortunately, those with a limited number of years of experience aren't as able to do this as people who have many years of experience. What these opposing viewpoints do point out though, is the value of continuing education and cross-training to develop expertise in a number of areas. It stands to reason that the more varied your skills, the better your chances of landing the job you want.

Assess Your Marketability

How you market yourself starts with a self-assessment of your skills. Be honest with yourself about your strengths and weaknesses. What you want to do is emphasize the former and work at beefing up the latter, through either additional experience, training, or a combination of the two. Decide what the job market is for your particular expertise. When it comes to factoring your experience into the equation, look for ways to project the experience you have that best fits the requirements of the job for which you are applying.

For example, if an open position emphasizes leadership skills, a resume that merely indicates you supervised people for three years isn't sufficient. It's best to show when and where you were a team leader on specific projects of importance to the company. The specific terms you use to demonstrate your talents go a long way toward selling you to prospective employers. The people who review resumes aren't going to play guessing games. Job titles held don't mean much to hiring authorities. The specifics of what you did on the job are what they are interested in. You have to respond to listed requirements directly, or risk being eliminated before you have a chance to showcase your talents in an interview. In the final analysis, you are selling yourself, and how successful you are in marketing yourself will depend upon how good a sales job you do.

You also have to determine what you are worth in the marketplace. As you increase your skills, your value increases. Always keep tuned to your current market value through salary surveys, people you know in similar positions in other companies, and so forth. When you have assessed both your expertise and value in the job market, the next step in marketing yourself is to determine the potential job market in which you can advance your services.

The type of position you are seeking to some extent dictates how you market yourself. For lower-level positions, employment agencies, newspaper ads, and sending out resumes is part of the process. For more senior positions, executive search firms and a network of contacts are the means to the end. You may decide to use a job counseling service, which for a fee assists people in resume preparation, interview preparation, and so forth. If you do, be sure to verify the firm's legitimacy, and check its success record through references. Most are legitimate, but it's your money and your career so you want to be sure of its credibility.

Before you actually start looking, narrow your base of prospective employers by determining the following:

* What size company are you interested in? There are pros and cons involved at all levels. Small companies may give you more responsibility, but both the pay and the level of support will be lower. Try to decide which best fits your needs so you won't be disappointed later.

* What are your geographical requirements? If you don't want to move more than forty miles from New York City, don't spin your wheels interviewing for jobs on the West Coast.

* What are your minimum salary requirements? No matter how good a job may look, you have minimum financial needs, so by establishing a salary floor, you won't waste time interviewing for jobs that won't pay your minimum.

Use Your Network of Contacts

One of the necessary elements of marketing yourself is having a solid network of people who know of you and your skills. Whenever you meet people who may be able to help you out at some point, keep a record of them. Incidentally, the social banter you conduct at association meetings, conventions, seminars, and so forth doesn't have to be wasted. If you keep track of people you meet, try to jot down a few of the personal facts you discover. People are always impressed by someone they met months ago, who after exchanging greetings again, mentions something personal, such as, "Is your daughter still playing the clarinet in the school band?"

To keep your network functioning, try to keep in touch with people periodically, either through a phone call, or getting together for lunch or a game of golf. With your out-of-town contacts, give them a call when you're in their area, and tell them to call you if they visit your hometown. Maintaining a base of contacts is a sure-fire way to garner job leads when you are looking for greener pastures.

Incidentally, doing favors begets favors. For this reason, make yourself available to do favors for people when the opportunity presents itself. Beyond the good feeling you get by doing this, the possibility of a more tangible payoff down the road always exists. Never make assumptions about who can or can't help your cause. Someone who may not be in a direct position to help you out may have a lot of influence with someone who can. This is a good reason not to underestimate the power of people. Be nice to everyone, since you never know who may be able to help you out in the future. Above all else, when you're in the marketplace for a job, be persistent, since that as much as anything is part and parcel of getting yourself settled in a good job.

SOME HANDY WAYS TO BUILD YOUR CREDENTIALS

No matter how secure and satisfied you may be in your current position, you should always be taking steps toward improving your ability to get another job, either with your present employer or elsewhere. One essential means of accomplishing this objective is to continually build your credentials to support your future quest for another job. It's all too easy to forget about the future when things are going well. However, when crunch time arrives and you have to go job hunting, the urgency then arises to present yourself in the best prospective light to potential employers. It's at this time that people start to think about their qualifications for various positions.

Unfortunately, the training and skills needed can't be obtained overnight. So people end up going with what they have, which may not be as much as they would like if they haven't been working hard at improving their qualifications. Therefore, it's never too early to start thinking about what sort of training and on-the-job skills would be beneficial to your future. Once you decide what you need to meet your future career goals, then it's time to start taking action to get the necessary education and job experience.

Improve Your On-the-Job Skills

Assuming you intend to stay in your present line of work, much of the experience and training you need can be gained in your present job, though you still have to think about what you can do to improve your credentials. This may mean taking the initiative to ask your boss for additional training in certain areas where you aren't satisfied with your present skills. As long as it's related to your job, there's every likelihood your boss will be more than willing to give you job assignments that will give you the needed experience, or approve any necessary courses. Naturally, you want to emphasize that the skills are needed to perform better on your present job. In actuality, you're accomplishing two things here. First, you're sprucing up your resume for the future, and second, you're demonstrating your dedication to learning how to do the best job possible to your boss. So you not only make your present employer happy, but you also improve your future prospects.

Become a Member of Trade and Professional Organizations

In terms of upgrading your skills, it's easy to get complacent if you have been doing the same type of work for a substantial period of time. The tendency is to believe you know all there is to know about a particular line of work. Yet it's important to keep current with the latest technology or trends in your field.

A good way to do this is to join any professional group in your field. These organizations typically sponsor courses and hold seminars which can keep your knowledge up-to-date. Some of them also offer professional certification programs which you may find listed in the qualifications of job advertisements. If your career field has a professional certification program, avail yourself of the opportunity to become certified. It will mean sacrificing some of your personal time to study for certification exams, but it's time well spent. Many prospective employers use these certification designations as a minimum hiring standard, since they know that anyone with the designation has met certain specific requirements.

Another advantage of such groups is their networking potential. By attending meetings of any local chapter you will get to know organization members in your field who work for other employers. This gives you an excellent opportunity to get a line on where the job openings are, what companies are expanding, and all sorts of other valuable career information. Belonging to professional associations also beefs up your resume, since membership indicates you are serious about keeping up with the knowledge base in your chosen career field.

Take Advantage of Continuing Education Opportunities

In looking for ways to improve your credentials, it's worthwhile to take courses or otherwise make efforts to improve those areas where you feel your skills are weakest. Computer skills, written communication, and public speaking are three representative areas which can be improved upon by taking a few courses at a local college to improve your abilities. If you anticipate the need for proficiency in a foreign language in the future, this again is an area in which you can seek out training.

Sometimes people want to improve their knowledge base through additional education, but never get started because they view a full-time job and part-time schooling as too grueling, or they adopt academic goals that will seemingly take forever. For example, people lacking a college degree think in terms of going to school at night for years before they will earn their degree. As a result, they may become defeated before they begin and dismiss the project as being too overwhelming.

It's far better to reach for something you can visualize as being doable in the short-term. For example, start by taking a course or two in areas which will build your job credentials. Don't look at it as an absolute must to have the degree. After you have taken a few courses, you may get in a routine where that becomes a viable option. If it doesn't, you are still learning skills that will make you more attractive to both your present employer and others. It also helps to be able to put on your resume that you are taking courses to improve your skills.

Do Volunteer Work

Various awards and other forms of recognition are nice credentials to have when you're job hunting. Obtaining these doesn't have to be a matter of waiting around to be recognized as a stellar performer. You can take action that will get you recognition. One such possibility is to volunteer for charitable campaigns or other civic affair endeavors, either at work or independently. Aside from the virtues of such undertakings, the exposure you gain within the community builds additional contacts, and you never know when you will find one of them sitting across from you at an interview. That, of course, is stretching it a bit, but the more people you know, the broader the network of contacts you have.

DO'S AND DON'TS FOR PREPARING YOUR RESUME

Unless you're applying for a job where the people doing the hiring know you personally, your resume will represent you to those doing the hiring. Therefore, what you put in it—as well as what you don't—dictates whether or not you are invited for an interview. For this reason, it's imperative to take the time to make certain your resume is complete, accurate, and professional in appearance.

Even if you choose to have a professional resume service prepare your resume for you, this doesn't relieve you of the responsibility for its contents. The best resume writers in the world can only work with the information you give them. Consequently, you should take great pains to put together all relevant information before you prepare the resume yourself, or seek someone to do it for you. The basics of a good resume are pretty simple, but careful preparation is essential, since a carelessly prepared resume isn't going to get you many job offers.

The one aspect of the resume that tends to cause the most confusion for people is the job objective. Some people advise using a general job objective covering your career goals, others recommend a narrow objective tied to the specific job you're applying for, while some resume experts suggest you don't use any job objective at all.

The respective arguments for each approach are that a general objective doesn't eliminate you from consideration for a variety of positions, while a specific objective allows you to address the needs of an individual job opening. As for not using any objective, the argument here is that for some positions—especially senior ones—you couldn't write a short enough objective to cover your strengths for the type of position you're seeking.

The best approach to take is to tailor your job objective to each specific job for which you're applying. The ease of revising a resume on a personal computer makes this entirely feasible. By doing this, you're able to target your resume to particular jobs, and the closer you can target your job objective, the greater the chance yours will be one of the resumes that's plucked from the pile for an interview. The best argument for using a well-defined job objective is that personnel people aren't going to waste time searching through a resume trying to figure out what position you're applying for. "When in doubt, toss it out," is probably the best way to define what happens to resumes that make life difficult for the people who have to screen them.

The next resume issue that's kicked around is how long the resume should be. You'll always find someone with a glib answer such as, "As long as necessary to do the job." This tells you nothing. A resume should be limited to one page if it's possible to do so, which is always true with people early in their careers. If you have been in the working world for a number of years and have accumulated varied experience, then a two-page resume may be necessary.

Shortening a resume isn't as hard as it seems once you get the hang of it. For starters, always leave out unnecessary information such as personal details of height, weight, and so forth. Working at tightening up your resume also has the advantage of forcing you to think about what you're saying in the document. Try reading your resume from the position of someone who didn't know you. Can you understand what the job experience listed is, and how it relates to the open position? If you can't, you better do some rewriting. Incidentally, when you list your experience, highlight your achievements, not the titles of the positions you held. The people reading the resume want to know what you did, not what your job title was.

There are a number of other resume basics that shouldn't be ignored. These are:

- *Don't use fancy colored paper.* White or off-white serves the purpose nicely.

- *Forget gimmicks.* People who sift through piles of resumes aren't impressed by poetry or perfumed resumes, much less odd-shaped paper.

- *Be neat.* If you're trying to prove how smart you are, it's pretty dumb to send out a resume with words misspelled.

- *Don't lie on your resume.* It's not worth taking the risk, and if you aren't caught until after you are hired, you could end up losing the job.

- *Avoid jargon which may not be understood by those who receive your resume.*

- *List your accomplishments—not your duties.*

Always include a cover letter with your resume. This should be as brief as possible, and serve primarily as an introduction to the resume you are forwarding. Don't put anything of substance in the cover letter for one very good reason. Cover letters are often detached from resumes, and even when they're not, they aren't always read. Therefore, don't spend a lot of time trying to construct the best cover letter in the world. Use the time instead to work on your resume.

HELPFUL HINTS FOR WINNING THE INTERVIEW GAME

For most job seekers, the interview process is a period of nervous apprehension with much time spent worrying about what to say beforehand, and a lot of thought afterwards as to whether or not the interview turned out well. It's understandable that this is so, since being grilled about your work history, no matter how pleasantly it's done, is a trying experience when a potential job hangs in the balance. The best way to keep worrying to a minimum is to be prepared adequately beforehand, since this alone will give you a greater degree of confidence. Fortunately, it's not that difficult to prepare for an interview as long as you know 1) what to expect, and 2) how to handle the questions that you're sure to be asked.

The starting point in preparing for an interview is to recognize that the objective of the interviewer is to find the person who is the "best fit" for the open position. Notice that it isn't the best qualified person, but the person who is the "best fit," and there's a distinct difference between the two.

Interestingly enough, most interviewers if pressed would say they are looking for the best qualified person, but that isn't really the right way to look at it, since it belies the personality issues involved in the hiring process. The bottom line is that the person with the job opening wants to hire the person who will fit in best within his or her group. Therefore, although someone else may have better qualifications on paper, the hiring authority may prefer someone with whom he or she feels more comfortable during the interview process.

For example, assume the final selection comes down to two candidates, both of whom have the capabilities to handle the job. One candidate has more education and experience, but acts disinterested during the interview and appears reluctant to handle some of the duties of the position. The candidate with the lesser qualifications displays enthusiasm, a willingness to learn, and appears to be someone who will be easy to work with. Even though this latter person has lesser qualifications on paper, he or she is capable of doing the job, and based on their personal attributes, would most likely be the one selected for the position. As a result, the starting point for successful interviews is to be confident of your abilities, and to project a sincere interest in the open position. Hand in hand with this is to present a good appearance, and neither intimidate nor be intimidated during the interview.

How to Answer the Tough Questions

When asked about your experience, always try to relate it as closely as possible to the job for which you are applying. To be successful at doing this, go over in your mind how you will answer these kinds of questions. Concentrate on your most recent job experience, not those from earlier periods in your career. Some of the types of questions you will be asked and the best way to answer them include:

"Can you tell us how your experience ties in with our job requirements?" Incidentally, you may get a helping hand if the person interviewing you describes the duties of the open position before asking you this sort of question. If that happens, you will be able to focus your reply to correspond with what you were told. Don't overdo it though, since if you grossly exaggerate your experience you are apt to be trapped by a follow-up question. For instance, if you say you have experience

using certain types of equipment, the interviewer may follow up with specific questions about the equipment. If you were just winging it and never used the equipment, it will become glaringly evident.

"Have you ever done any . . . ?" Here the interviewer keys in on a specific function which applies to the job in question. For example, budget preparation, systems analysis, programming, purchasing, and so forth are the types of things an interviewer might focus on depending upon the type of job that's being discussed. There are usually two reasons this question is asked. First, it's one of the requirements of the position to be filled, and the interviewer is probing your ability in this area. A secondary reason is that even though it's not a major requirement of the job, you listed expertise in this area in your resume, and the interviewer wants to find out how much you know about it.

In answering this type of knowledge-testing question, display your expertise, but don't overdo it since you don't want to trip yourself up. This also points out the wisdom of not padding your resume with a list of areas in which you have experience unless the claims are valid. If you have negligible knowledge in an area and include it in your resume, a question may be asked on the subject. If you stumble around, and can't answer the question intelligently, the assumption may be that you don't know much more about anything else. The end result is that unfavorable conclusions will be drawn by the interviewer that wouldn't have been if you hadn't tried to pad your resume. You can avoid this by including in your resume only those areas in which you are accomplished, and avoiding those areas in which your experience is weak.

"Can you give me an example of one or two of your major accomplishments on your present job?" If you prepared properly beforehand, you should know what you're going to say in response to this question. This is a standard question, so you should decide well in advance of any interview what you will emphasize. If you don't, and the question hits you cold, you may be hesitant and vague in your response.

Assuming you are ready for the question, there are only two things to watch out for. First, don't overrate your contribution to a project. This is something that you also have to watch when doing your resume. Saying to the interviewer, or writing in a resume, that you increased sales 20% during the last fiscal year is great if it's true. However, if you were one of ten salespeople who contributed to the 20% increase, it's something else again. A little bit of puffery will be overlooked by most interviewers, but someone who implies that a group accomplishment was an individual achievement isn't going to impress anyone. Another point you want to be sure to address is the highlighting of accomplishments that are relevant to the type of position you're seeking.

NOTE: When you're talking about your accomplishments, it's great to have some written documentation with you to confirm what you're saying. This doesn't have to be a formal award, since a "well done" memo from a manager, customer, and so forth is just as good. The advantage of this is that it provides independent verification of what you're saying. This gives you credibility with the interviewer, and it can carry over to other aspects of the interview. Therefore, if you have such documentation, make sure you bring it with you.

"Can you tell me why you're looking for a job?" Don't try to avoid the obvious here. If you lost your job, give an understandable answer. For example, "There was a reorganization, and the customer service function was consolidated at our main location. I didn't want to relocate." If you were involved in a layoff, if possible, try to give a valid reason as to why you weren't one of the people retained on the payroll. For example, "The company had a reduction in force and I was one of the junior people in our department."

On the other hand, if you're still employed but are looking for another position, give a reason that indicates you're not just bouncing from job to job. After all, even though everyone wants to get ahead in their career, the people interviewing are looking for someone who will be around for a while. So just saying you're looking for a better job doesn't cut the mustard. Instead say something such as, "I like my present job, but I'm looking for a position in which I can make use of my computer skills." The specifics aren't as important as giving a reason you're looking for another job which won't paint you as either a job-hopper, or a dissatisfied employee.

Incidentally, always remember not to bad-mouth your present employer or boss. It smacks of disloyalty, and even though you may feel justified, the people interviewing you don't know the facts and aren't likely to be empathetic. No one wants to hire someone who may cause dissension, so employers will be cautious about hiring someone who complains about a prior employer.

There is one final point relating to interview questions to keep in mind. You may have a number of interviews with the same employer and be interviewed by different people. Obviously, these individuals compare notes, and one of the things they're looking for is to see if you give consistent answers to questions. This is one more reason to stick with the facts in answering questions, so you won't be caught giving one story to one interviewer and a completely different pitch to another.

Getting Your Questions Answered

It's certainly necessary to be ready to answer the questions interviewers are sure to ask you. What many job candidates overlook, however, is to get their own questions answered. Don't go into a job interview on the defensive. It's a major decision to accept a new job and you want to know as much as possible about your prospective employer before you're hired.

First of all, why is the position you're applying for open? You sure want to know if it's because five different people have failed in the job in the past six years. Naturally, something such as that isn't going to be answered anyway, but if you can't get a handle on why the position is vacant, and you have other doubts, you may be better off passing on the job. Frequently, if you inquire about the opening, the interviewer will be forthright about telling you why the position is available. This is particularly true if someone retired, or was promoted. It may also be obvious, as in the case of a new position that has just been created.

It's also handy to know why the position isn't being filled from the inside. The logical reason is because no one is qualified to fill the slot, but if it's because no one is interested in it, you may be buying into a thankless position. Other questions you need answered are on the specific duties of the position, as well as the need for and extent of any required overtime and business travel. Don't be pushy if you encounter reluctance in having your questions answered, but keep this in mind if and when you have to make a decision about accepting a job offer. The company interviewers are expecting you to level with them, and they should be equally forthright with you.

Aside from getting your questions answered, be sure to observe what goes on during the interview. Are the people you interview with friendly? Do the employees you see seem upbeat and full of energy, or do they look like they would like to be somewhere else? Does anyone who interviews you allude to something negative about the company without being specific? None of these signs may be conclusive, but if after the interview process you have a gut feeling that the prospective employer isn't one you want to work for, perhaps you should go with your instincts. If you're picking up bad vibes that easily, then there's probably something behind your suspicions.

SIMPLE STEPS FOR SALARY NEGOTIATIONS

One of the hardest issues for many job candidates to understand is how to go about asking for and getting the salary you want. Although the subject of salary negotiations seems to be cloaked in mystery, it's really very basic, as long as you know what to expect and how to deal with the situation. The first step is to put yourself at ease as to any expectation you might have that you need to be a super negotiator to get the salary you want. There's nothing complicated about how to achieve it. The important point is to control the process correctly so you maximize your chances of getting the best salary deal possible.

Do Your Homework to Determine What You're Worth

Job candidates sometimes think that asking for too much money may cost them the job. That isn't likely to happen when salary demands are reasonable and in line with marketplace rates for similar positions. If a prospective employer does balk at paying you what you're looking for, then you're better off not getting the job in the first place.

The starting point for negotiating your salary is being prepared before the prospective employer's representative even makes you an offer. This requires you to do some research to see what you should be asking for. You shouldn't simply rely on your present salary and then factor in another ten or fifteen percent as your asking price. For one thing, your company's salary scales may be higher or lower than industry averages. Furthermore, if you are considering a position in another part of the country, geographic differences can influence the salary structure.

Many other factors can influence salaries; business prospects for the prospective employer have to be considered, and supply and demand in your occupational field can affect the going rate for jobs. If you're lucky enough to be in a field where there is a shortage of qualified candidates, your chances for a higher salary are improved substantially. The size of the employer can also enter into the picture. Smaller firms often pay lower salaries.

On the other hand, a smaller company may have more flexibility in setting the salary for someone they really want, since they are less burdened by the more rigid bureaucratic structures typical of larger firms. The possibilities for rapid salary growth after you're hired may also be greater with a small firm that is growing fast. As the company expands, your responsibilities—and salary—can increase rapidly. Therefore, you can't assume blindly that larger employers are certain to offer you a better salary, either to start with or in the future.

Checking salary figures isn't difficult, for the most part. Professional associations often publish surveys for their members, so if you belong to such a group this is a first-rate source of information. Employment agencies can also give you going rates for different jobs. Remember though, if the job is in another part of the country, get figures from agencies in that area. Personal contacts can also be useful in dredging up salary information relative to other employers.

There are also all kinds of surveys published in magazines as well as government publications. You have to be cautious about using these figures, since they may be outdated. They may also be national in scope and not accurately reflect the salary range for the local area.

Position Yourself to Get the Salary You Want

Once you have salary information in hand, the next step is to determine what your asking salary will be. General guidelines are to seek a salary 10% to 15% higher than you're presently earning. You might even want 20% or more if you're relocating. But be flexible about your salary, since the attractiveness of the position and the benefits offered may justify accepting something less. Other factors can also come into play. For example, if you're switching careers, you may have to accept a starting salary which is less than you are making on your present job. The bottom line is not to accept a position for anything less than the minimum salary you consider to be acceptable.

Somewhere during the interview process the subject of salary will come up. You're better off waiting and letting the interviewer raise the issue, since you don't want to appear to be overanxious. Furthermore, salary isn't likely to come up until the employer's representatives have settled on you as the candidate they want. Once they do that, they are more committed to wanting to hire you than they might have been earlier.

Most of the time the interviewer will ask you what your salary requirements are. Instead of just giving a figure, the best bet is to respond with a question such as, "What is the salary range for this position?" That way, you get to know the salary scale, so when you do give a number, you can make it near the top of the range. Of course, savvy interviewers may thrust the ball right back in your court by responding with something such as, "We're flexible, what are you asking for?" If this happens, don't antagonize the interviewer by continuing to be coy. Give a figure somewhat above what you expect to get. For instance, if you're looking for 10% more than you are presently earning, ask for 15%. The reasoning here is simple. It's a lot easier to lower your demands than it is to raise them after you have put a number on the table. Even if the interviewer does come back with a lower figure, you are still likely to be able to get your 10%. However, if you give a figure 10% higher initially, and the interviewer comes back with a lower number, it is much more difficult to get what you want.

Many people are afraid that if they ask for too much money they will lose out on the job. As long as the figure is reasonable, there's little danger in that. You have to keep in mind that the company has chosen you as the final candidate. Therefore, they want to hire you, and aren't about to lose their prime candidate over a few dollars. Even if the interviewer does come back with a lower figure, if you can make a convincing case of what you can contribute to the company if you're hired, then you may still get what you want.

THINGS YOU SHOULD CONSIDER BEFORE ACCEPTING A JOB OFFER

You have gone through the interview process successfully for what looks like a promising position and finally the phone rings with a prospective employer making you a job offer. The temptation may be to immediately accept the job and be done with it. After all, it's pretty much what you wanted in terms of both the salary offered and long-term career opportunities. The typical thought process is that there's really nothing to do but agree on a starting date, assuming that hasn't already been done during prior discussions. This is fine if you have no doubts about the position. If, however, you have some hesitancy about whether or not this is the right job for you, it's much wiser to postpone the moment of truth to give yourself a day or two to think matters over. Why do that? Won't it jeopardize getting the job if the offer isn't accepted right away?

Naturally, you can't keep a prospective employer on the hook for an extended period, but every employer will wait a day or two to give you time to consider a job offer. Why take the time? For one thing, the euphoria of receiving the offer may cloud over some judgments you have to make about whether or not this is the job to which you want to commit.

All too often, the job hunt is such a time-consuming and frustrating experience that when the first offer comes along there's a natural tendency to accept it and put an end to job hunting. This initial relief may obscure some real doubts you have about the job. As a result, taking a day or two to consider the offer will give you ample time to reflect on the pros and cons before you make up your mind. After all, this is a decision that will significantly alter your work life, so it shouldn't be made on the spur of the moment. How do you handle this with the person on the other end of the phone? Say something such as, "I'm very interested in the position, but I would like to take a day or two before making my final decision. Does this present a problem?" The other party in all likelihood will agree with your request. Then agree on when you will get back to the person with your decision.

This sounds simple enough, but many people worry that if they don't accept the job right away the prospective employer will start looking elsewhere. That's foolish for one simple reason. The company has gone through a lengthy process to find their best candidate for the open position, and you're it. As a result, they aren't going to write you off because you want a little time to think the offer over. Having succeeded in gaining time to mull your decision over, what are the factors you should be thinking about?

First of all, are the duties of the job ones you can live with? You certainly don't want to take a position in which you will be bored quickly. The flip side of the coin is not to put yourself in a position where you will be swamped with work and stressed out continually. If you will be taking over an existing position, the duties will be pretty clearly defined. Conversely, if it's a newly created position, the precise nature and extent of your responsibilities may rest partly on what you make of the position after you start the job. What you determine to be good or bad for you depends pretty much on your own personality. Some people like structure, while others like a position that gives them more of an opportunity to freelance.

Aside from the job itself, how comfortable do you feel about the person for whom you will be working? You can't learn much from just sitting down for one or two interview sessions, but even in that short span of time you will have a gut reaction to your future boss. Was the person genuinely friendly during the interview process, or did he or she come across as cold and aloof? Were there numerous job interruptions during your interview? If so, it may indicate your future boss doesn't plan very carefully, since he or she should have arranged an uninterrupted segment to conduct interviews. Did you develop any sort of rapport during your discussions? All these factors aren't particularly significant taken individually, but if you have several nagging questions about your future boss, don't jump too quickly to accept the job. Remember, you'll be working for this person on a daily basis, and if an interview or two left you with doubts, think of what might develop on a regular basis.

What about the company as an employer? Are you satisfied with the salary offer, and does the new job offer hope for career growth? Is the company expanding in a growing industry which holds out promise for some degree of job security? Finally, what about the more personal issues that may affect your decision? Will your commute be unreasonably long or difficult, or will the working hours be different than what you have been working? If the latter is true, will this require any adjustments in your personal life?

Although you may experience some hesitation about the new position, some of this may be attributable to the fear of change itself. Everyone experiences doubts about any major decision, but unless your consideration of the possibilities turns up something substantive, take the job and shake the cobwebs of doubt from your mind.

POSITIVE WAYS TO JUMP SHIP GRACEFULLY

Landing a new job leaves some people harboring thoughts of settling a few scores on the old job on the way out the door. This is especially true if you've been given a pink slip, or have suffered in silence under a tyrant of a boss. If these thoughts should enter your mind, put them to rest. You might gain a little personal satisfaction out of telling someone off, but in the long run it can come back to haunt you. Career paths take some strange twists and turns and you never know when the boss you blasted will be reunited with you in another company, much to your dismay. Even if that doesn't happen, gossip travels well, and you never know whether or not you might incite someone to bad-mouth you with your new employer. Subdue any urge for vengeance and enjoy the fact that your new job is offering you a new beginning.

Beyond settling scores, there are other advantages to leaving your job gracefully. In fact, if you go about it the right way, you can cement relationships with your present contacts as good insurance for the future. After all, it can bring a measure of satisfaction to tell a boss you can't stand how much you enjoyed working for him. If it's more than you can muster to do that with a straight face, then at least part on a friendly basis.

Handle the Formalities

There are several other actions you can take to leave a job in good standing. First of all, always try to schedule interviews on your own time. This may not always be possible, since interviewers may not want to forgo their lunch hour, or work after regularly scheduled business hours. Therefore, you may have to use vacation or personal time for interviewing. In addition, don't advertise to your co-workers that you're looking for another job. It's virtually guaranteed that this information will find its way back to your boss. This in itself may not do you any harm, but it certainly won't do you any good. A boss isn't going to go out of his or her way to do favors for an employee who is looking for a job elsewhere.

Once you accept a job offer, it's time to take care of the formalities. The first thing to do is to tell your boss you have accepted another position. Give sufficient notice, which is two weeks for most jobs. Also let the boss know where you stand on any open projects and which ones will be completed before you leave. At this time, take the opportunity to let your boss know how much you enjoyed working for him, even if that doesn't happen to be true. After all, you won't have to work for the s.o.b. much longer, so why not be magnanimous?

You should also sit down with your co-workers and thank them for all the assistance they have given you in the past. Some of them may be friends, but even those you dealt with only infrequently will appreciate your thoughtfulness. This is a good way to continue your networking activities, since in the future many of these people will go on to work for other employers. Therefore, it's a good idea to let people know where you are going and to maintain contact after you leave.

Beware of Exit Interviews and Counteroffers

Some larger companies conduct detailed exit interviews, in which they seek to learn why employees are leaving, and what you think can be done to improve the company. This *is not* the time to be candid. Anything you say that is negative about a boss or anyone else may not remain confidential. Therefore, there's nothing for you to gain by being vindictive. Even if there are aspects of the company about which you feel constructive suggestions for improvement can be made, keep them to yourself. You're not being paid to be a consultant, and your suggestions probably won't be appreciated. In providing a reason, offer some innocuous answer which doesn't reflect on your present employer or your boss.

One dilemma some people face when they give their notice is a counteroffer from their present employer. For the most part, it's unwise to accept an offer of increased pay to stay. For one thing, you had good reason for wanting to leave or you wouldn't have been job hunting in the first place. Furthermore, if the company thought you were worth more, they could have raised your pay before you went looking elsewhere. There's also no guarantee that if you accept the counteroffer, your employer may not wait a long time before giving you another raise.

Therefore, over the long haul you won't gain anything. Besides that, your relationship with your boss and others may shift subtly if you change your mind and stay put. Nothing may be said, but there may be an underlying belief that you're not very loyal to the company, and that won't bode well for you in the future. So once you make a commitment to another job, follow through and move your career along.

WHAT TO DO IF YOU LOSE YOUR JOB UNEXPECTEDLY

A sudden termination, for whatever reason, can leave you in a panic wondering what to do next. First and foremost is to collect your thoughts, as hard as it may be to regain your composure. This may sound unrealistic five minutes after someone has told you to clean out your desk and not return tomorrow. Nevertheless, as difficult as it is, when times are toughest is when it's most important to have control of your emotions. As for what to do when you have been told you're losing your job, the first step is to determine what you have coming in terms of pay and benefits. Chances are a personnel representative will explain these things to you. Listen carefully, since your mind may be elsewhere and you want to be alert to ask all the questions necessary to understand your rights fully.

The tendency when you suddenly lose your job is to panic and rush to find something else right away. This won't solve much for the long haul, since taking the first job that comes along may put you in a position you wouldn't have taken under ordinary circumstances. Instead, take the time to find the type of job you want for the long term. Be honest with yourself about this, and ask yourself this question: "Would I take this job if I wasn't out of work?" If the answer is "no," then you're not solving anything by taking a position just to be working.

Sure, you still have to pay the bills that keep coming in, but with severance pay, unemployment benefits, and cutting back on expenditures, you have some time to look for a job you can live with. In fact, if your financial situation becomes a problem before you can secure a new job, you might want to consider doing some part-time work just to bring in a little money. However, don't do this at the expense of limiting your search for a job, since that is—and should be—a full-time proposition.

Sudden unemployment can have a hidden benefit for some people. It forces action on long-held dreams to try a new career. If you have harbored thoughts of starting anew in another career field, this may be just the time to do it. Many people ignore this possibility and go on looking for another position in the same field. But if someone is going to switch careers, they might as well do it from a base of being unemployed. Otherwise, it's unlikely a steady job will be abandoned to start off fresh.

The biggest hurdle to avoid if you lose your job is to fall into a rut. Searching for work while being unemployed is more traumatic than doing so from the security of a job. There's a tendency to give up if you don't find another position in a short period of time. For this reason, it's useful to take advantage of any outplacement assistance your employer may have furnished. This will help set you firmly on your way toward another position. It's important to keep a daily routine, if for no other reason than to avoid dwelling on the loss of your job. If necessary, do some volunteer work to fill up any empty spots on your calendar. It may not seem like it at the time, but eventually you will look back on losing your job and realize that it was just a minor blip on the radar screen of life.

TWELVE QUICK WAYS TO REDUCE EXPENSES BETWEEN JOBS

If you lose your job suddenly, the chances are you will experience a period of unemployment before landing a new position. Since you can't be certain how long you may be unemployed, one of the first actions to take is to cut back your spending to stretch your budget a little farther, since your regular source of income has ceased. Incidentally, chapters nine and ten cover financial planning on a long-term basis and regular tactics for saving money. Following these measures throughout your career will give you the financial security you need no matter what happens.

The focus in this section is on temporary measures to tide you over a period of unemployment. If you're getting little or nothing in terms of severance benefits or other monetary payments from your employer, this may be an absolute necessity. This is certainly true if you don't have much in the way of savings.

On the other hand, some people receive a hefty severance payment and may also have substantial sums vested in a 401(k) plan which they have the opportunity to cash out or rollover to an IRA (Individual Retirement Account). Alternatively, some folks may have substantial savings on which they can live. There's a very real temptation to use this money to tide you over the period of unemployment, but this is unwise if it can be avoided. It takes a long time, as you know, to accumulate savings in any form, and using it for living expenses can burn it up quickly. Even if you have funds available from other sources, it's still prudent to cut your expenses to the bone.

Naturally, you may have to use some of your existing funds for emergencies, but the main idea is to tighten your belt as much as possible until you start a new job. Depending on your circumstances, there are all sorts of ways to cut costs. Here are twelve possibilities for cutting back on your expenditures on a temporary basis, and you can undoubtedly add your own ideas to the list.

- *Go from two cars to one.* Use the proceeds from the car you sell to help with your living expenses until you land another job. If you have only one vehicle, and it's a late model car which is paid off, you may want to sell it to come up with some funds to pay your bills. You can then pick up an older used car for basic transportation. In fact, if you have good public transportation where you live, you may even be able to get by without any car for a while. On those occasions when you need one, use a rental car. These may sound like drastic suggestions, but next to housing, cars are the biggest expense for most people. Therefore, in a time of dire financial need, it's an area that has to be looked at to reduce expenses.

- *Eat in—not out.* Dining out may be one of your few pleasures, but when you're trying to conserve funds, preparing meals at home is a lot less expensive. Don't just assume that since you don't eat at fancy restaurants, this isn't an area where you can cut back. Fast food or having pizza delivered several times a week can eat up a big chunk of cash. One of the main reasons people give for eating out is that they don't have time to cook. This argument isn't so valid while you're between jobs.

- *Cut your heating and cooling bills.* Adjust the thermostat and live with it being a little cooler at home in the winter. If you have central air conditioning, reduce its use and adjust the setting to make the indoor temperature a little warmer. Turning off TV's, fans, and lights that aren't being used will also lower your utility bill. Cut your hot water bill by washing clothes in cold water.

- *Put your credit cards away.* Use cash for everything you buy. That way, you're forced to think about what you spend. If you have outstanding balances on your credit cards, reduce your payments to the minimum due each month until you have a paycheck coming in again.

- *Don't write checks for nonessentials such as magazine subscriptions, various mail order solicitations, or membership dues.* You can revive these at a later date.

- *Shop at discount outlets.* For necessary expenditures, do your buying at discount outlets, or at special sales. Compare prices so you know whether or not you're getting a good price.

- *Reduce your food shopping costs.* Cut back on convenience foods, snack foods, and brand name items which tend to be more expensive. Instead, buy items on sale, use coupons, and purchase store brands. Make out your shopping list before you go to the store and stick to it. That way, you won't be tempted to buy things you don't need. It also helps not to go grocery shopping when you're hungry, since your appetite may induce you to buy more than you would if you were shopping on a full stomach.

- *Look for ways to scale back on regular expenditures.* For example, lower cable TV costs by eliminating premium services, and cut your automobile insurance premiums by opting for higher deductibles.

- *Look for a way to temporarily reduce your housing costs.* If you rent, perhaps you can ask your landlord for a temporary decrease in the amount of rent you pay, which you will repay when you begin working again. If you own, depending upon the interest rate on your mortgage, you may be able to refinance and lower your monthly payments.

- *Look for chores you can do yourself that you were paying others to do.* Lawn and pool maintenance, house cleaning, and washing your car are typical areas in which you can cut costs by doing the work yourself.

- *Entertain yourself inexpensively.* Look for free or inexpensive entertainment instead of paying for high-priced theater or sports event tickets. Watch TV movies instead of renting videos.

- *Look for substitutes to spending money for something you want.* For instance, if you need tools for work around the house, borrow them from a neighbor or relative.

FIFTEEN RULES FOR A SUCCESSFUL JOB SEARCH

Prior sections of this chapter covered various aspects of searching for and landing a new job, and the following chapter covers all the elements to consider if you plan to change careers. Since it sometimes helps to be able to quickly summarize the steps you need to take for a successful job search, the following fifteen rules are furnished with this thought in mind. They are not meant to be all-inclusive, nor will all of them be useful in every situation, but collectively they represent the most important factors you have to consider when hunting for a new job. As you will see from the list, some aspects of searching for another job are of a continuing nature, such as networking, while other measures won't come into play until you actually decide to pursue a job lead.

1. *Determine what your specific goals are in terms of the job you are seeking.* Usually, people just generalize in doing this by saying they want a better-paying job with greater career opportunities. That's fine as far as it goes, but it isn't specific enough to narrow your search, nor does it contribute to making an intelligent decision regarding accepting or rejecting any forthcoming job offers.

For example, how much additional money would constitute a better-paying job? What is considered to be a better career opportunity? These are questions that you have to think about in specifics before you start your job search. Not only will it save you time and effort in looking for a position that fits your criteria, but going through this exercise forces you to contemplate your career goals in depth. Doing this will give you a better handle on what you are looking for in a new position. It also prepares you to better articulate your desires during the interview process. A good way to go about establishing your goals is to sit down and write them out. Be as specific as possible when doing this. For example, what is the minimum salary you will accept? What size company do you want to work for? Are you willing to relocate? What kind of job responsibilities are you looking for? Make this list as complete as possible and don't ignore seemingly minor items such as the length of commute or working hours.

Naturally, some of the items will have more significance than others. Furthermore, you may be flexible about waiving your requirements with some items if a job offers numerous advantages in some other areas. For example, you may be willing to accept a longer commute if the salary is high enough. When your list is complete, put it in order of your priorities. If salary is most important, put that first and go on down the line. You may also want to note any items where you are flexible about waiving a requirement if the position offered meets most of your other needs.

2. *You should continually avail yourself of opportunities to establish contacts.* There are a variety of ways to do this, such as professional association meetings, conventions, trade shows, or by actually joining a networking group. Don't hesitate to let people know what your career interests are. You never know when a casual contact may lead to something significant. Once you decide to look for a specific position, let the people in your network know what you're looking for. By the way, don't be shy about helping other people with their job searches, since this is a pretty good way to invest in your own future.

3. *Decide upon your specific search methods.* It's in your best interest to explore all possible avenues in your job hunt, but you don't want to waste energy by spending time on what may be unproductive. For example, senior positions aren't filled through want ads listed in the daily paper, so it would make little sense to send resumes out in response to help-wanted ads. This may be a viable approach for lower-level positions, but never make this your sole source for a job search. Furthermore, avoid answering blind ads, since you never know whether or not it might be a help-wanted ad placed by your present employer.

4. *Line up your references.* Naturally you want to give references who will give you a strong recommendation. However, just lining up three good friends doesn't add any credibility to your credentials. Therefore, whenever possible, try to cite references who have a connection to the job you're seeking. For example, a noted expert in your career field can carry some weight as a reference.

   Something else to consider is the prestige trap. Some people like to find the most influential people they know to use for a reference. This can cause problems if they know little or nothing about your capabilities, since this may become obvious if they are contacted. Furthermore, not everyone will be impressed by the stature of the individuals you may list. In fact, this could work in reverse if you, for example, gave a noted politician for a reference, and the person reviewing the application happened to be a supporter of the opposing political party.

5. *Update your resume and reword it as necessary to tie your accomplishments to the requirements of the job for which you're applying.* What you want to do is emphasize the experience you have that meets the responsibilities of the open position. Be honest in doing this, since the job you get is the job you'll have to work in day after day. So if a job requires substantial experience in an area you know little about, even if faking it gets you the job, it won't help you keep it.

   What you should do is present a resume that details your relevant experience in the priority of the job requirements. For example, if the requirements for the open position emphasize teamwork, this is the experience you should highlight on your resume for this particular position. The next position you apply for may emphasize specific expertise in your field of work; this would be what to highlight.

6. *Prepare a cover letter to accompany your resume.* If you're replying to an inquiry requesting your resume, personalize the letter, since no one likes to receive what is obviously a boilerplate letter. Avoid putting important information in a routine cover letter that accompanies a resume. The letters frequently get separated from the accompanying resume, and in any event, most reviewers pretty much ignore the cover letter and go right to the resume. So if you have included significant information in a cover letter, it may not be seen.

7. *Prepare for your interview.* Aside from preparing yourself to answer questions, don't neglect to think about questions for which you will want answers. Job candidates get careless in this area. They are conscientious enough to consider how to field questions from an interviewer, but they neglect to ask their own questions. Don't be hesitant in doing this. It's not a one-way street where the prospective employer gets to ask all the questions. It may be the company's job, but it's your career, so don't shy away from asking questions for fear of annoying someone.

If you're interviewing with the type of boss for which you want to work, they will be more than willing to discuss your concerns. If not, then you probably don't want the job anyway, since reticence to respond to your queries may be a sign that the job isn't as good as advertised. From another perspective, a prospective boss who doesn't answer your questions *before* you're hired isn't going to change after you take the job. So a failure to communicate at an interview may signal a boss who doesn't communicate with employees. If so, you're better off discovering this at the interview stage, rather than as an employee who can't get answers from the boss.

8. *Research any prospective employers with whom you plan to interview.* When companies call the final few candidates in for interviews, their qualifications have already been screened. Therefore,

most of the time there's very little in terms of qualifications and experience to differentiate between the individual prospects. If you are the only one who has shown the initiative to learn something about the company, this can help swing the hiring decision in your favor.

9. *Don't neglect your appearance when you are going for an interview.* This isn't a factor that will override qualifications in getting you a job, but it is certainly a factor that can exclude you from consideration.

10. *Negotiate your needs in terms of what you can live with when you are going through the interview process.* As long as you are reasonable, the prospective employer will be willing to consider adjustments. For example, don't say salary doesn't matter if you're asked by an interviewer, then come back later after receiving an offer and say the salary is too low. The same holds true for relocation benefits and any other aspect of the position that is open for discussion. The only thing that will really irritate an interviewer is a candidate who says nothing until an offer is forthcoming and then wants to bargain about everything. During the interview process, you expect the company to level with you, and you should do likewise.

11. *Within twenty-four hours of an interview, send out a "thank you" note to the people who interviewed you.* This seems like a simple formality, but many job applicants don't bother to do this. If you take the time to express your appreciation, it will set you apart from less considerate applicants. This can mean something to the boss you will ultimately be working for if you get the job. It signals that you appreciate what people do for you, and this is an attribute a prospective boss can respect.

12. *After the interview, spend some time thinking about what you learned.* Do this before your thoughts on what transpired get stale. What were you pleased with about the job and the people you were interviewed by, and what, if anything, wasn't satisfactory? Doing this will give you the basis for deciding whether or not you will accept any offer that may be forthcoming.

13. *Field any job offers you receive.* Generally this will be by phone with a written confirmation. Most of the time the person making the offer

will ask if you want a day or two to consider the offer. You may want to take advantage of this if you are on the fence about the job. If so, let the person know you will be in touch with them by a mutually agreeable date.

Another reason for hesitating may be that you have another offer pending. If you haven't received it yet, then contact the other prospective employer and let them know you have received an offer. Say something such as, "I'm very interested in the position you have open, and wondered whether or not you will be making an offer to me in the next day or so?" This may prompt this prospective employer to get back to you with an offer if they are considering you as their prime candidate. You then have a couple of offers to choose from.

Assuming you have no valid reason for taking time to consider the offer you get, you might as well accept it when you get the initial phone call. Ask for confirmation if the other party doesn't mention it. You will probably also agree on a starting date at this time. Barring some unusual circumstance, you should always give sufficient notice to your present employer. As a guideline, two weeks is sufficient for lower-level jobs, while higher-level positions should be longer, with thirty days being reasonable for mid-level positions. This allows for a smooth transition and gives your employer time to start the process toward hiring your replacement.

14. *Give notice to your employer in such a way that you leave in good standing.* The first person to know you have another job should be your immediate boss. That's basic enough, but what can happen is in the excitement of hearing the good news, upon hanging up the phone, the happy camper blurts out his or her news to everyone. As you know, this sort of scuttlebutt travels like wildfire and it could reach your boss before you do. So if necessary, subdue your urge to let the world know of your good fortune until you have told your boss. Incidentally, as a matter of diplomacy, it helps to subdue your joy about getting the other job. After all, your boss and peers may

be quite happy where they are and it's poor taste to imply that you didn't like your job or your boss.

15. *You will contact many prospective employers in the course of a job search, have a number of interviews, and meet many different people.* You will also experience a number of rejections which may arrive as a form letter. Even though you may not be selected by a prospective employer this time around, there's always the future to think about. Therefore, even with rejections it's a nice touch to send out a note thanking people for considering you. It involves a little bit of effort, but it may pay dividends in the future. There's a tendency to neglect this formality once you have landed a new position. Never forget though, that in the future you may be applying for another job. If that happens and someone remembers your thoughtfulness from the past, it can't hurt your cause.

Last but not least, don't let rejections during your job search slow you down. Sometimes a number of rejections can be depressing and lead to discouragement. This can lead to a slacking off in your job hunt. You have to keep in mind that rejections aren't a reflection of your qualifications. The final decision on filling a position always comes down to a subjective decision no matter how objective people try to be. Therefore, the people doing the hiring ultimately base their decisions on who they feel is the "best fit" for that particular position. Whether or not they are ultimately right is something with which they will have to live. If they didn't select you, you already know they didn't get the best candidate.

Chapter

6

CHANGING CAREERS THROUGH CHOICE OR NECESSITY

There may come a time when you decide for one reason or another that a career change is in your best interest. This is a decision that isn't made lightly, particularly if you have spent a number of years gaining experience in one field, and are now considering starting a new career in an unrelated field. There are, however, sound reasons for switching careers. Perhaps you're in a field where future prospects aren't very bright. Or you may be losing a job because of cutbacks and for the first time have a real opportunity to pursue a long-standing dream. Whatever the reason, there are numerous factors to consider when making a decision to switch careers.

First and foremost, you have to weigh the financial considerations of a career switch. Are you in a financial position to take the risks associated with a change in careers? What are the long- and short-term risks of a career switch? These questions can't be answered hastily. In fact, it's important to plan a career change well ahead of time, carefully taking these and other factors into consideration.

179

There are other aspects of career changes that shouldn't be overlooked. For example, is it feasible to explore a new career by taking advantage of part-time job opportunities? And if your long awaited goal is to start your own business, what are the pros and cons you have to consider? All these topics are covered in this chapter, beginning with how to assess your career alternatives should you lose your current job.

ASSESSING YOUR CAREER ALTERNATIVES IF YOU LOSE YOUR JOB

The best time to make a career change is from a position of being gainfully employed. However, it's often when one suddenly loses a job that the decision is made to start over fresh in a new career. Although this isn't the ideal way to make a move, if it's viable for you to do so financially, it's certainly a good jumping-off point for starting out fresh in a new field. Even if your finances aren't in the best of shape, circumstances may dictate that now is the time to think about a different career. For example, you may be losing your job because you're in a field with a bleak employment outlook. If so, your prospects for landing another position in this field may be slim to none, so you might as well bite the career-change bullet now.

The financial factors involved in a career change are covered in the following section, but to some degree no matter how shaky your finances are, it may still be the wise choice for you to change careers now. The alternative of waiting until you feel financially secure to make a change may be an elusive goal which you never quite seem to reach. Financial security can also be used as an excuse for not making a career change, which is a lot harder to do in reality than when you are thinking about it in abstract terms.

Nevertheless, the loss of a job isn't as bad a time as you might think to make a career switch. It's easy to visualize saving money while working in a secure job and then pursuing your dream job when the moment is right. Unfortunately, most folks pretty much live up to the level of their earnings. Therefore, when you're in a secure job that pays fairly well, it often boils down to not having sufficient savings to make a career switch.

Other folks, even though they may have the financial resources, don't want to risk a comfortable lifestyle for the unknowns associated with a new line of work. As a result, many people spend their working lives in jobs they hate without ever exploring career alternatives. So all in all, being out of work is an opportune time to bite the bullet if you want to make a career change.

Being suddenly unemployed after losing your job usually sends people scurrying to find another job in the same field as fast as they can. This can even happen when all signs point to a dismal future in a particular occupational field. However, when you're out of work, it helps to be brutally honest with yourself as to your future prospects in your present line of work. If the outlook is dim, or you hate what you have been doing, then it's worthwhile to assess your career alternatives.

Decide what other career fields interest you, and what the job prospects are in those areas. It makes little sense to leave one career field where the future is bleak for another which is equally gloomy. There's no shortage of information sources about the occupational outlook for different kinds of jobs, with both government and industry sources publishing such information. Trade and professional journals in different fields have a wealth of information on careers in the fields they cover, and they also publish salary surveys. Unless you are willing to relocate, you also have to factor in the local job market for the career field you're interested in. With some occupations, the jobs are clustered heavily in certain geographic areas.

Many people have long harbored a desire to enter a particular career field and with them there's no decision to be made as to what they want to do. For other people who aren't sure what sort of career choice might interest them, career counseling might be in order. You may be able to get this for free if you are entitled to outplacement services with your former employer. If so, take advantage of this to determine where your aptitudes lie.

Once you have your career choice in mind, decide what skills you have that are transferable to that particular field. Often people get discouraged and think, "Gee, I don't have any experience in that field, so I don't have anything to offer." That's usually far from the truth. You may not have the specific technical skills for a particular job, but many of your best traits may be transferable to another career field. For example, good communication skills are sought out almost universally, and anyone who is adept at working well with other people is a desirable asset in any field. Rather than assume you have little to offer prospective employers, sit down and analyze those talents you have which would be readily usable in another career field. Play up these skills in your resume when you send it to prospective employers.

One career alternative that some people give thought to is striking out on their own. Starting your own business is something people do all the time, but it requires a lot of hard work, persistence, and the ability to survive for an extended period of time with little financial return. It's certainly an alternative that can't be ignored, and if you plan on going that route you will be interested in the later section in this chapter on starting your own business. Whatever you do, don't fall into the trap of starting your own business as a substitute for hunting down a new job in your present career field, or beginning over in a different career with another employer.

IDENTIFYING THE FINANCIAL CONSIDERATIONS OF A CAREER CHANGE

It's one thing to harbor thoughts of pursuing a lifetime career dream. It's quite another to have to deal with the reality of whether or not this is a financially viable alternative. This involves considering not only what jobs are available in the field you want to enter, but also what the pay scales are. Beyond that is the need to deal realistically with your position in life. Your responsibilities, in terms of both family and finances, can't be ignored. What is a viable alternative for someone who is single with substantial financial resources is not realistic for someone living on the financial edge with three children and a hefty mortgage.

What can't be overlooked is your present financial condition, as well as your income potential in your new career field. First and foremost is your present situation. Generally, a career change means accepting a cut in your income, at least until you become firmly established in your new field. This means hard financial choices have to be made. If you have available financial resources, then your first decision may be how much of this nest egg you will use to augment income as you start out in a new field. As part and parcel of this decision, you have to decide whether or not you want to cut your standard of living to adjust to a lower income level on a regular basis.

The best approach, of course, is to use as few of your existing financial resources as possible to finance daily living expenses. Therefore, it's prudent to plan how you can cut your expenses to reflect your new income level more closely. To do this successfully, you first need to determine what your income potential would be in your new line of work. You have to figure out what you will earn realistically during your first year or two. There is plenty of available information on starting salaries in different career fields, including both government and non-government sources. Don't overlook the fact that if you have experience or training that's transferable to your new line of work you may be able to command a starting salary that's above the entry level for the field. But be honest with yourself in what you can expect to earn.

Once you have a handle on what you can expect for a starting salary, look at how this compares with what your earnings are in your present job. The difference between what you're currently earning and your expected income is the differential you have to adjust for in your future lifestyle. This means cutting back on your spending, or supplementing your future earnings from savings and other available funds.

If you have been planning a career change for some time, you may have worked hard to save money for this adjustment period. Perhaps you will have funds available from a retirement plan at work, or a generous severance package if you lost your job. If any of these factors apply, then you may not have too much difficulty supplementing your earnings during the early stages of your new career. Nevertheless, even with substantial financial resources, you can't continue to use these funds indefinitely to augment your earnings. If the new career field you're entering will never bring you to your current earnings level, you will have to live more frugally in the future than in the past. This adjustment is part of the price you have to pay for switching careers. Although it's not a simple adjustment, it's certainly doable, and you may well find yourself a lot happier earning less money in a new career than you could ever be in your former job.

For some people, a career change may only require a temporary financial belt-tightening, since the long-term earnings prospects in your new profession may far exceed those of your current position. If this is the case, then any adjustments in your standard of living will be easier to make knowing that the financial rewards will be forthcoming in the future.

The specific financial considerations of a career change will differ due to personal circumstances. In general, if you're making a career switch early in your career, the pay differentials won't be as much as in later years when you are well established in a job. At the other end of the ladder, someone who is entering another field of work after retirement may have a steady stream of income from pensions, social security, investments, and so forth on which to rely. In these circumstances, a pay differential may not even be a consideration.

The extent to which you can transfer your experience and knowledge from one field to another will also influence the starting salary you will receive in your new field. So the financial impact of a career switch will vary, but the important point is to assess beforehand how it will affect you beforehand. If you do this well before making a career move, you will be in a better position to prepare yourself for any eventuality.

WEIGHING THE SHORT- AND LONG-TERM RISKS OF A NEW CAREER

There's a double-barreled reason why it's easy to overlook the risks involved in switching careers. These consist of being unhappy in your present job, along with visions of how wonderful a career in your dream field would be. This emotional baggage can cause you to make a career switch without fully assessing the risks involved in doing so. Conversely, although you should weigh the pros and cons carefully before changing careers, the potential pitfalls shouldn't be overemphasized to the extent that they paralyze you into staying put. It all boils down to putting the emotional aspects of making a career switch on the back burner and concentrating on an honest assessment of the short- and long-term risks and rewards.

Explore Options with Your Current Employer

The best place to look when you decide you want to do something different may be your present employer, assuming there are positions within the company in your chosen field. If you like the company you work for, there's no point in pursuing opportunities elsewhere until you first explore your internal options. This can be tricky though, so you have to be careful about how you proceed. Some bosses take offense at the notion of an employee not wanting to work for them anymore. Others who are more enlightened may assist you earnestly in your endeavors.

If you're able to transfer to another position with your present employer, you lower the risks of making a career change. With a new employer, not only do you run the risk of not liking the job once you're working in it, but also the risk of being unhappy with the company for which you work. This latter risk is eliminated if you are able to secure an internal transfer.

There are a couple of ways you can ease the passage into a new career with your present employer. First, be sure you can perform the duties of the position adequately. If possible, network within the company to become familiar with the department in which you want to work. Get to know the people who do similar work, and find out how they like both their jobs and their boss. By doing this, you minimize the risk of putting yourself into a bad situation. You should also get to know the department head and learn about future openings. When a job slot opens up, bring the subject up with your current boss, but do it in such a way that it doesn't indicate unhappiness with either your job or your boss.

Weigh Future Job Prospects in a New Career Field

One of the reasons people switch careers is to escape the insecurity of an occupation which has bleak prospects for the future. Therefore, it follows that you don't want to switch careers, only to find out later that prospects in your new field aren't much better than in the occupation you left behind. This can be easy to do if you're enamored of working in a job you have always dreamed about. As a result, your emotions can obscure the fact that job prospects in the field aren't very good.

You also have to look at the job prospects in a new field from a long-term perspective, since sometimes current openings in the field may be high, but technological change, or some other factor, may dim the outlook for the future. Forecasting the long-term risks of job security in a field isn't easy, since such crystal-balling isn't always on the mark. Therefore, you shouldn't base any career decision on this one factor. But if government and industry predictions for future job growth are bleak in a field you're hoping to switch to, you should take this into consideration if job security is one of your major motives for a career switch.

One of the biggest impediments to switching careers is the fear of taking on the risk of changing your career field. This translates into thinking, "What happens if it doesn't work out?" Yet with careful planning beforehand, most career switches can be successful. The danger lies in having expectations that are set too high. This is especially true when someone visualizes the new line of work as being the solution to unhappiness in their present job. This can lead to unrealistic assumptions that the new job will solve all their career problems. Unfortunately, every job has its ups and downs, so it only makes sense to approach a career change with a level-headed assessment of what can be expected. Otherwise, when the career change is made, the realities that were ignored beforehand may cause discouragement and a conclusion that the career switch was a mistake. Therefore, the greatest risk of a career switch may be in expecting too much from your new field before you even begin. Fortunately, this problem can be overcome by planning a career change well in advance. This isn't always possible, but it's very practical for people who have had long-standing ideas about career opportunities they would like to pursue.

PLANNING THE PLUNGE WHEN CHANGING CAREERS

Once you make a final determination to change careers, unless circumstances such as a layoff force you into action, you should take time to plan your move carefully. There are many factors to consider, such as what sort of additional education or training you will need, what the financial impact will be, and how long it will take for you to establish yourself in your new field. There may even be geographic considerations involved, since jobs in some career fields tend to be concentrated in certain geographic areas. By planning your move ahead of time, you will be able to make the switch with full knowledge of what to expect, and a minimum of disruption in your life.

You Have to Plan to Get Where You Want to Be

Many people have a dream goal in the back of their minds for years and never act on it unless they are forced to by a sudden job loss. Then, not having done any planning, they suddenly face an opportunity to change careers, but don't know how to go about it. The reality of the working world is that many people will work in two or more careers over a lifetime of work, either by choice or necessity. For this reason alone, it's imperative to always be planning your next move, even though you may be perfectly content at the moment. After all, at the same time you're coasting along engaged happily in your work, the corporate hierarchy may be planning a reorganization that eliminates your job. That's a scary thought which usually brings self-denial to everyone's mind. Yet it happens all the time, so it's better to take control of your career yourself, than to be at the mercy of corporate planners.

The starting point for planning any career change is to be candid about what you are looking for in terms of a career. Is it money, job security, prestige, or any of a number of other factors? The specifics aren't as important as determining what matters most to you. If you have a broad-based image of what you would like to do, but little first-hand knowledge, then your first step is to become informed about the career field in which you're interested. Read up on the field as much as possible to glean a general overview. In fact, if you're unsure of your career interests, then it may be worthwhile to have some career counseling. With this, you can determine where your aptitudes lie.

Glean Practical Knowledge Before Changing Careers

Assuming you have a career in mind, a great way to decide whether or not your choice is a good one is to gain some practical insights into the field. There are several ways to go about this. From a general standpoint, talk to as many people as you can who work in the field. Find out about their likes and dislikes. You can garner a wealth of inside information this way, and it's not difficult to do. Your greatest fear may be a hesitancy to ask people about their jobs, but keep in mind that people usually love to talk about themselves. They may exaggerate and complain, but if you learn to recognize this as a given, the information you gather will be of value.

If there are opportunities to explore the field by doing part-time work, by all means take advantage of it. Not only will you learn the working details of the field you want to enter, but there are other advantages to this tactic. First, you will be able to make contacts in the field which you can use when you start to look for a job. Second, you will gain a measure of experience that you can use on your resume. Even beyond that, when you do start to look for a job, prospective employers will see that you're serious about the field from your part-time work experience. This is a plus for your job hunt, since there's skepticism occasionally on the part of employers regarding someone looking for a job in a different career field. By having worked in the field part-time, you will be pinpointed as someone with a serious commitment.

Two other aspects of switching careers that benefit from long-term planning are educational requirements and financial considerations. If your career plans are aimed at an occupation or profession that will require additional schooling on your part, then you have to decide how to go about getting it. Since this is covered at length later in the chapter, suffice it to say that you have to plan ahead if extensive educational requirements have to be met in your chosen field. As far as financial considerations go, planning ahead of time will allow you to save the funds that will give you the opportunity to switch career fields.

Above all else, your future depends upon the amount of time and energy you're willing to expend in planning your career. You have to recognize that there may be sacrifice involved in switching from one career field to another. You also have to look for ways to continually enhance your value in the job market. For example, many skills are interchangeable among jobs within one career field, as well as in different fields. The more skills you're able to develop, the more valuable you become to employers—whether you change careers or not.

TEN QUESTIONS TO ANSWER BEFORE STARTING YOUR OWN BUSINESS

Many people spend a lifetime dreaming of owning their own businesses. Some of these people scrimp and save until they have the money to give it a shot. Others may not have even given it a thought until they are handed a pink slip and early retirement. Then, with the assistance of a generous severance package, they see themselves with the financial wherewithal to become entrepreneurs. Either way, what everyone who ever strikes out on their own soon learns is that your own business usually means long hours and little money for the foreseeable future.

There's a "glorification" process attached to starting a business that associates small business owners with being the last of the pioneers. Everyone knows the success story of some computer whiz who made millions, or a retailing giant who started out with a corner store. Very few people stop to think that for every success there are far more failures. Admittedly there are rewards in running your own business, and if you think the decision through carefully, you have a fair shot at succeeding if you're willing to put in the hard work that's necessary. However, before you consider your own business as a viable career alternative, let's look at some of the questions you should answer first.

1. *Do you have the perseverance and commitment to succeed?* Starting and running a business require long hours and hard work, and success doesn't happen overnight. Therefore, if you're thinking about becoming an entrepreneur, make sure you are doing so for the right reasons, not because you're unhappy with your present circumstances. Being unhappy with a boss at work doesn't mean being your own boss will be any better, only that you may have a different set of problems with which to deal. Quite simply, if you want to start a business, do it because of some burning desire to do so, not to get out from under an unpleasant situation where you work.

2. *Can you function without the support services of a corporate employer?* In a corporate environment there are support and staff services available for every conceivable function. When you're on your own, you have to handle these chores yourself. This may not seem like such an insurmountable problem, but it's easy to overlook how easy certain aspects of your working life are until you have to do them yourself, or pay someone else to do them.

3. *Have you determined the market for your product or service?* Who will your customers be and what is your competition? You should carefully study the type of business area you're going to enter to determine its growth prospects. The greatest product in the world will be of little value if there's no market for it. One mistake some folks make is trying to expand a hobby into a business. This isn't necessarily bad, but because of passion for the hobby, it sometimes leads to going ahead without first determining if there's a valid business opportunity.

4. *Will you be happy in the business you're planning to enter?* As opposed to folks who try to expand a hobby, some people decide to start a business because they see it as the road to riches. Never start your own business in the hopes of becoming wealthy. People sometimes succumb to this temptation after reading about entrepreneurs who have made millions. What they neglect to realize are that these people are a distinct minority, and that many businesses fail completely, while others barely eke out a living. With all the effort involved, if the business isn't one you can enjoy working hard at, you're better off not getting started.

5. *What approach to your own business are you planning to take?* Have you carefully thought through both the type of business you want to start, as well as the best way to do it? You may be able to buy an existing business that meets your needs, or perhaps start your own business from scratch. Perhaps you are considering a franchise, which may give you support in getting started, but will also limit your freedom to run your business the way you want to.

6. *What about money?* You have to carefully plan your financing well in advance so you have the necessary funding in place when it's time to make your move. The amount of money you need will vary

with the type of business you're planning. If, for example, you're going to be running a business from a home-based office, your initial outlays will be less than if you're planning to buy a going concern. One thing you shouldn't do is minimize the amount of money you will need. Among the factors to consider if you will be seeking to borrow funds from lenders are the following:

- Be able to show that you have the expertise to run the business.

- Be realistic in your financial projections. A typical business starts off slow and gains momentum over time, and your numbers should reflect this.

- Pinpoint how you will cope with the inevitable downturns in business that every company must confront eventually.

- Be reasonable in your funding request. Don't try to struggle by on a minimum of capital, or make an unreasonably high request that can weaken your credibility with prospective lenders.

- An accountant can provide invaluable assistance in preparing the financial projections you will have to make. What's more, accountants lend the sort of credibility to a financial proposal for which bank loan officers and other financial sources are looking. By the same token, before you make any firm commitments with a financing source, be sure to bring your lawyer on board to protect your legal interests.

7. *Have you drawn up a viable business plan?* One of the first tasks every entrepreneur undertakes is the preparation of a business plan. Yet despite the importance of such a plan, there are often misconceptions about both its preparation and its use. As for the latter, many prospective business owners view a business plan as nothing more than a tool to secure necessary financing. Of course, a well-conceived plan is essential in this regard. However, there are a number of other equally important reasons for preparing a plan.

First and foremost, the preparation of a plan may reveal potential problems that will lead you to decide that the venture isn't worth pursuing any further. If so, then the plan serves its purpose by preventing what might ultimately be a financial disaster. Even if this worst-case scenario doesn't arise, a good plan should be able to anticipate the questions of prospective lenders and address them accordingly. The plan should also be useful as an ongoing management tool once the prospective business is launched.

In terms of actually preparing a plan, the initial work is best done by you. This forces you to think through all the pros and cons of the prospective endeavor. Only after a first draft has been completed should professional assistance be sought. However, it's wise to avoid the temptation of going ahead without professional help in attempting to secure financing.

In general terms, your business plan should include both financial and business operations sections. The financial part should demonstrate the financial potential and viability of the business, while the operating plan should describe the undertaking, as well as identify the specifics of how you will accomplish your objectives. Don't assume knowledge of your type of business by anyone who will be reviewing your plan. Make it as complete as possible to cover not only the product or service you will offer, but also include information on marketing, pricing, and customer-service strategies. In addition, the success of a business rests largely upon how much competition it faces, so be sure to identify both the competition and how you intend to beat them in the marketplace.

Assembling the facts and figures for a sound business plan is a complex and time-consuming task. Unfortunately, your effort doesn't end when this has been accomplished. To convince a financial source to part with funds for your project requires a selling job. As a result, your plan must not only be complete, it must also be easily understandable by anyone who reviews it. This means it must be both presentable and convincing. As for the visual design of your plan, neatness and organization are far more important than having a fancy brochure with disorganized content.

Although there's no perfect length for a plan, it should be long enough to contain all the relevant information, and yet not be overwhelming. It's important to include a brief summary at the beginning to provide an overview. It's also helpful to put most of your financial details in separate exhibits, since intermingling them with the text tends to be confusing. And a confusing presentation can lead not only to annoyance, but also to outright rejection.

The work required to thoroughly prepare a plan will force you to think through all the details of your prospective business. This will assist you in identifying potential problems before operations begin. As a consequence, you will prevent costly mistakes from occuring after your business is up and running.

8. *Do you have business advisors lined up?* Before you launch a business, you should have a team of advisors lined up to assist you in getting the business up and running. These include accountants, lawyers, bankers, as well as potential investors and partners. Incidentally, your accountant and lawyer should be involved from the start, rather than be brought on board at the first sign of trouble.

9. *Do you have your financial safety net in place?* Before you make the plunge to start a business, you should first be certain that essentials such as health insurance and living expenses are covered adequately. The money to cover living expenses should be set aside and not be intermingled with that of your business. Once you start off in a business you may become so involved at first that the nitty-gritty details of your personal finances get short shrift. Therefore, by paying down your bills, and putting a lid on your living expenses before you take the plunge, you will be less likely to encounter time-consuming problems that detract from running your business in its early stages. It will also lessen the need to rely on profits from your business during the early going.

10. *Do you have a fallback position if things don't work out?* No one likes to think about failure when they're thinking about starting their own business, but doing so can give you some peace of mind. Decide what you will do in terms of employment if your venture should fail for any reason. Will you go back to your old line of work, or seek employment in another field? Assessing the possibilities beforehand will give you confidence that your future will still be secure if the venture doesn't pan out. Incidentally, this is one reason why you will want to leave your present employer on good terms, since you never know when you may want your old job back. Thinking about a fallback position may not be foremost in your mind, but knowing you have alternatives down the road can give you the impetus to take a crack at starting your own business.

USING PART-TIME AND TEMPORARY WORK TO ASSESS OTHER CAREERS

It may not always be feasible to do so, but if the opportunity presents itself, one of the best ways to check out other career fields is to find part-time or temporary full-time work in your desired field. Needless to say, the type of part-time or temporary job opportunity you get may not be the type of job in which you would be interested. Nevertheless, it should at least give you a close-up perspective of what you will encounter. Plus, there are other advantages to seeking part-time or temporary job opportunities to explore career possibilities. You may be able to make valuable contacts who can assist you in getting a job in your new career. If you're really fortunate, you may even get a full-time job offer that meets your transitional career objectives.

For the most part, a part-time job would be the route to follow if you're presently employed and want to explore other career fields. Unfortunately, your ability to do this is somewhat limited by the kind of part-time openings that would be available during your nonworking hours. Assuming your regular job is of the nine-to-five variety, and the jobs in the field you are interested in are mostly during the same hours, then your chances of finding a part-time position are slim.

In a few career fields, your regular working hours won't be as much of a handicap. Retailing is the most obvious example, so if you're looking for a part-time job in this field, then it's easy enough to get one that doesn't conflict with your regular job. Aside from using a part-time job to explore career opportunities, it's also a good way to gain some insight into starting your own business. If that's your goal, then working part-time at a business similar to the one you hope to open gives you an opportunity to see both the risks and rewards first-hand. It will also give you a basic understanding of some of the problems associated with running a business. Incidentally, if you have been thinking about buying a franchise, there's no better way to gain experience than to spend some time working in the trenches. Seeing the problems first-hand can not only help you decide whether or not to go forward, but can also help you avoid some mistakes you might otherwise make.

In terms of exploring other careers, full-time temporary assignments offer many advantages. Temporary-help agencies can place people in all kinds of occupations, so all you really have to do is hook up with an agency that specializes in your line of work. One big plus when looking to change your career through the temporary job route is that a prospective employer may be more willing to overlook specific experience in the field as a qualifying factor. This is because it's a lot easier to take a risk with a temporary position than to fill the position permanently.

The temporary employment route, then, may be an easier way to get your foot in the door in another career field. Naturally, this doesn't mean a full-time position will result but it does accomplish several things. It gives you valuable experience in the field you're seeking to enter, and enables you to make contacts in the field, some of which may become valuable in the future even if they can't help you right now. Then, there's always the possibility that by working in the field this way, you may decide that this isn't what you want to do after all.

There's both good and bad news associated with using temporary employment as a means of looking for a job in a new career field. From the positive side, many businesses do hire temporary workers to ultimately fill permanent positions. Some companies, in fact, use temporaries as a positive way to observe prospective hires without having to make a permanent commitment on the basis of an interview or two. Seeing the individual on the job not only gives the company the opportunity to observe job skills, but also lets the company see if the individual will fit in with the people with whom he or she will be working. On the downside, many companies use temporaries to augment their regular work force and seldom hire temporaries for permanent positions. So although a temporary job has many advantages in terms of exploring other career fields, it's no guarantee that you will land a permanent position this way.

Aside from its use as a means to explore other career fields, a temporary position can be beneficial in a number of other ways. For some people, who value the flexibility of having more control over when and where they work, temporary assignments are a permanent way of life. Other people prefer them for the variety of assignments they offer. After all, boredom is often one of the hazards of many jobs, so the ability to switch from one company to another on a new temp assignment can be appealing. Some folks use temporary jobs as a steady income base while they are looking for a permanent position, or as a supplement to other income sources, as in the case of retirees. So whether you use a part-time or temporary position to explore new career fields, or for other purposes, these are two more tools for your career-planning toolbox.

WORK FORCE RE-ENTRY: GOING BACK TO WORK ON YOUR TERMS

For one reason or another you may have been out of the work force for a period of time. Perhaps you were devoted full time to raising a family, or maybe you retired early but have decided to return to the work force. Whatever the reason may be, you don't want to jump at the first job that comes along. After all, since you have been away from the business world, you might as well take advantage of that to carefully plan your return so your next job amounts to more than daily drudgery. How you go about that is contingent upon your personal circumstances and goals.

For instance, if you're harboring thoughts of having a different career, then why not prepare yourself by securing any needed training while you have the opportunity. Alternatively, you may just want to take a course to bring your skills up to date. With the rapid technological changes that are taking place, it doesn't take much time for your skills to become outdated. This is especially true if your experience is in a high-technology field, where yesterday's hot technical breakthrough is obsolete tomorrow. Starting off fresh also gives you the opportunity to explore a variety of different jobs which you think might be of interest. Working for a temp agency or accepting part-time employment will also give you the chance to sample the alternatives available to you.

Another advantage of improving your educational credentials while you're out of the work force is that it gives you increased value in the marketplace. It also counters the impression that someone who hasn't worked for a year or more isn't as sharp as someone who has employment continuity. This may be an erroneous impression, but like a lot of other things, whether it's valid or not doesn't matter if someone perceives it to be true.

Planning your re-entry into the work force should be done with care in order to maximize the chances of finding a job opportunity that best fits your circumstances. The first thing to do is to establish your priorities, which will vary from person to person. For some people, it may be the resumption of a career already embarked upon before an extended absence from the working world. Someone else may be more concerned with flexible hours than with either the job itself or the pay. Others may just want to work at something they planned to do once they retired, and now have the opportunity to do just that.

Whatever your individual focus may be, the first step is to define your goals and then develop a strategy to reach your objectives. For example, if your primary interest is to secure a position with flexible working hours, then you obviously want to avoid jobs that won't give you that option. On the other hand, don't arbitrarily write off certain positions because you don't think flexible hours would be an option. For example, perhaps you took early retirement and want to get back in the business world without making a long-term commitment to a permanent position and long working hours. One option might be consulting, and your former employer may even be a potential client. Another approach would be taking a part-time position with a small business that is looking for certain expertise, but can't afford to fund a full-time position.

The bottom line in going back to work is finding a job that best meets your personal needs—so be clear about your preferences. Sometimes people ignore the advantages of a position that best suits their desires because it doesn't offer the pay or prestige of another position. Then, after being back at work for a while, reality sets in and there's dissatisfaction over aspects of the job that weren't considered beforehand. For instance, someone might take a job that pays more only to realize later that commuting costs more than eat up the differential from that offered by an employer closer to the employee's home.

This seems to be pretty basic, but unfortunately there's always been a tendency to measure jobs strictly in terms of how much money they pay. That's fine if your top priority is money, but if it isn't, you shouldn't let salary alone be a determining factor. Don't ignore the minor matters that can make a job a much better fit for your circumstances. It may be working hours, commuting time, leave policy, fringe benefits, or any of a number of other factors. Being honest about what you're looking for will put you in a better position to find a job that meets your needs.

EVALUATING YOUR CONTINUING EDUCATION NEEDS

There was probably a point in your life when you decided you had all the formal education you needed or wanted. This is certainly understandable, but it isn't necessarily practical these days. The learning process is never-ending, for work or life in general. So from the time you decide that your educational needs have been fulfilled, others who continue to seek educational opportunities will position themselves to bypass you in terms of career growth. Consequently, you should continually search for and take advantage of training opportunities that will enhance your career needs.

Further training can be useful to you in two ways. First, it can be used to increase your knowledge and potential in your existing job, along with providing the necessary credentials for you to advance within your career field. From a different perspective, continuing education can be used to give you the flexibility to change careers if that is one of your future objectives.

One area in which it pays to take the initiative is to keep abreast of the skills needed in your career field. In technology-driven areas in particular, your knowledge can be outdated rapidly if you don't stay abreast of the trends. This may mean taking short courses or seminars. Frequently, professional organizations offer various courses that are of value in keeping people up to date. Neglecting to keep pace can mean seeing those who are better prepared moving ahead of you in their careers. Those who lag behind in staying current with the latest developments in their field are also setting themselves up as prime prospects for the next layoff.

Many people shudder at the mention of furthering their education, assuming that means long nights of schooling over a period of years to obtain one or more degrees. Yet some of the most valuable training you can receive isn't lengthy or time-consuming. Taking advantage of short courses in a particular subject tied in with your job can be worth far more than your investment in time. Not to be overlooked are on-the-job training opportunities which many employees tend to avoid. In short, sprucing up your knowledge doesn't have to be either lengthy or expensive. Furthermore, in many instances if the courses are even remotely related to your work, your employer may pick up the tab.

If one of your eventual goals is to switch careers, then you should first establish what the educational requirements are in the field you plan to enter. If formal education is a prerequisite to a position you aspire to, then you may want to start working on getting the necessary education on a part-time basis. Many people say things such as, "I want to retire early and teach" or "I'm going to work at this job for several years until I save enough money to get a college degree." However, they never bother to get started with the educational requirements and down the road never realize their dreams.

If you're gainfully employed with future goals in mind, start working on your educational requirements on a part-time basis. That way, you can steadily accrue the educational credits you need to accomplish your objective. A good way to approach it is by taking it a course or two at a time without thinking about all the courses you have to take to reach your goal. In this way, the prospect of obtaining your education won't seem to be so daunting.

Another useful aspect of continuing education is to increase your flexibility in terms of qualifying yourself to do jobs other than the one you presently hold. Even if you don't harbor any present thoughts of making a job switch, taking a course or two to learn something in another field gives you added flexibility. It may even help you in your present job, but even if it doesn't, it provides you with some job insurance for the future. It's a lot easier to job hunt when you can qualify for a number of different jobs, rather than having to look for one that fits your rather limited experience. Community colleges generally offer a wide array of courses in various vocations. Even if you don't have a particular job in mind that you would like to train for, why not take a course or two that just happens to interest you. It wouldn't be the first time that a future career started by someone taking a course just for the fun of it.

LEARNING TO BALANCE WORK, LIFESTYLE, AND FINANCIAL PRIORITIES

One factor that can't be overlooked if you're thinking about changing careers is the demands on your time. In fact, many people start to think about changing careers due to the heavy time demands of their existing job. To have a well-balanced lifestyle with a minimum of stress, it's important to establish your priorities. The amount of time you want to spend on your career pursuits can't be determined without looking at the priority you place on your personal time. Beyond this, financial factors also come into play. Let's look at some of the considerations involved in determining how you can balance your business and personal life to your satisfaction.

Balancing Family Priorities

One of the biggest juggling acts for working parents is balancing work and family priorities. There is the almost constant struggle for competent child care, but as difficult a hurdle as that is, it's only the first of many hurdles facing working parents. Coping with emergencies, spending time with the children, and even routine visits to the pediatrician are all part of the problem for parents facing the competing demands of managing careers and children. And, as the traditional family of the past has given way to two working parents, neither business nor government has kept pace in adjusting to this trend. This leaves mom and dad in a dither as they struggle to maintain their sanity in a never-ending cycle of near chaos. Even though each situation is different, there are some basic approaches that can help you cope.

Plenty of planning is necessary to prevent every problem from erupting into a crisis. For example, after searching long and hard for competent child care, it's easy to breathe a sigh of relief when that necessity is fulfilled. Emergencies, however, have to be factored in. Children's illnesses, doctor's appointments, and any number of unexpected events have to be anticipated.

Even with a good primary source of child care, it's important to establish an emergency network as a backup. Relatives, friends, and neighbors are all obvious potential providers of child care when the unexpected occurs. And don't overlook other parents where you work as prospects for trade-offs in emergencies. After all, many of them are facing the same problems. For example, if you can establish a network of three or four parents to alternate days off during school holidays or vacations, you can cut down on your own time off from work. In any event, the important point is to have as much backup as possible planned ahead of time so you don't get caught short.

Another factor for career couples to consider is that coping with hectic schedules requires flexibility. It's not possible for working parents to maintain a household as if one of them were at home handling the chores on a full-time basis. That means expectations have to be lowered, both in terms of home and work.

It helps to use time-saving techniques as much as possible in doing routine household tasks. It may mean less cleaning and combining the shopping to eliminate the number of trips you make to the supermarket. This seems insignificant, but combining, postponing, or eliminating chores can give you what is in short supply—time. Always try to establish priorities and stick with them. In the final analysis, you can't do everything, so don't try to.

One of the most underutilized assets in alleviating the burdens of dual-career parents may be good old dad. Fathers seldom volunteer to take time off from work for parenting duties. The fact is that fathers share an equal responsibility for raising the kids, and unless they participate fully in sharing this burden, working mothers are the victims of this neglect.

Make Your Needs Known at Work

Another area of importance in managing both children and career is getting recognition of your family responsibilities at work. Unfortunately, some executives still adhere to the traditional family concept as the norm. That's why both where you work, and whom you work for, are vital elements in minimizing the stresses associated with parenting. If your immediate boss is sensitive to the demands placed upon working parents, it makes it easier to deal with difficulties when they arise.

Whatever the circumstances may be in terms of your employer, it's up to you to take the initiative in asking for time off to attend to parenting responsibilities. Sit down with your boss and openly discuss both your career concerns and parental duties. And don't be hesitant to point out what you bring to the party. After all, someone juggling both a career and a family has a lot to offer an employer. They're less likely to job-hop to advance their career, they exhibit a high level of resourcefulness, and are adept at getting tasks done quickly.

An employer's personnel policies are crucial to aid you in successfully balancing work and family priorities. A company that offers flextime so you have control over working hours is a distinct benefit. But even more important are the demands of the job itself. For example, any position that requires extended travel is going to have built-in liabilities.

Equally frustrating is the need to work extended hours. It's possible to get caught up in a self-imposed trap, since working late often results more from peer pressure than the requirements of an employer. Nevertheless, if you have concerns about this, it's worthwhile to be honest with your boss about your parental obligations. You may want to offer to take work home when necessary, rather than do it at the office. A little practical politics doesn't hurt either, such as occasionally letting the boss know that you have been working on a project at home.

Even if you decide that you can't maintain your present schedule, don't just assume you have to change jobs. If you point out the advantages of having more flexible hours, you might be able to work out a satisfactory solution to the problem with your employer. After all, the workplace hasn't yet adapted to the reality of dual-career parents. Since you're in the vanguard of this change, you may have to do a little modern-day pioneering to get your problems recognized.

Even if you don't have family responsibilities, you may place a high priority on your leisure time. Whatever your personal circumstances are, take these into consideration if you're planning a job or career change. It's a given that certain professions and jobs require long hours or extensive travel. These are not favorite employment choices if you value your personal time. Along with avoiding these as future employment possibilities, it's imperative to seek out a position with family-friendly employers who have policies in place that incorporate flexibility in dealing with employee concerns.

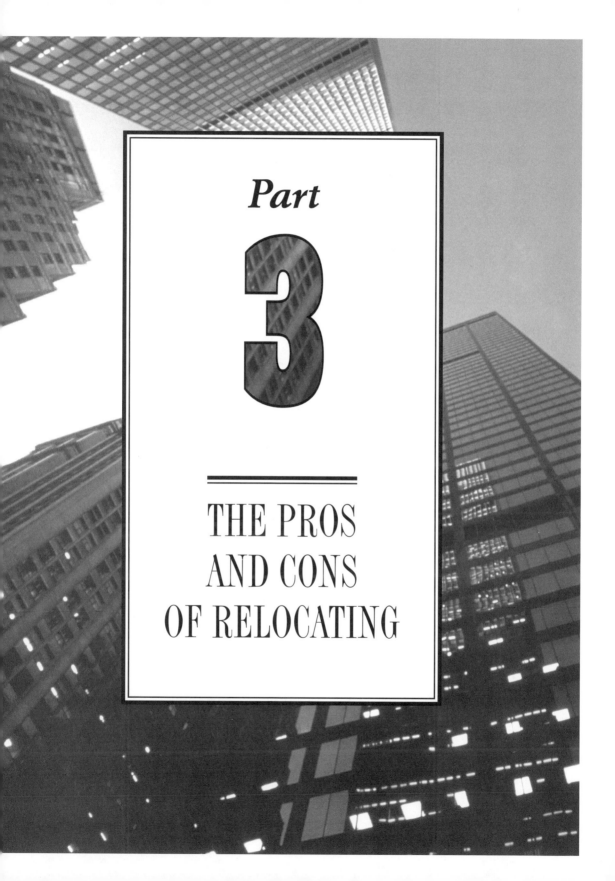

Part

3

THE PROS
AND CONS
OF RELOCATING

If you're looking to change jobs, one of the considerations you may have to deal with is whether or not you will relocate. A long-distance move is an adventure welcomed by some people, and studiously avoided by others. Yet as job markets shift from region to region, relocating may be a necessity even if you don't relish such a possibility. In certain situations, your choice may even boil down to unemployment or underemployment, or a move to a distant locale.

Despite any misgivings you may have, relocating isn't as daunting as you might imagine. Nevertheless, it does require careful consideration, not only from a career standpoint, but also for its personal impact on you and your family. Although you may not be planning an immediate move, careful consideration of the factors involved will allow you to make a better decision either now or in the future.

If you do decide to relocate, the question then becomes a matter of where you will find an environment in which you would be comfortable. Everyone has different lifestyles, and an area perfectly suited to one person wouldn't work for someone else. Knowing how to evaluate your preferences, and relate them to potential areas for a job search, will narrow the odds of your making a bad move. The two chapters that follow cover all the information you need to know in deciding whether or not to relocate, and how to evaluate the locations best suited to your needs.

Chapter

7

EVALUATING POTENTIAL JOB LOCATIONS

Relocating to another area of the country for employment purposes is a difficult decision for most people. It means leaving behind friends and family and starting over in a new area with which you may not be familiar. It presents additional burdens for dual-career couples and families with children. Furthermore, different areas offer different lifestyles, and an environment that works well for one person may not be suitable for another. Therefore, a relocation decision can't be made in haste, no matter how bad you may want a particular job you have been offered.

This chapter covers a wide variety of considerations you should evaluate long before you decide whether a particular location is the right place for you to pursue your career. Among the questions you will find answered in this chapter are how to analyze cost-of-living differences in different locales, as well as how to evaluate quality-of-life factors. Also covered is how to job hunt long distance, and the right way to negotiate salary and relocation expenses when you are making a geographical move. First of all, however, it's important to establish whether or not you want to move, and if so, how to decide upon the areas best suited for your job search. So let's start by considering your options in terms of weighing the practicality of moving to specific areas that will best meet your needs.

SOME BASICS TO CONSIDER IF YOU'RE THINKING OF MOVING

If you're considering the possibility of relocating to take advantage of job opportunities, before you even start a job search in distant locales, there are a number of basic factors you have to take into account. These include everything from deciding where to relocate, to the impact on yourself and your family. Not to be overlooked, of course, are the costs involved, and what happens if you relocate and things don't work out as planned.

Relocation is one of the most important career decisions anyone has to make. Yet whether it's by personal choice, or the request of an employer, there's usually little advance planning. The issues faced in relocating go far beyond an increase in salary, or even long-term career objectives, and the personal adjustments extend beyond learning new names and corporate cultures. Therefore, a well-thought-out decision can't ignore either the personal priorities of your lifestyle or the trade-offs involved in moving out of state.

What every long-distance move boils down to is assessing the pros and cons of moving from both a family and financial standpoint. The benefits and liabilities of such a move should be looked at, both on a short-term basis, as well as for the long haul. Given the initial euphoria surrounding a lucrative job offer, it's sometimes easy to ignore something as simple as the relative ease or difficulty of moving back home if things don't work out as planned. Beyond this is the need to face the reality of the value you place on your present lifestyle. Your current interests have to be considered, and this includes everything from losing a good golfing partner, to uprooting your family from a familiar environment.

In the past, there was often a tacit acceptance of relocation as a necessity for career advancement. Therefore, individuals didn't find it necessary to think about the consequences of moving to another part of the country. In today's environment, there are added influences that have a significant impact on relocation decisions.

One such factor is the dual-career family. As hard as it is to plan for relocation where one career is involved, when both marriage partners are pursuing career goals, the problems are multiplied. For example, the type of job a trailing spouse is seeking may be in short supply in the city where the marriage partner has a job offer. In order to cope with such dilemmas, career couples need to sit down and carefully consider how to balance their respective careers. This may necessitate turning down job offers in locations that don't offer sufficient opportunities for both partners to pursue their careers simultaneously.

A greater emphasis on personal priorities is also influencing job transfers than in the past. Family, friends, and a spouse's career may take precedence over even the most attractive job offer if it requires a change of residence. As a result, it's become even more difficult than in the past to accept a job offer that requires relocation to another part of the country, or perhaps even a foreign assignment.

The financial aspects of a job offer in a different geographic area also require close scrutiny. Among the factors to be considered are:

- *The overall cost of living in the new area.* Certain metropolitan areas such as the Northeast and the West Coast tend to be higher cost areas, so any salary offer you receive should reflect that.

- *Housing costs.* This is the major budget item for most people, and housing costs are substantially higher in some areas of the country than they are in others. The important point is to be sure you pin down what they are before you move. Otherwise, you may suffer from housing price sticker shock when you land in your new location.

- *Local taxes.* State taxes vary, and some cities and counties have local sales taxes. This shouldn't be a major consideration in most cases, since tax rates are always subject to the whims of the political climate.

- *Employer-paid relocation costs.* Be sure you establish precisely what your future employer will and won't pay in the way of relocation expenses. Otherwise, you may find your wallet substantially lighter if you find yourself paying for expenses you hadn't contemplated.

- *Tax aspects of moving.* Such items as the deductibility of moving costs, and the tax aspects of selling a residence shouldn't be overlooked.

- *The prospect of incurring unforeseen expenses.* The need for private instead of public schooling for your children, or the need for a second car are the sort of hidden expenses that can crop up unexpectedly when you move to another area.

It's not a topic that people are inclined to think about, but you can't ignore the possibility that a job move won't work out for one reason or another. If that happens, there will be costs incurred to move back to your former place of residence. Furthermore, if you owned your own home for a number of years, you may have a large capital gain when you sell it. On the other hand, if you later move back to your former place of residence, you'll be buying back into the market at current prices.

All in all, relocating for career advancement can be both personally and financially rewarding. To a large extent, a successful relocation will depend on your personality. Some people treat relocation as a career necessity, others enjoy periodic moves, while many people have some degree of apprehension about making a move. Whatever your feelings may be, don't relocate without weighing all the pros and cons before you make a decision. By taking the time to do this, you will be better prepared to make the decision that's best for you.

PINNING DOWN WHERE YOU WANT TO LIVE

One of the hardest decisions you have to make when considering relocation is deciding just where you want to live. This isn't as easy to do as it might seem initially, since you then have to factor in the job possibilities in any area you consider to be acceptable. In a worst-case scenario, you might find that the locations that are acceptable to you aren't necessarily the ones that have the available jobs.

There are a number of issues that can make one location more desirable than another, but irrespective of that, your personal preferences can't be ignored. After all, no matter how attractive a potential area may be from a cost-of-living or job availability angle, you're the one who will be living there. Consequently, you don't want to ignore your personal preferences. That is, of course, unless you're one of those rare people who can pretty much settle into any environment. Even if you think you are, be totally honest with yourself about this, since you don't want to have regrets after you've relocated.

In evaluating places you're willing to move to, it helps to list those qualities you're looking for in your new surroundings, as well as those aspects you find to be totally unacceptable. For example, if you hate cold weather, you can quickly eliminate large regions of the country. You also have to be realistic in your assessment of different areas. No place will be perfect, but some will fit your expectations a lot better than others. The trick is to establish which is which before you start to do any serious job hunting.

"Almost anywhere" might be a great place to live for some people, but that doesn't necessarily mean you. Relocation is a very personal decision that goes far beyond the salary and perks of a good job offer. So a well-thought-out decision—one way or the other—must include your personal likes and dislikes. If you receive a great job offer, the first inclination might be to accept the job and downplay your doubts about the geographic location of the position. Unfortunately, you may discover after relocating that a good job won't substitute for the absence of the friends and family you have left behind.

Involve Your Family in the Decision

One of the first things you have to do when you think about relocation possibilities is to assess the probability—pro or con—that you will be able to adjust to your new surroundings. It's important to do this in conjunction with your family members, since they have an equal, if not greater, stake in any relocation decision. After all, you will be occupied during the week with your work, which will also give you an outlet for at least minimal socializing. They, on the other hand, won't have this luxury, which may make their adjustment a lot harder. For this reason, it's imperative to sit down and discuss the nitty-gritty details of relocation with your family, including job prospects for a trailing spouse, and schooling for the kids. This aspect of relocation is, of course, easier for you to cope with if you are single and don't have family obligations to consider.

What you are actually doing in performing this evaluation is making an assessment of the relative likelihood of success or failure if you do relocate. If you feel that the risk of relocation being unsuccessful is relatively high, you may decide that relocation is out of the question. Nevertheless, if it's more a nagging doubt than a firm conviction, you might want to determine the relative ease or difficulty of moving back to your hometown if the relocation doesn't work out. If moving back won't be an insurmountable burden from a financial and practical standpoint, then there's no reason why you shouldn't give relocation a chance.

Naturally, whatever your feelings are about relocation it pays to be financially conservative when you first move to another location. This can prevent adding a financial burden to the other stresses of a job move. It can be easy to overspend, especially as a form of compensation for missing your former surroundings. It's wise, however, not to spend any windfall from a generous severance package from your former employer on a new car or expensive home furnishings—at least until you're sure things will work out.

Research Relocation Possibilities in Depth

Aside from the job offer itself, your relocation decision will be largely influenced by the environment in the city to which you may move. The only way to fully inform yourself so as to be able to make an intelligent decision is to do as much research as possible. Some of the information can be gathered from published sources, one of the most valuable of which is the local newspaper. From the paper you will be able to garner such disparate information as facts about real estate, local politics, crime, entertainment, education, and so forth. Many larger cities also have local and regional magazines which can give you an overview of the local lifestyle. The local chamber of commerce is another source for all sorts of community-based data.

Another excellent tool for research is your computer, to collect information from sources in the community you have under consideration. In fact, this is a good way to establish contacts in a distant city before you even set foot in it. If your present job gives you the opportunity to do so, you may be fortunate enough to have business contacts in a city you are thinking about relocating to. If this is the case, then take advantage of them to learn everything you can.

There's nothing like visiting a community that may become your future place of residence; at the interview stage you will get this opportunity. If you harbor long-range plans of relocating, take advantage of business and vacation trips to scope out future possibilities. Don't be shy when you do this. Talk to as many locals as you can to get their thoughts. The more people you talk to, the better your chances of getting an overall viewpoint that is realistic. Along the same lines, if either through personal knowledge or contacts you can locate people from your hometown who have relocated to a community you are considering, take advantage of any chance to talk with them. After all, they have already made the move you are thinking about, so they're in a position to give you some tips that can save you both time and money.

Another route is the social or civic organizations to which you belong. See if your local chapter can put you in touch with members in the city in which you are interested. This also gives you a source of contacts after you move, which will help ease your transition into the new environment.

No matter what the source of people who are giving you advice about another community, you have to view it from the perspective of the person giving the advice. For example, someone who has lived in a distant city for a short time and didn't like it may well downplay the community in conversations with you. You can't overlook the fact that this person may be downgrading the community as personal justification for not having been able to adjust to living there. The person's unsatisfactory adjustment, incidentally, may have been for reasons entirely unrelated to the community itself. Other people tend to see themselves as an authority on any community in which they have done nothing more than pass through the airport. The point is simply not to place too much weight on the individual opinions you receive. It's the cumulative evi-

dence that's of more value, and then only if you hear one or two negative factors repeatedly.

DETERMINING WHERE THE JOBS ARE

Once you have pinpointed the areas of the country you find to be
acceptable for job-hunting purposes, your next step is to determine the
availability of jobs in these areas. Once you start to do this, you will
quickly eliminate many areas from further consideration. If you have only
a limited number of geographic areas to start with, by the time you weed
out those with few job possibilities, you may find your relocation options
to be fairly limited.

The areas with available jobs will depend upon the nature of the job
for which you're looking. If you're looking for a relatively low-paying job
calling for a minimum of experience, they will be widely available in
most areas. On the other hand, some highly-skilled professional positions
tend to be concentrated in certain geographic areas, or large cities. What
you want to do is determine where the best prospects are for the type of
job you're seeking among the different geographic areas to which you're
willing to relocate. You also can't neglect the job prospects of a working
spouse, since even if *you* can land a good job somewhere but your
spouse can't, then you may end up with a lower standard of living.

Use Research Sources to Target Your Search

Knowing where you want to live then leaves you to determine the job
prospects in the area. This isn't too hard to determine, since magazines
and newspapers frequently publicize the fastest-growing areas of the
country for new jobs. This at least gives you a general overview from
which to start. Statistics published by the government on employment is
another data source. Don't place undue emphasis on unemployment
rates though, since the employment picture in the specific field you're
interested in may be quite different from the general job picture in the
community.

To pin down specific types of jobs, contact employment agencies in
the city you're interested in, and ask about the availability of jobs in your

line of work. The help-wanted ads for the newspaper in the area will also alert you to the possibilities.

Finding areas that offer numerous job opportunities in your field obviously gives you a better chance of landing a job, but there's another advantage as well. If you plan to stay in the area, the wide availability of positions in your field gives you future employment opportunities. This can come in handy in the long term if you want to switch employers, or if the job with the company you initially sign on with doesn't pan out.

Once you start your search for locations that present the best employment opportunities, you may discover certain patterns. For example, technology and other knowledge-based companies tend to congregate in areas where there are one or more large research universities. The reasons for this are obvious if you think about it. First of all, the university serves as a resource for the companies, providing not only a steady stream of graduates to fill vacancies in growing businesses, but also the consulting services of faculty members. The university may also be engaged heavily in the type of research that serves the employer's field of technology.

Employers in certain fields also tend to congregate in close geographic proximity because of formal or informal relationships. For example, suppliers often locate facilities convenient to large buyers of their products and services. Regional cost differences and development incentives offered by state and local governments also entice employers to locate in certain areas.

What all this means for you if you're looking to relocate for work is that it's fairly easy to identify a small number of geographic areas in which a relatively large number of prospective employers in a particular field are located. Once you do that, it's easy to concentrate your job search efforts in these areas.

HOW TO JOB HUNT LONG-DISTANCE

Looking for a job at distant locations can be a trying experience if you don't go about it the right way. There are a number of alternatives you can use, such as employment agencies in the area of interest. Many positions are advertised nationwide in large metropolitan dailies as well. So if you're living in a large urban area, your local paper may have classifieds for positions in the area you're considering. However, this is pretty much a hit-or-miss proposition, since it's pure chance that you will find a position you qualify for in a distant city being advertised in your local paper. Other possibilities include employment ads in a number of national publications, such as *The National Business Employment Weekly, The Wall Street Journal,* and *The New York Times.*

Diversify Your Approach to Job Hunting

Don't stop there though, since the secret to landing a job long-distance is to explore every possible avenue. This approach is also best even with a local job search, but it's much more imperative when you're job hunting from afar. One good approach is to obtain the local paper in the areas in which you're interested. Many of the larger out-of-town papers are available at local newsstands that specialize in carrying them. If you don't have one in your immediate area, you can always subscribe to an out-of-town paper. This can be of value not only for job hunting purposes, but also for a wealth of other local information that will be of value to you. In fact, reading an out-of-town newspaper on a regular basis will acclimate you to a new community quicker than most other avenues.

Aside from help-wanted ads in the local paper, the business section will contain news of companies that are expanding in the area. This type of information can also be obtained from the regional business publication serving the local community. Professional trade journals also contain help-wanted ads for jobs in the field which they cover.

One good way to scout positions long-distance is to use any contacts you may have with suppliers or customers of your present company. If you work in a position where you're in contact with these people, don't hesitate to ask them about job possibilities. Don't limit it to the particular company the individual works for, either, since someone may be aware of openings elsewhere in the area. Say something such as, "Frank, I'm thinking of moving to Memphis. Do you know of any available positions in my field down there?"

You may be pleasantly surprised how helpful someone may be in response to such a query. They may even go so far as to suggest you send them a resume which they can circulate. Of course, how much assistance you get will depend primarily upon how well you know the individual who's helping you. Even casual contacts can be very helpful, and some people take it as a compliment that you have an interest in moving to their hometown.

If you have relatives or friends in the area, look them up since they can provide you with a wealth of assistance. Along this line, it can be a distinct advantage to have a local address when you're job hunting. Many companies shy away from hiring people from out of state since they don't want to pay for relocation expenses. This is especially true if you're looking for a lower-paying job for which there are an ample supply of potential candidates in the immediate geographic area. Therefore, if you have the chance to use the address of a friend or relative as your local residence, take advantage of it to overcome this hurdle.

In fact, even if you are looking for a highly skilled position for which a company might pay relocation expenses, it may still be to your advantage to forgo this option. This would be true if you are single and really don't have that much in the way of personal belongings to move. By doing this you lessen the chance of losing out on a job because an employer doesn't want to pay relocation costs. Using a local address can overcome this handicap.

As an alternative, you can let prospective employers know when you send in your resume that you're not looking for relocation expenses. Use your discretion though, since if you're applying for a position at a level where relocation expenses would normally be paid, an employer who sees you decline this assistance may think you can be bought cheap. As a result, any salary offer may also be lower than might otherwise have been the case. Furthermore, some employers might draw a conclusion that you are trying to sell yourself cheap to cover up other inadequacies. In any event, this is a judgment call which you have to make based upon your particular circumstances.

The key to job hunting long-distance—or locally for that matter—is to avail yourself of every possible way to hook up with a prospective employer. Your college placement office is a good source for searching long-distance, as many colleges work closely with older alumni in their placement efforts. Aside from that, if the college you attended is local, visiting the office will give you access to a ton of information on employers in the area in which you're interested.

Just as the three most important aspects of buying real estate are often quoted as being, "location, location, location," in job hunting it's "contacts, contacts, contacts." The more contacts you have, the greater the possibility of one of them paving the way to a job opening. So when you're job hunting, ask friends, relatives, business acquaintances, and anyone and everyone in any network you have built up over the years. You might be surprised at the leads you get using this approach.

Incidentally, even if you're familiar with the city you're looking to relocate to, it pays to travel there to job hunt firsthand. And if you aren't familiar with it at all, then it's imperative to visit to gain firsthand knowledge of the locale. If you're staying with relatives or friends you may not be constrained by time limits. However, if you're picking up the tab for a hotel, you will want to maximize your efforts within a short period of time. If it's feasible, try to line up interviews before you go. You may not be able to get any definite job commitments on your first trip, but you can lay the groundwork for a future visit.

SEVERAL WAYS TO CHECK OUT POTENTIAL EMPLOYERS

When you're job hunting locally, it's a lot easier to become knowledgeable about prospective employers. You may already be familiar with many of them, but even if you aren't you can easily check them out through contacts you may have. These can be people you know who work for them, or in some way or another have knowledge of the company. This is a more difficult proposition when you're job hunting long-distance. If it's a major international or national company, then it presents no great difficulty for you. The problem is with smaller and mid-sized firms of which you have never heard, much less know anything about. Yet you have to be able to evaluate the company as a prospective employer. You may find a bit of research is necessary to find out what you need to know.

What's the value of doing this? If you're going to uproot yourself and your family to accept a job offer at a distant location, then you want to be sure what you're getting into before you sign on the dotted line. After all, if you're going to do something as routine as buy a car, as the saying goes, you probably insist on kicking the tires before you buy.

With something as important as relocating for a job, you want to be at least equally positive about what you're approving.

What should you be looking for in terms of prospective employers? Ask yourself the following questions:

- *Is the company in a growth business?* You have to keep in mind that even companies in declining industries hire people. However, you don't want to put yourself in a position of moving for a job which may be eliminated in a year or two. Therefore, the long-term prospects of a prospective employer can't be ignored.

- *Is the company profitable?* There are companies that fail no matter how good the overall industry outlook may be, so you don't want to land with an employer who may be going bankrupt.

- *Is the company growing rapidly?* A company that's expanding will offer plenty of opportunities for advancement, so your career will move along a lot faster in such an environment.

- *Is the company's business cyclical?* If the company is in a business that experiences sharp ups and downs in a cyclical pattern, you could find yourself out of a job at the next economic downturn.

- *Does the company have a history of avoiding layoffs even when business isn't at its best?* Some employers go to great lengths to avoid layoffs, and if you can land a job with such a company, your job security worries will be minimized.

- *What kind of personnel policies does the company have in place?* Is it an employer who puts people first? For example, companies that offer flextime, job-sharing, child-care assistance, and so forth, and show a recognition for the personal needs of their employees. These are indications of an employer who treats people with respect.

- *Is the company a leader or a laggard in terms of pay and fringe benefits?* Not all companies are competitive in terms of pay and benefits, and as a result they are likely to have a higher rate of employee turnover. This also means they have more job openings at any given time, so you want to be certain you're not being offered a position with such an employer.

These are some of the general questions you want to answer about a prospective employer, although you may well have others that fit into your specific situation. Of course, how any employer rates on an overall basis depends to some extent on your personal vision of what constitutes a good employer. For example, one person may place a top priority on an employer who pays high salaries, while someone else may value a company that offers greater job security. In any event, you have to realize that no employer is perfect, and your objective should be to seek out those employers who best fit your personal profile of a company for which you want to work.

Doing the research to answer your questions on potential employers can be time-consuming, but the reward comes in having assurance that you will be working for a company that offers you the chance to realize your career potential. As for doing the research itself, a considerable amount of information on which companies are good employers can be gleaned from published sources such as articles and surveys in business magazines. For the most part, however, you will have to do some digging to come up with a fair evaluation of a company.

As far as the business prospects of a company are concerned, one good place to start is with the same information you would use to make an investment decision. What do the investment pros think of the company? These people are paid to assess the future prospects of businesses, so you might as well avail yourself of this advice in terms of evaluating them for employment purposes. Check with your broker for investment recommendations on companies in which you are interested. Send for annual reports, and use your local library to research investment reports.

For specific information as to whether or not the employer is a good one, it's useful to talk with employees or ex-employees. Use all the networking sources you know to put you in contact with these people. Even if you don't know anyone personally, perhaps you can make connections with people by personal computer through any of the on-line services that are available. Other potential sources of information include any business contacts you have, such as suppliers, buyers, and others who may do business with a company. These people may not have the specific details that an employee can offer, but their business dealings may give them an overall inkling of the merits of the company. It may take some digging to track down people who know anything about a distant company, but the information you get will make the effort worthwhile.

USING BUSINESS OR VACATION TRIPS TO EXPLORE JOB OPPORTUNITIES

It's a good idea never to assume you will work in one area of the country for your entire career. Circumstances may be such at the moment that you have no intention of ever relocating; however, it doesn't take much more than a layoff to have you reconsidering where you will live and work. The desire for a regular paycheck can make a distant area more attractive rather quickly. Because circumstances may change, it's always good to use business and vacation trips to research job opportunities in other areas. This doesn't mean you should cancel your February Caribbean cruise to explore job options in Buffalo. Nevertheless, when you're in an unfamiliar area, either on business or vacation, it doesn't hurt to assess its livability for employment purposes.

The idea of a "vacation" often has folks conjuring up dreams of landing a job, or starting a business, in their favorite resort area. What better way to combine the need to work with the pleasure of leisure, or so the thought process goes. Before you put forth any effort in pursuing such a dream, it may be useful to consider the downside of looking for work at a popular vacation destination.

Most resort areas don't have a lot to offer in the way of jobs, so it's unlikely that you could even land a position in your chosen field. The available work is generally tourism-related, and many of the jobs are low-paying. Furthermore, even these jobs may be seasonal if the location isn't a year-round resort area. As for the possibility of starting a business, the choices tend to be limited to those that would appeal to vacationers. And if you haven't noticed, most resort areas don't seem to need another restaurant or ice cream stand.

Beyond the job difficulties in relocating to a resort area are the problems that go hand-in-hand with living in such a locale. In fact, some of the very attributes that make a place attractive as a tourist destination serve to make it less so as a permanent residence. The beaches, mountains, or whatever else that draws tourists to an area, also brings about tourist-related problems for permanent residents. For example, traffic congestion and crowded restaurants aren't pleasant to endure on a daily basis, nor are the sudden turns and quick stops of drivers unfamiliar with the local area. Furthermore, those high prices you see in the stores at a vacation spot are what you have to pay on a regular basis if you live in the area. From both a career and personal standpoint, these resort areas may be nice places to visit, but less preferable as a spot in which to live and work.

Many vacation destinations such as large cities are also prime prospects for employment. Therefore, if a vacation is taking you to—or near—a large metropolitan area, it doesn't hurt to check it out as a future relocation possibility. This doesn't mean you have to spend your vacation researching employment opportunities or checking out housing in the area. In fact, just being aware of the relocation potential is sufficient, since this alone will have you making observations about the city you wouldn't otherwise notice. This awareness also applies to business trips that you make for your present employer. If you have developed a more serious interest in a specific location in terms of employment, you can use a business or vacation trip to do even more detailed research on the area and its employers.

WEIGHING COST-OF-LIVING CONSIDERATIONS IN DIFFERENT LOCALES

One important element that can't be overlooked in any job relocation decision is the cost of living in an area you're considering relocating to. This is something that can prove to be substantial if it's ignored, since even an increase in pay may not compensate for much higher living costs. There are a number of factors to consider, but the starting point is to determine if there is a major variance in the cost of living between where you presently live and where you may decide to relocate. It's essential to perform this analysis before you sit down to negotiate a salary with a prospective employer, because living costs may influence the salary you are willing to accept.

The bottom line in considering variances in cost of living in different areas is that it's not how much money you make, but the purchasing power the money gives you. And the truth of the matter is that it's a lot cheaper to live in some parts of the country than in others. As a matter of fact, even within the same geographic region, you don't have to travel too many miles to lower your living costs. The best example of this is with the housing market in many metropolitan areas. As a general rule, the further away you get from a major city, the lower the price is for comparable housing. The same is often true for local property taxes.

Other factors can balance this financial advantage out—such as the costs associated with a lengthy commute. And arguably, there may be reasons which you can't put a dollar figure on that make the more expensive suburb a better bargain. Quality of life issues, such as better public schools, are often cited in this regard. Yet on the other hand, the less expensive area may also have its own quality of life advantages, such as a quieter rural environment with less traffic, lower crime rates, and so forth. Frankly, when you get into these kinds of arguments, it pretty much boils down to what it is you truly want, and how much you are willing to pay.

The differences in cost of living for long-distance relocations are much starker than for any local variances. There's no getting around the fact that it will cost you a lot more to live in New York City than it will in a small town in mid-America. The same applies to many other cities and regions of the country. What often happens to the good or ill fortune of many transferees is that they are relocated by their employer and suddenly realize there's a huge difference in housing costs. If you're going from selling a house in a high-cost area to buying one in a low-cost region, then its time to break out the champagne and celebrate. Conversely, if you're faced with buying into a high-priced housing market, you may discover that the proceeds of the sale of your old house aren't going to go very far.

The personal aspects of this sort of scenario can result in seriously altering the lifestyle of those involved. It is no laughing matter to someone moving to a high-housing-cost area to discover that the only houses they can afford are ones they wouldn't have considered living in where they previously lived. Sometimes, even when there's an overall awareness of the price differentials beforehand, they aren't taken seriously until actually experienced in person. After all, it's hard to visualize it when someone tells you the house you're now living in will cost $100,000 more to duplicate somewhere else.

Beyond housing costs, there are other living cost differentials from region to region. State and local taxes are one variable, but a great deal of emphasis on this factor probably isn't warranted. Where one form of taxes are low, frequently other forms of taxation make up the difference. For example, a high sales tax in one state may be offset by low property taxes. Therefore, any relocation decision shouldn't stand or fall on this issue.

In fact, cost-of-living differentials, aside from the areas of the country with extremely high housing costs, are less of a factor than your individual lifestyle and spending habits. Lower costs on any specific item can be offset easily by other items. For example, gasoline may be a few cents a gallon cheaper in some areas than others, but you may find yourself driving many more miles, which will more than offset any savings. Therefore, these minor variances generally aren't worth considering.

The major difference in living costs will be when you transfer to or from a high-cost region such as the Northeast to a relatively low-cost area such as parts of the South or Midwest. And any rural or small town environment will tend to offer lower costs than a large metropolitan area. If you are faced with this sort of choice, then it behooves you to do some research as to the differences in living costs. Local chambers of commerce can provide you with information, and many of the larger relocation firms do cost-of-living surveys for different cities. Even then, the best way to get a feel for what it will cost you to live somewhere else is to pay a visit to the community. Then, and only then, will you be able to get firsthand knowledge of what the costs will be to maintain the lifestyle to which you're accustomed.

EVALUATING QUALITY-OF-LIFE FACTORS IN OTHER AREAS

There's more to life than work, but if you move to the wrong location you may discover that there isn't much other than work. What constitutes a satisfactory quality of life in a new community depends to a large part on your viewpoint, as well as your personal circumstances. A quiet rural setting may be idyllic for one person, and nerve-wracking frustration for someone else. From another angle, a community with good schools may be essential if you have school-aged children, and not be a factor at all if you don't have children in school.

Therefore, to some extent, whether the quality of life in a new community is adequate for your needs is a personal decision. For the most part, there are a number of fairly common elements that most people would consider to be essential in appraising the relative merits of a community. Let's look at each of these and see how you can evaluate them, both individually and on an overall basis.

1. *The availability and make-up of the housing in the area.* Does the community offer an adequate supply of the type of housing with which you will be comfortable? Are house prices available within your budget, and are there established neighborhoods which will help maintain housing prices?

2. *Accessibility to shopping, schools, and other community services.* Be careful with this, since the housing you find desirable may be remote from both community services and your place of work. Since the amount of leisure time is a priority quality-of-life issue for most people, you don't want a location where you will be spending a great deal of time either commuting to work or driving long distances to do your shopping and other chores.

3. *Availability of recreational activities.* Considerations here include both individual recreational needs, as well as spectator sports. If you have children, of prime consideration are the quality and quantity of youth programs in the area.

4. *Availability of cultural activities.* Libraries, museums, theater, opera, the arts, and other cultural needs aren't always available in smaller communities. This isn't necessarily a problem if it's only a relatively short drive to the nearest big city.

5. *Reasonable access to hospitals and other medical services.* This can be especially important if you or a family member has medical needs that require access to specialized medical facilities.

6. *A low crime rate.* No one wants to be a victim of crime, and although that fate can befall you anywhere, an area with a low crime rate puts the odds of avoiding such a fate in your favor.

7. *Good public schools.* If you have school-aged children, this is a prime consideration. It can also be a major pocketbook issue, since if you're not happy with the public schools, you will have to foot the bill for private schools. If that possibility exists, then determine what the status is for private schooling in the community.

8. *A climate you can enjoy.* This is more of an issue with some people than with others. Obviously, if you can't stand the sight of snow, you don't want to move to a snowbelt area. On the other hand, not everyone likes the long hot summers that certain parts of the country endure.

9. *Population density.* This is the city versus small town or country argument. There are people who thrive on living in the hustle and bustle environment of a big city, while other people prefer the tranquility of country living.

10. *Public transportation.* In some places it's easy to evaluate the public transportation—there really isn't any. On a more serious note though, don't disregard something such as the proximity to the nearest major airport, especially if you have the type of job which requires a lot of travel. Otherwise, you may find yourself spending predawn hours on the road to a distant airport to catch early morning flights.

Coping with Changing Lifestyle Considerations

Once you start to settle in within your new community, you may discover that your lifestyle isn't the same as it was in your former place of residence. Many of the adjustments you will have to make will be minor ones. You may find yourself missing everything from sports teams to your favorite supermarket. Over a period of time, many of these changes will fall into place, and you will start to discover things that you like better about your new environment. Initially, try to be as positive as is possible about all the minor adjustments you have to make. That way, it will be easier to cope with some of the more significant changes you may face.

NEGOTIATING SALARY, FRINGES, AND RELOCATION EXPENSES

As you recall, salary negotiations were discussed back in chapter five, so what we're dealing with here only concerns negotiating salary when relocation has an impact on the salary you are willing to accept. In general, most of the basic principles for negotiating salary previously discussed also apply here, with the additional element of asking for adequate compensation to cover any increase in the cost of living resulting from your move.

The same applies to fringe benefits, which for the most part will be the same as if you already lived in the new area. However, in some situations, you may be able to negotiate a one-time bonus or some other quid pro quo to compensate you for money you may have spent in relocating. Naturally, the one essential element that has to be negotiated when you move to a distant job are relocation expenses. For the most part, companies have a standard policy in this area, but there is flexibility involved and the more flexible you can encourage your new employer to be, the better financial shape you'll be in after the moving van drives away.

In terms of using cost-of-living differentials as a negotiating wedge for a higher salary, bring the issue up. Although employers tend to pay salaries that are competitive within the geographic area, if someone relocating faces substantially higher housing costs, some adjustment may be worked out. In lieu of adjusting the salary offer upwards, many employers will provide some form of assistance with housing. This can vary considerably from employer to employer. The basic point is not to put yourself in a position where you will be lowering your standard of living by accepting a job offer in an area where housing costs will price you out of the market.

As for relocation expenses in general, you might want to talk to other people who have relocated with your employer to see what sort of relocation costs were paid by the company. Companies have set policies, but they tend to be flexible in this area, so it can't hurt to ask. Everyone's needs vary somewhat when it comes to relocation expenses, so the company's representative will probably try to accommodate your needs. Be reasonable about it, and don't expect the company to foot the bill for stays in the presidential suite of a five-star hotel while you're on a house-hunting trip. You'll know when you're pushing your limit if the company relocation coordinator starts to get a little bit testy.

THE PROS AND CONS OF OVERSEAS ASSIGNMENTS

As difficult as the problems may be in relocating within the company, they are relatively simple compared with the problems involved in an overseas assignment. Then again, this depends both on your personal outlook and the location and duration of the assignment. There are generally two routes to working overseas, one being looking for such an assignment, and the other being offered one by your employer. If it's the latter, then the first question you have to deal with is whether or not to accept the offer.

Some employers routinely rotate managers overseas, with the expectation that it's a necessary ingredient for career advancement. Others are more flexible, and strive not to coerce those not interested to take such a position. Employers also differ in terms of the support they offer to those being assigned abroad. So for starters, if you work for an employer who is offering you an overseas assignment, the first consideration is whether or not it's to your advantage to make the move.

If the company you work for is determined to expand its overseas presence, then an overseas assignment will certainly strengthen your advancement potential. It's also a credential that serves to distinguish you from your career competition. After all, everyone may get a shot at production or marketing assignments, but few get the call for overseas postings.

Whatever you do, when you are first asked about a willingness to accept a job overseas, sit down with your boss and discuss the pros and cons. Make sure you know the length of the assignment. Look at where you are going to be assigned from both a practical and business standpoint. Is the country you would be going to one of the company's best markets, or is it a marginal operation in which the company doesn't show a lot of interest? This is meaningful, since it gives an indication of how much visibility you will have in your job. You don't want to spend a year or two in a corporate backwater where you will be all but forgotten.

Equally important is to get some form of commitment as to where you will be assigned after you complete your foreign tour. What you want to prevent is going overseas, and then ending up in a dead-end job when you come back because there is no desirable position available to you. It makes no sense to do an overseas tour to further your career, only to discover it has been set back by your absence when you return. You can get a general idea of your future when you return by looking to see where previous job holders were placed upon completing a similar assignment. In this regard, it also helps to have a good mentor stateside to keep you informed as to what's happening, and to look out for your interests as much as possible.

Foreign assignments can also have their drawbacks, not the least of which are family adjustments. As hard as it is for a family to adjust to relocation within the country, the trauma is even greater with a foreign assignment. In fact, the language barrier alone presents a hurdle that many employees and their families find difficult to handle. Beyond that are cultural differences that present additional challenges.

Some companies have programs to help employees cope with the difficulties of a foreign tour, but as helpful as they may be, if a family isn't committed to trying to make a foreign assignment work, then it will likely fail. In fact, some people never finish foreign assignments because of an inability to adjust. The situation is even more complicated than it used to be, since so many families are dual-career households. As hard as it is to seek out a new job for a spouse in a domestic relocation, it can be impossible to accomplish with a foreign assignment. The alternative is for the spouse to put a career on hold for the duration of the overseas tour.

Learn the Language

The surest route to success in a foreign assignment is an understanding of the local culture. It's a given that an understanding of the local language helps, so see if your company will foot the bill for foreign language courses. If you work for a company which routinely assigns executives to a specific foreign country, you may want to take the initiative to get language training well before you even get an overseas transfer.

This not only gives you more time to gain proficiency in the language, but being fluent in it will give you a leg up in being able to land the assignment.

Incidentally, even if you have to foot the bill yourself, it's worthwhile for family members to learn the language of the foreign country. Your ability to successfully complete a foreign assignment will be tied closely to the ability of family members to adapt to the local culture. This is especially true if there will be few other American families living near you in the foreign country. You will have your work to keep you occupied, but a spouse and children can be extremely isolated if they are unable—or unwilling—to immerse themselves in the local culture.

For this reason alone, every attempt should be made to look at going abroad as both a learning experience and an extended vacation. If the family is involved in learning all about where you will be living, it can turn what might be a disaster from a family perspective into an adventure. In this way, the assignment can be of value beyond just adding valuable business experience to your career.

On the other hand, you have to be realistic if you're offered a chance to work at an overseas outpost. If the family isn't likely to adapt well, then the business experience you gain won't be worth it. In fact, it could even be harmful if you're forced to come back early because of family problems. If there's little likelihood that the posting will be a success in this regard, you are well advised to decline such an offer. Most businesses are understanding about this, since with the large sums of money involved, they are happy to minimize any risk of someone not being able to complete the assignment. If you have school-aged children, or a spouse with a career, these are considerations that anyone can understand as a valid reason for not wanting to work overseas.

Chapter

8

WEIGHING THE ADVANTAGES AND RISKS OF MOVING

Even when you have established that certain areas meet your needs in terms of accepting a job offer, there are numerous other ingredients that go into any successful relocation. And unless they are resolved, a promising career opportunity elsewhere runs the risk of creating more problems than it solves. This chapter explores many of the risks and rewards of relocation, including the impact on family members and the problems of a dual-career move. You will also find assistance in dealing with many of the financial considerations of relocating.

Any relocation effort requires adjustment to a new community as well as maintaining ties with friends and family back home. Some helpful hints on how to do this are offered in this chapter. Plus, not every relocation works out for the best, so you'll find some assistance on what to do if a move doesn't work out quite as well as you had hoped.

ASSESSING THE IMPACT OF MOVING ON FAMILY MEMBERS

Moving to meet the needs of your employer or to seek a new position may not be much of a problem for you personally. On the other hand, it may be a real hassle for family members. Aside from the problem of dual careers which will be discussed in the following section, there are very real problems that moving can create for family members. Children's schooling can present a real problem, and one or more family members may have social or civic organization ties that can't be easily duplicated elsewhere.

It's usually a lot easier for the person being asked to relocate to adjust. After all, if he or she will be working for the same employer there is a great deal of familiarity associated with the working hours. And even if it's a job with a new employer, the sense of anticipation adds an element of satisfaction to moving. This isn't true for other family members, and so some serious discussions about relocation should take place before you jump the gun on the assumption everyone will be as happy as you are.

There are any number of details, large and small, that have to be addressed, and working them out beforehand will ease the transition when you move. Then again, some difficulties may be such that a decision is made that relocation isn't the right choice at the present time. If this happens, then it's a lot better to find it out before you make a move that doesn't work out.

Schooling is something that has to be considered from several angles. For example, if you or your spouse are enrolled in a part-time degree program at a local college, will it be possible to continue this education at your new location? This is a question that has to be researched beforehand. First, there may not be a college that offers the same program of study, and even if there is, will the credits earned be transferable?

Don't casually make assumptions about these matters, since you may overlook significant problems. As an example, you may find out either independently or through a prospective employer that the same program of study being pursued locally is also offered by a college at your new place of residence. Unless you check the details, you may discover later that the college is located some distance from your new job site, or that the courses aren't offered in the evenings, which is when you or your spouse would be planning to attend.

Various aspects of schooling can arise concerning your children. Your research may discover that the public schools in your new area don't offer a program in which one of your children is presently enrolled. From another angle, the quality of the schools may not be quite up to the level of your expectations. If this is the situation, does private schooling become a possibility, and if so, is it readily available and affordable? Paying for private versus public schooling can erase any financial advantage you might gain from relocation.

Another school-related factor that can't be ignored are the grade levels of your children. If you have a son or daughter in their last year of high school, it's obviously not an easy choice to move them to a new school. This factor alone might give you pause about accepting a relocation offer at the present time.

One of the most difficult aspects of relocation is the prospect of leaving close relationships with family members and friends. In fact, there may be problems in this area that make it unwise to relocate. For instance, if you or your spouse have aging parents whom you look after, circumstances may make it impossible to relocate. Perhaps your parents have no desire to move, and you wouldn't feel comfortable not being nearby to care for them. Sometimes when a distant job offer beckons, the reality of these situations doesn't surface until you think them through. You may be reassured by parents that they have no problem with you relocating, when you know full well that isn't true. So if you have nagging doubts about this, or other aspects of relocating, you should deal with them openly. Otherwise, they will continue to bother you after your relocation.

Although you may be in a position in which there are no insurmountable obstacles to making the move from the standpoint of your present residence, your concerns shouldn't end there. If the area you are relocating to differs substantially from where you live now, you have to consider the impact of this on both yourself and other family members. Everything from a different climate, to moving from a city to a rural environment, can cause plenty of headaches after you move. Therefore, it pays to deal with these issues well before any decision about moving is made. The optimum choice is for yourself and family members to visit any potential relocation site before a final decision is made.

DEALING WITH THE PROBLEMS
OF A DUAL-CAREER MOVE

Apart from the overall impact of moving on family members, as discussed in the prior section, one of the most difficult hurdles of a relocation is its effect on two-career households. Although a relocation may advance the career prospects of one member of the household, it can sidetrack a spouse's career. A couple faces the quandary of trying to turn a win-lose situation into a win-win situation. This isn't easy to do, especially if both people are well-established in their careers. It's further complicated when the job prospects for the trailing spouse (a term used to identify the person who will accompany the one being relocated) aren't favorable in the new area.

Some employers who routinely transfer people are attuned to this problem and will provide assistance in obtaining employment for the trailing spouse. Even so, there's no guarantee this will occur. So for the most part, the burden of deciding what to do falls squarely on the individuals themselves. The starting point for minimizing problems is to carefully think through the job possibilities beforehand, and to devise a strategy for landing two positions in the new area. It may also require you to further limit your geographic relocation preferences to areas which can best satisfy the career needs of both parties. Then again, you may decide jointly that for now the best move is no move at all.

If your employer is relocating you, some form of spousal assistance may be available. This can vary from employer to employer, with some offering minimal assistance in the form of resume preparation and job counseling, while others go so far as to search for in-house jobs and to pay for spousal job-hunting trips. Yet for the most part, couples are pretty much left on their own to resolve dual-career conflicts.

Some careful planning is needed to properly manage two careers, and this should be started long before a relocation problem makes hasty decisions necessary. Both marriage partners should sit down and work out their joint short- and long-term career goals. None of this will be etched in stone, since people's goals change for any number of reasons. However, a little planning can simplify things somewhat.

In discussing relocation prospects, the occupations of both parties must be considered. By doing this, you can immediately render large areas of the country invalid as relocation possibilities because of the lack of job opportunities in the career field of one or both spouses. By the process of elimination, you can narrow your potential relocation choices to a limited number of cities. These will be the ones that have a reasonable number of potential jobs in both career fields. This way, you will at least have a predetermined idea of where relocation will work best for both people. Naturally, this depends upon the type of job each person has, since in some occupations opportunities may be fairly universal, while in other fields they may be more restricted.

Although the objective is to treat both careers as deserving of equal consideration when decisions are made, at any given time the circumstances may be such that one career should take priority over the other. One example might be where the spouse being relocated will be moving into a senior management position, while the trailing spouse has been thinking about switching jobs anyway. Naturally, the circumstances could be such that the reverse is true.

Incidentally, a move or stay-put decision shouldn't be based strictly on monetary considerations. This is the sort of argument that goes something like, "Well, the money is too good to pass up." When you're working together to maintain two careers on track, the issues go beyond dollars and cents to what is the best way to make both careers work. In the end, it's not the money that counts, or any one job offer, but the commitment of both marriage partners to mutually support and accept the other's career ambitions—even if that sometimes means subordinating your own career goals on a temporary basis.

SEVERAL HIDDEN RELOCATION PITFALLS YOU SHOULD KNOW ABOUT

While some of the problems associated with relocation are obvious, there are a number of hidden pitfalls that aren't always apparent. Since these can surface after you've moved and cause considerable distress, it's worthwhile to at least recognize them beforehand. Otherwise, you may find yourself joining the ranks of others who have relocated only to end up saying, "I wish I had thought of that before I moved." When it comes to relocation, you're better off erring on the side of caution, since unnecessary hassles can add stress to an already stressful situation.

The first thing to recognize is that it's inevitable that unexpected problems will occur no matter how carefully a relocation is planned and executed. It can be anything from the mover showing up late with your belongings, to not being able to move into your new home as scheduled. Many of the unexpected hassles will be minor, but you may have the misfortune to encounter a major headache or two along the way. Being aware and ready to accept the fact will help you in dealing with any major or minor hurdles that come along.

The best way to minimize potential pitfalls is to practice prevention. This should start the minute your company asks you to relocate. Also, find out precisely what the company will contribute in terms of relocation assistance. This will provide you with the baseline of what you have to handle yourself. Your employer may also set you up with a relocation firm which will provide various forms of assistance to you in terms of both selling your existing home, and locating new quarters in your future place of residence.

Have Questions Answered Before You Move

Aside from the obvious hurdles of relocating, such as selling an existing home and buying or renting at your new location, there are many minor details that have to be handled. Take the time to make up detailed lists of what has to be done, and then check off what has been accomplished. Otherwise, things will be overlooked, and this can prove to be more difficult to resolve at a later date.

You will find that many of the questions that you need answers to concern the availability of specific services at your new location. For example, perhaps someone in your family sees a medical specialist on a regular basis. You obviously have to locate another physician in your new area. Rather than leave this until you move, ask your existing specialist for a referral. That way, you will have this problem resolved before you move.

There are all sorts of questions you will likely have in your mind concerning your new location, ranging from how to get a new veterinarian for your pets, to lining up a new dentist, to knowing just where the best places are to shop for home furnishings. Some of these questions can be answered by relocation experts if you have access to them. Others can be answered by people you know who live in the new locality. You may even find your personal computer to be an asset in finding answers. Through one of the on-line services, try to establish contacts with people who live in the new community and are willing to answer your questions. You may even get some solid advice that you wouldn't have thought about otherwise.

Bring Necessary Documents with You

A number of nuisance issues can cause you concern after you move if you haven't thought to take care of them before leaving your old location. Make sure you have birth certificates with you for all members of the family. If you have school-aged children to enroll in a new school system, find out before you leave for your new destination what documentation will be required for registration. It's worth a long-distance phone call to obtain this information. Otherwise, you may try to enroll your kids in school only to be told that they need immunization records, school transcripts, birth certificates, and the like. What's worse, you may meet with an enrollment refusal until this documentation is provided. This can cause difficulties if school is about to start and the papers you need are a thousand miles away. You will find yourself scrambling to have everything sent to you in a hurry. Although you may be in a rush, the clerk charged with digging the records out and sending them to you may not have the same sense of urgency. The end result may be that your children start school late because of a paperwork snafu that could have been prevented.

All important personal records that might be needed should be assembled before you move. It's also important to carry them with you, or otherwise make sure they will be available when you need them. In no event should you pack them away to send with the mover. They could get lost or misplaced, or the mover may not get to your new home by the date you are expecting. In either event, you're left with a major problem.

Although it's not a necessity, there are many other details you can expedite by making some phone calls in the days and weeks before you move. Ask ahead about telephone and utility services, registering your automobiles, driver's licenses, and all the other incidentals you will have to deal with on your arrival. Knowing the procedures you will have to follow and the documentation you need will make it a lot simpler to settle in at your new location.

Setting up your banking connection at your new location before you move can save you a lot of inconvenience when you first arrive in town. By opening accounts ahead of time, you won't have to deal with the hassle of merchants and others who don't want to accept out-of-state checks. It also simplifies transferring funds from your old bank to your new one. Along the same line, you may want to arrange for your brokerage account to be transferred to the local office at your new location.

One of the pitfalls of relocating that can be overlooked is the new job itself. All the hassles associated with a long-distance move can preoccupy you to the extent that little or no thought is given to the new job you have. After all, relocations often include both a promotion and a hefty pay raise, so the tendency is to temporarily forget about that aspect of your new life and concentrate on the moving hassles. Yet, as with any other new job, your initial effort should concentrate on whether the job itself will be beneficial in advancing your career.

Frankly, since you're uprooting yourself and your family by relocating, job satisfaction is even more important than if the new job was a local one. How much responsibility will you have? Who will be reporting to you, and who will be your boss? Is your new boss someone with whom you will feel comfortable working? These are questions you shouldn't lose sight of in the excitement over a relocation opportunity.

SELLING THE MOVE TO FAMILY, FRIENDS— AND YOURSELF

Once you start giving serious consideration to relocating, the doubts will start popping up in your mind. It's pretty easy to fall victim to the temptation to just forget about the whole thing the minute this happens. This tendency is likely to be reinforced the minute you mention relocation to family members or friends. Even people you work with are likely to emphasize the negative. After a while, you may start to wonder if there's anyone you know who doesn't have an unhappy tale to tell about living in some other part of the country.

Although it's prudent to carefully explore the potential problems associated with moving, the flip side of the coin is not to dramatize the downside and ignore the positive points. This is easy to do when most people seem to be emphasizing the negative. You have to take these comments and put them in perspective. Many of the people are looking at your relocation from a selfish point of view. Even though they may not be doing it consciously, they raise negative issues in an attempt to discourage you from moving. After all, your friends won't want you to leave, and your family members who will be staying behind will be even more disappointed at your relocation. And finally, your spouse and children may dread leaving the familiar for the unknown.

For these reasons, it's to be expected that initial reactions may weigh in on the negative side. For this reason, you have to separate pure emotional reasoning from any hard facts you hear as to why relocation isn't a good idea. You may also encounter one or more people who have lived in the area to which you will be moving. They may not have been happy there for reasons entirely unrelated to the location itself. Alternatively, they may have had unfortunate relocation experiences due to poor prior planning on their part. These folks will undoubtedly weigh in with all of the wrong reasons as to why you shouldn't relocate.

Apart from these individual negatives, everyone will be subconsciously reflecting the "hometown factor" when they voice an opinion. This unspoken reasoning is something like, "Since I'm living in this community it's obviously better than anyplace else, since if it wasn't I wouldn't be living here." This sort of parochialism makes sense only to the person thinking that way, but it does help explain why you will find people living in places you would consider to be the end of the earth.

Apart from the naysayers, you may run into a few "see the world" types who think any move is a good one. These people will be just as quick to tell you what a smart move you're making. The long and the short of all of this unsolicited advice is that most of it won't be of much value in helping you make a sound decision. The important point is not to let it bother you too much. Remember that you're the one doing the moving, not someone else. Even if you don't want to convince every casual acquaintance that you're making the right move, you do want to be in a position to point out the positives. For one thing, this will tend to quiet those who persist in telling you what a mistake you're making every time they see you. Beyond this, you want to be able to reassure family members and close friends of the benefits of the move. Once you're able to do this, they will tend to be supportive of your decision.

Beyond those staying behind, the first people to sell the move to should be those people, if any, who will be accompanying you. There is no way to avoid the initial sorrow associated with leaving behind friends. Children will miss their old schools and playmates, and someone such as a good child-care provider won't be easy to replace. To ease the transition, it's helpful to stay in touch with those left behind and share with them the adventures of moving. It may initially result in a pretty steep long-distance phone bill, but it will be worth it if it helps to ease the adjustment.

To make the adjustment as painless as possible for everyone, it's important to get involved in the new community right away. Whenever it's feasible, pursue the same activities as the family members were involved in at the old location. Beyond anything else, it's important to communicate openly with family members about the move. Give the kids their say, and explain the situation to them. It's also useful for the whole family to take a familiarization trip to the new location. In the end, everyone may not be enthusiastic about the move, but generally everyone adjusts within a short period of time.

HOW TO DEAL WITH RELOCATION STRESS

If there's one thing that you can be sure of, it's the stress that can be associated with relocating. Changing jobs alone can be stressful, and unless you're a sucker for punishment you know how trying it is to move your household. When you add a long-distance move into the equation, the stress possibilities multiply. Unless you're someone who is extraordinarily calm in any situation, the chances are you will find yourself losing it occasionally as you battle the pressures of relocation.

The very newness of the job and your home can cause stress by itself. The littlest things are initially much harder to do when you don't know where everything is located. Not only are your surroundings new, but your status as a known quantity at work is also missing. Until you have worked in your new location long enough to prove yourself, you may experience the feeling of being on trial. To add to the discomfort, you no longer have a handy network of friends outside the office with whom to share your feelings.

To counteract being new to the area, be friendly and strive to make new acquaintances both at work and within the community. At the same time, don't push too hard to get everything done at once. Don't forget you're pursuing two major challenges at the same time, one being a new job and the other being setting up your household in a new location. Recognize that the job will become routine after you get used to it, and don't try to master everything at once.

On the home front, every last box doesn't have to be unpacked right away. In fact, if you did a good job of packing, the nonessentials have been placed in separate boxes. These doo dads, memorabilia, and fifteen-year-old unused wedding gifts can be left packed—if not for the duration, at least for the immediate future. Instead of rushing to unpack every last box, make time to check out your new surroundings, and enjoy a little leisure time.

To cope with relocation stress, you may want to try the following:

- Take up your favorite activity, such as golf, tennis, bowling, and so forth as soon as possible after you settle into your new location.

- Have plenty of rest, instead of pushing yourself to get acclimated to your new surroundings.

- Call your friends back home and catch up on the news.

- Treat yourself by trying out the restaurants in your new community.

- Talk out the adjustment problems with your spouse. It will be a lot easier to adjust if you both are able and willing to express your concerns.

One of the most important ways to reduce relocation stress is to give yourself enough time to complete the relocation process. Selling one home and buying another one is in itself time-consuming, but when you add the problems of a distant move the situation becomes even more difficult. Start-to-finish usually can't be crammed into a thirty-day period, and to rush the process only adds to the possibility of frayed nerves. Sometimes, in coping with the transition from one locale to another, you may have to make hard choices. For example, if you have children near the end of a school year, it might be wiser to let them finish out the term where they are. This may mean leaving your family behind temporarily while you go ahead to start your new job. This isn't the best of circumstances, but in the long term it may be the appropriate choice.

TAX ASPECTS OF A JOB MOVE

Tax considerations shouldn't be a major determinant in any relocation decision you make. This doesn't mean, however, that you should ignore any tax implications of a job move. Your career moves are based on long-term factors, and as you know, politicians are adept at talking about tax cuts, while simultaneously managing to take more money out of your pocket.

Aside from this, a state or community with a relatively low tax structure today may be headed toward raising taxes in the future. This is especially true if you're relocating to a place that is growing rapidly. The need to provide infrastructure such as schools, public safety, and so forth to meet the needs of a growing population probably means increased taxes may be in the future for such localities. So don't stake your career on living somewhere just because you may save a few dollars in taxes. In fact, even where taxes are low, you may find yourself paying more in the form of fees, licenses, and other local assessments, which somewhat offset any tax savings.

Although taxes shouldn't be paramount in your decision, your circumstances may be such that you can fare much better in one locality than another. If you have a relatively high income, then a low or no income tax state may give you a substantial monetary advantage. This is especially true if you currently reside in an area where state and local taxes are relatively high. So it's certainly prudent to figure out what your net gain or loss will be on the tax front if either your present or future residence are on the high or low end of the tax scale.

There are three major areas in which a relocation may involve tax considerations. One is in selling and/or buying a home, the second is the moving expenses themselves, and the third is the impact of state and local taxes at your new location versus your former place of residence. There can be some real intricacies involved in these areas, so it's of paramount importance that you consult your attorney and tax adviser for professional advice in dealing with your tax issues.

One general consideration you shouldn't overlook when you hunt for a home in your new community is property taxes. These can vary widely from one town to the next in some parts of the country. For this reason, if local property taxes are high in your relocation place of residence, you want to make sure you know the impact of property taxes in the area in which you're buying a home. You can also find variances in sales taxes between cities and counties in the same general area. By itself, this shouldn't be enough to influence you to choose one community over another. But a high sales tax combined with a lofty property tax, and perhaps even higher fees, can put a dent in your budget. As a consequence, this is something to keep in mind when you do your house hunting.

You may decide to rent, at least temporarily, at your new location. If so, high property taxes won't be a direct consideration for you. Your landlord will be paying these, so indirectly at least they will be factored into your rent. If you rent, you won't be paying a mortgage, and from a tax standpoint you won't have the tax deductions associated with home ownership. Last, but certainly not least if you're affected, is the matter of foreign assignments. If you're relocating overseas, the complexities of your tax situation will be magnified.

The bottom line on this and any domestic relocation is that your tax status will vary with your individual circumstances. But whatever your situation, there are a number of details with which you will have to contend. Therefore, to get off on the right foot when doing this, consult your attorney and tax adviser early on in the relocation process so you can minimize any tax problems down the road.

SOME NOT-SO-OBVIOUS RELOCATION EXPENSES TO CONSIDER

Such items as moving expenses and housing costs will obviously get your attention when you start to assess the cost of relocating. Consequently, you should spend a considerable amount of time in working to keep these to a minimum. If you have an employer who is picking up the major portion of the tab, this will lessen any anguish you may have over this topic.

Aside from this, with or without relocation expenses being paid for by an employer, there are some not-so-obvious costs associated with relocating. If you don't recognize and budget for these beforehand, you can find your financial picture becoming much less favorable than you had contemplated initially. Since this isn't the best way to get off to a good start in your new location, it's worth the effort to explore some of the possible monetary pitfalls lurking in wait.

Although your individual situation will dictate whether or not particular expenses apply to you, there are a number of fairly common ones that most people can encounter. Let's look at what some of these are and what you can do to avoid or minimize them.

One major financial headache that can put a crimp in your finances is trying to pay two mortgages if you can't sell your house right away at your former location. This may not be a problem for you if your employer, either directly or through a home-buying company, is going to buy your house. Unfortunately, this doesn't hold true for everyone, and if you're on your own in selling your house, don't take it for granted that it will sell quickly. Changing economic conditions can quickly throw the housing market for a loop. In other instances, homes can be overpriced in the eyes of buyers, even though the home seller doesn't think so. Frequently, people become very attached to a house and fail to notice some of the liabilities involved with selling the property. If you price your house realistically, you will avoid falling into this trap and will be less likely to find yourself having to deal with two mortgages.

Another major unforeseen expense may be the cost of private schooling for your children, which can put a serious dent in any budget. If you don't investigate the public schools in your new community before you move, you may not even anticipate this expense beforehand. On the other hand, don't arbitrarily panic if your youngsters experience initial difficulty in a new school. They also have relocation adjustments to make, and as they start to make friends and participate in school activities their conduct and grades may improve. You certainly don't want to assume they will do better in private school if it's a temporary adjustment problem, because you will only be adding to the problem by putting them in another new school environment.

Lifestyle Changes Can Be Expensive

One major expense you might not anticipate when you relocate is a change in your lifestyle which results in higher living costs. You may find yourself living at a higher standard than was true at your former place of residence. This can happen if you're promoted and find that those you socialize with at work live a life of greater extravagance to which you are not accustomed. This can also come about by virtue of the neighborhood you move to, as you unconsciously adopt a "keeping up with the Joneses" philosophy. Needless to say, if you can't afford it, pull in your financial horns when you see this happening.

One of the biggest financial shocks of a relocation experience is the loss of a spouse's salary. This may only be temporary until a new job is found, but in the interim it can mean some serious belt-tightening is in order. It can also create longer-term problems if your spouse isn't able to get another job that pays as much as his or her previous position. This is just one more reason why dual-career relocations aren't easy to pull off without hitting some snags along the way.

A lack of planning can also result in dishing out unnecessary cash in some circumstances. For example, utilities often require a deposit from new customers. These payments can be avoided if you arrange for a credit letter from your former utilities attesting to the fact that you paid your bills on time. Based on these, utilities will waive new customer security deposits. Be sure to handle this shortly before you leave your former place of residence, so the notification will be received before you apply for service at your new residence.

A relocation can also result in other expenses you may or may not contemplate. At least initially, you can expect your long-distance phone bills to be higher with calls to keep in touch with family and friends. And just as with a local move, a new home brings with it the need for new furnishings. Some of these may be necessities, such as window treatments in the form of curtains and blinds. Others may result from decisions made prior to moving, such as not bringing along older furniture with the idea of replacing it at your new location. If you do this, just make sure you factor replacing furniture and other household possessions you don't bring with you into your financial equation.

Sometimes you can overlook what in retrospect would be an obvious expense. For example, if you move from the south to a northern state during the summer, you may forget about the fact that you will be buying a lot of cold-weather clothing as soon as the chill of the fall air arrives. A change in climate can also bring about other expenses besides clothing. Ice skates and skis may be new additions in a south-to-north move, and the cost of maintaining a swimming pool may be added if the move is in the other direction. Overall, even a local move can result in unforeseen expenses, but the possibilities are multiplied if it's a long-distance move, so keep your checkbook handy and be ready to be surprised by something you forgot to factor into your budget.

RENT OR BUY: EXPLORING YOUR HOUSING OPTIONS

One of the biggest hurdles you face when relocating is finding a place to live. If you are relocating at the request of your employer, you may have the good fortune to have a lot of assistance in doing this. Otherwise, you will be pretty much on your own in terms of finding a real estate agent and so forth.

You may only be interested in renting an apartment under any circumstances, but even if you plan to look for a home you may want to rent initially. This is especially true if you're unfamiliar with the area you're moving to, and the move is on short notice so you haven't had time to check out the local housing market.

Research Where the Best Schools Are Located

In assessing the specific area you want to live in within your new community, a number of considerations come into play. If you have children in school or a year or two away from that, then the local schools are an important determinant. These can vary widely from one area to the next, so you have to be certain which ones are favored by the locals. This isn't hard to do, and local real estate people will be able to pin this down for you. Don't rely on one opinion though, since if someone is selling houses in a particular area, they aren't likely to spotlight the fact that the best schools are somewhere else. Actually, you can figure this out for yourself by just checking the real estate ads in the local paper. Houses for sale in an area where there are good schools often emphasize this point in the classified ads, so when you see the same schools mentioned again and again in real estate ads, you know they are probably the cream of the local crop.

Incidentally, if you're moving to a rapidly growing area, school district lines can become an important consideration. You may buy a house close to a school district line which is changed after a year or two as enrollment starts to exceed capacity. To your chagrin, you may then find yourself with a notice in the mail advising you that in the next academic year your children will be assigned to a new and distant school. To prevent yourself from getting caught in this dilemma, contact the local school board and ask what if any redistricting actions are contemplated. Better yet, get yourself a map of the school district boundaries. Then don't buy any house that's close to the existing boundaries, since those are the areas most likely to be affected if school district lines are redrawn.

This is the sort of issue that can be overlooked when you're relocating. It can create serious problems though. Remember, you're already uprooting your school-aged children to relocate. You don't want them settling into a new school only to be uprooted again in a year or so. This is an area in which a little bit of legwork initially can save you some big headaches down the road.

Making the Rent or Buy Decision

One of the first issues for you to decide upon when you are relocating is whether to rent or buy a home at your new location. For some people, particularly if they are single, this doesn't require a decision, since they may not have any desire to purchase a home. For others, if the relocation by an employer is for a relatively short period of a year or less, they too may decide to forgo home ownership.

Most others would prefer to buy a home, and will eventually, but might prefer to wait temporarily. There are any number of valid reasons for postponing purchasing a home right away at your new location. One reason can be preferring to wait until your existing home is sold before committing to purchasing another residence. It puts you at a distinct negotiating advantage to put a condition in a purchase offer for a new home that's contingent upon selling your present home. It can also put you in the position of being so eager to sell your home that you accept a less than fair market price. A bridge loan, which is based on the equity in your existing home, can help you in this dilemma. However, a bridge loan may be more difficult to get with a relocation, since the lender may not be familiar with the market area of your new home.

Another reason for renting temporarily at your new location is not to lock yourself in if the new job or surroundings don't work out. This is something you will have a handle on within a relatively short period of time, so a rental situation may be preferable until you feel secure enough to commit to a home purchase.

The most common—and practical—reason for renting is that it will give you sufficient time to familiarize yourself with your new community. It will allow you to appraise the various neighborhoods, assess relative selling prices in these areas, and decide upon the area in which you want to purchase a home. If you buy a house quickly to have a home to move into when you relocate, you may find later that it isn't either the house or the neighborhood in which you prefer to reside.

If you only want to rent long enough to get settled in and spend some time house hunting, you don't want to tie yourself down with a long-term lease. One for five or seven months is probably sufficient, or you may choose to rent on a month-by-month basis. If you aren't planning on buying a home in the near future, a longer-term lease may give you a lower monthly rental.

If you are going to rent, then you have to decide what type of accommodations you want. If the arrangement is just for a few months, then you might as well look for accommodations as close to your work as possible. Something else you have to consider if you are moving from a home to an apartment is what to do with all your home furnishings. It's unlikely you will find, or even need, an apartment big enough for all the belongings you had in a house. Your best bet may be to put some of them in temporary storage until you eventually buy a house.

If apartment living, even on a temporary basis, isn't for you but you don't feel secure committing to buying a home right away, then you may want to consider a lease-option home purchase. Under this arrangement, a certain percentage of each month's rent is allocated as a credit to be applied to the down payment if the option is exercised. Generally, there's also a lump sum option amount paid upon signing the agreement which also goes toward the down payment if the option is exercised. Although in most instances, a lease-option is used where a buyer doesn't have funds for a down payment, it can be used if you don't want to lock yourself into a house until you are certain the relocation will work out for you. It's not always easy to have the seller go along with a lease-option provision, so this isn't a route you can count on with any certainty. You also stand to lose any up-front option money if you don't exercise the option within the stated time period.

Assuming you're going to go the home-buying route right away, take advantage of all the help you can get from the relocation people at the firm your employer uses. If you're on your own, then hook up with a real estate agent you feel comfortable with at your new location. Rather than establishing a price range and looking at homes on that basis, first pin down the area in which you want to live. This means you have to spend some time touring your new community, but you would be surprised how closely you can zero in on prospective areas of the community even before you set foot in it. Get the local paper by mail, request information from the local chamber of commerce, real estate agents, banks, and others.

Using this information, it's not hard to figure out where the best schools are, which areas have the lowest crime, and which are the most convenient to shopping as well as your place of work. This way you can at least make an initial determination of potential areas to concentrate your house hunting in. If you do this, by the time you make your house hunting trips, you will be better prepared to make intelligent decisions. Inevitably, you will find you have to make trade-offs, such as sacrificing proximity to work for a good school district, but if you have established your priorities beforehand, then this shouldn't be difficult to do.

SEVENTEEN WAYS TO MAKE MOVING EASIER
ON YOURSELF

If your employer is picking up your moving costs, then you don't have a lot of worries, as long as you stay within any preset limitations. It's a different story though if you have full responsibility for your moving bill. The costs of moving can add up rapidly if you're not careful, so not only do you have to get the best price you can from a mover, but you had better decide early on to plan what goes and what doesn't. It's virtually guaranteed that if you haven't moved in some time, you have a lot of household possessions that you never use. In fact, you may be surprised to find how many things you dig out of basements and attics you didn't even know you had.

Beyond the expense of moving is the stress that it can create. Much of this anxiety can be overcome if you plan your move well in advance so that everything goes smoothly. So let's look at some actions you can take to lighten both the burdens and expense of moving:

- *Go through all your possessions and decide what you aren't going to keep.* Anything that you haven't used in a long while isn't likely to be needed in the near future, so why pay to move it?

- *Large items that are expensive to move may not be worth it if they are nearing the end of their useful life.* Old washing machines, dryers, and other large appliances are examples of this sort of item. There's little point in spending money to move any large item that isn't likely to last much longer.

- *Make certain you will have space in your new residence for your household goods.* If you are moving to smaller quarters, then weed out what you don't need. Otherwise, you will end up paying the cost of keeping it in storage at your new location.

- *Hold a garage sale to earn some money from all the usable odds and ends you're not taking with you.*

- *Remember not to bring items you won't need to your new locale.* For instance, if you're moving to a warmer climate where central air conditioning is the norm, you may not need to bring a portable air conditioning unit. You may also have items that come with your new home that are duplicates of your current possessions. For example, if a refrigerator comes with your new home or apartment, then you can sell yours rather than pay to move it.

- *Fill out a change of address notice at the post office.* You will also want to notify people independently of your new address.

- *Collect your valuable personal records, including medical and dental records, immunization forms, school records, and so forth.* Carry these with you so you'll have them readily available.

- *Arrange to close any safe deposit box and complete all other transactions at your present home.*

- *If you're arranging for a mover, get several estimates.* Make sure they are binding quotes before you sign any agreement.

- *When you pack—if you do it yourself—put those things you won't readily need together.* Do the same with those items you will want to unpack right away. This seems like a minor detail but when you get to your new location, you don't want to be scrambling around opening boxes to find something you need. It's very helpful to clearly mark the outside of each box to identify its contents. You can also do this to identify the room in which the contents of each box belong. That way, the movers can be directed as to where the boxes go. It also saves you a lot of work lugging boxes all over your house before you empty them. A good way to identify them by room is by using different colored labels or stickers.

- *Make an inventory of the items you're moving.* You may not want to record every single item, but as a minimum know how many boxes you have, as well as all the unpacked furniture, appliances, and so forth that are being moved. Often on long-distance moves, loads are combined and something belonging to you could inadvertently get delivered to someone else. If you don't record what you moved, it's not easy to discover what's missing before the mover leaves.

- *Transfer magazine subscriptions to your new address, and notify utilities at your old address where to send a final bill.*

- *Notify credit card companies, the holder of any auto loans and mortgages, and others you owe money to of your new address.* Your mail will be forwarded by the post office, but there is a delay involved. In the meantime, the clock is running on the due date for bill payments. By letting your creditors know your new address by phone, they can immediately mail statements to your new address, or send a duplicate if the latest statement was sent to your old address. Doing this will prevent the possibility of late payments being recorded because you didn't get statements in time to pay by the due date.

- *If your automobiles need any servicing or repairs, get them done locally before you move.* That way, they will be in good repair if you're driving them to their new destination. Even if they will be hauled or towed, it's still better to service your car at your old location where you know the dealer and mechanic. When you first arrive in your new community you won't know a mechanic you can rely on, so you don't want to be in a position of needing repairs right away.

- *You might want to bring a local phone book with you.* You will not have to use directory assistance this way, and it will simplify finding the phone numbers of places and people you have to call. You may not think there is anyone you will need to contact other than those people whose phone numbers you already have, but for one reason or another, you will likely have to contact stores and such with which you did business.

- *Contact your auto insurance company and let them know of your change of address.* You may also have a premium adjustment, hopefully in your favor. Also get in touch with the company holding your homeowner's insurance and arrange for either homeowner's or rental coverage at your new location.

- *What may be the most important tip of all is to have the phone number where you can contact the mover with you at all times.* Also give the mover a number where you can be contacted. Once you and the mover part company from your prior residence, you won't know where your possessions are until they show up at your door. Everything doesn't always go according to schedule, so you don't want to be in a panic wondering where your possessions are if they don't arrive on the morning they're scheduled. Doing this also allows for easy contact if there are any changes in plans by either party which could cause potential delivery problems.

SIMPLE STEPS FOR ADJUSTING IN YOUR NEW COMMUNITY

If you, or other family members, experience difficulty in adjusting to your new environment after the initial impact of the move has worn off, then you have to take some measures to adapt to your new surroundings. It's not as hard to do as it might seem, but it requires taking the initiative to get involved in social activities or community organizations. The longer you wait to do this, the harder it becomes. So take advantage of every opportunity that comes your way to make new friends and acquaintances. There are all sorts of approaches you can take to do this, but inevitably you have to take the initiative to become part and parcel of the fabric of your new hometown.

The first impulse upon moving to a distant location is to immediately notice the differences from your former home. Even the most insignificant item will be mentioned as being different than back home. Family members will comment on what's missing in the way of favorite stores, and so forth. These comparisons present no problem in themselves, but if they persist it can signal a refusal to let go of the past and to accept the new location as home.

The amazing thing once people get beyond the initial feeling of newness is how similar so many things are. Your first trip to the local shopping mall will tell you that. Marketing is international, so you will find many of the same stores wherever you go. Even when the store name has changed, the products inside will be the same. The simple fact is that there are far more similarities than differences when you move from one area to another. This is significant, and it helps to point this out if one or more family members bemoan the change in environment.

Cultivate Your Children's Routine

One of the biggest relocation concerns falls on families with children, especially those of school age. It can be hard for kids to adjust to new schools and have to make new friends. The best solution to this problem is to get them involved as soon as possible in the same interests they held in their hometown. Whether it's gymnastics, dance classes, baseball, or something else, find out about the local programs and get them signed up as soon as possible. This will not only take their mind off moving, but will also give them an outlet to make new friends. It's natural as a parent to worry about your children adjusting to their new home, but although it may be difficult at first, most kids adapt very quickly.

If you have a choice in the matter as to timing your move to a new location, it helps to move shortly before the school year begins if you have school-aged children. That way, your kids will be involved quickly in the school routine which will keep them busy. It also gives them a better opportunity to meet other kids their own age. If you move early in the summer, then the kids may have a month or two before school starts. Even though they may make friends in the new neighborhood during that time, the kids they meet may be in a different grade or even go to a different school. If that happens, then not only have your kids had to adjust to leaving their friends in their old hometown, but they may also lose the new friends they make over the summer when school begins again. This may not happen, but if it does it can be a traumatic experience.

Relocation, at least as far as adjusting to a new community, is usually easiest for someone who will be starting their new job right away. In fact, between the turmoil of moving, and the excitement of a new job, not much time is left to dwell on the past. There's also the opportunity to meet people at work and form new friendships that may extend beyond working hours. And even though kids miss their friends initially, they soon make new ones. Where adjustment problems are often the hardest is for a nonworking spouse.

It's not easy to make new friends without an outlet outside the home to meet people. So if the at-home spouse is just temporarily between jobs because of the relocation, it's worthwhile to begin a job hunt as soon as possible. On the other hand, if the at-home spouse isn't planning to work outside the home, then it's useful to explore volunteer activities as a source for meeting people. In fact, being a school volunteer will not only give you a chance to make new friends, but will also give you a quick and up-front appraisal of the new schools your children are attending.

On an overall basis, adjusting to a new community can be made much easier by duplicating the lifestyle of your former home. Whatever the interests of family members were at the former location, concentrate your efforts on doing things the same way in your new environment. This isn't difficult to do, unless your move is to an area where it's impossible to pursue some of the former family activities. For the most part, these would consist of activities impacted by a change in climate, such as avid skiers moving south, or year-round boating or fishing enthusiasts moving to an area where such a form of recreation isn't popular or practical. If a former activity is no longer feasible, try to take up the slack by substituting activities that are popular in your new place of residence. In the final analysis, adjusting to a new community isn't difficult, but it does require making the effort to move the process along.

HOW TO BEAT THE HOMESICK BLUES

Some people start to miss their former hometown the minute they pull out of the driveway. For others, the initial excitement of a distant move overcomes this for a short period of time. Then, they too begin to talk aloud about all the things for which they long. It's certainly positive to talk openly about what's missed, since it helps to cope with homesickness. It won't really become a problem unless it's dwelled on to the point of being unreasonable. Nevertheless, there are measures you can take to ease the transition from your former residence.

Naturally, the extent to which your former place of residence is missed will depend largely on how long you lived there. If it was the place in which you grew up, the ties will run deep, whereas if it was just a one- or two-year assignment at a corporate outpost, then there may be no problem at all. Your experience with relocating is also a factor. If this is your first long-distance move, then the adjustment process may be harder than if it's your fifth or sixth.

It's important to be realistic about your outlook. It is frequently only after someone relocates that they suddenly discover how wonderful the place was where they were living. Overlooked are the many negatives, some of which may even have contributed to the decision to relocate. So for starters, it pays to be honest with yourself about the pros and cons of your old hometown.

Aside from taking measures to adjust to your new community, there has to be a recognition by each family member that this new location is now home. It won't come instantaneously, and it won't come at the same moment for everyone. Yet over a period of time, the daily routine and current activities will slowly work to overcome lingering homesickness. In the meantime, it helps to keep your old hometown in some sort of focus, since you can't just arbitrarily forget it ever existed, and most likely you won't want to. You still have friends and perhaps family there. If so, visits back and forth will become commonplace.

One good way to maintain contact is to subscribe to your old hometown newspaper. It will provide news about what was familiar to you until you become entwined in the activities of your new community. More than likely this paper will be read with avid interest at first, but receive less and less scrutiny by household members with the passage of time. In fact, by the time the first year's subscription is up, you may well decide not to renew because of lack of interest.

Although your first long-distance phone bill may give you pause, don't discourage family members from calling their friends to keep in contact. You may have to set some sort of time limitations with youngsters who can easily talk for two hours at a time. These conversations help people overcome the gap of geographic separation. As with the local newspaper, the passage of time will produce fewer and fewer calls as your youngsters make new friends.

Another way to overcome the homesickness gap is to invite family and friends to visit. One advantage of doing this is that both you and family members may unconsciously adopt the position of being a goodwill ambassador for your new community. In the process of telling and showing visitors everything you like about the new community, you may be aiding your own acceptance of the location. This works especially well with your kids, who you may be surprised to hear bragging about aspects of their new home to visitors, when all you were hearing were their complaints. Above all else, time alone will serve to cure any homesickness blues, at least in the majority of cases. With some people the inability to move somewhere different is deep-seated, and it's in these situations where relocation may not work out.

WHAT TO DO IF THE MOVE DOESN'T PAN OUT

From the minute you commit to relocating there's no certainty it will turn out to be a successful venture. All sorts of problems can crop up, some of which have been anticipated, but couldn't be overcome, and others that weren't even factored into the equation. Whatever the reason may be, every relocation won't be a success, and you may be forced to finally concede that it just won't work out. This is one good reason not to burn your bridges behind you when you leave a job. You never know when you may be back knocking on the door. Hopefully, that won't happen, but the possibility can't be ignored.

If a move doesn't work out and you decide to move back to your old stomping grounds, try to maintain a positive outlook on the entire experience. Treat it as a learning experience, which it is, and not a foolish decision on your part. However, before you throw in the towel always try to tough it out at the new location long enough to overcome the initial hurdles associated with relocating. Some people don't invest enough time in a new area to give relocation a chance to succeed. Almost from the minute they arrive, they're ready to turn around and head the other way. When this happens, it's usually because not enough thought was put into relocating before the move was made.

Once it's obvious that a relocation isn't going well, the first thing to do is identify the problem and assess the possible solutions. The reasons aren't always as apparent as you might think. For example, a spouse may be extremely unhappy, yet when confronted will deny that the relocation has anything to do with it. Another possibility is that youngsters will start having difficulty in school, or get into more than their share of mischief. Here too, there may be a denial that the move is in any way responsible. Denials are a natural enough reaction, since no one wants to feel they are responsible for the relocation not working out.

Good communication is essential in making relocation work, so encourage family members to share their thoughts as to how they are faring in their new surroundings. If someone is having problems, talk it out and explore the possibilities for resolving the difficulty. The source of the difficulty could be almost anything, but try to look for areas where the person's circumstances have changed radically from what they were used to. For youngsters, the problem might be that they are now in a large school, while they were formerly attending a smaller school in which they knew everyone. The solution might be to enroll them in a smaller private school, which would give them a more close-knit environment.

A spouse might be experiencing concern about being isolated with no family or friends to visit. A possible solution, aside from joining local organizations, may be a part-time job. It's a good way to start forming a network of new friends and pick up a little cash at the same time.

Another good alternative is to enroll in one or two continuing education courses. It's a far more serious problem, though, if a spouse has given up a career temporarily to make the move. Here, the emphasis should be on re-establishing the career as soon as possible.

It may be that the problem adjusting has nothing to do with either your family or the new community, but is instead your own unhappiness with your new job. Perhaps you haven't been given all the responsibility you were led to believe you would have. Maybe you're having real problems getting along with your new boss. Problems with a new job can come up, whether the job is a few miles or several hundred from your former place of employment. The difference being that in the relocation situation, you've moved yourself, your possessions, and your family a long way for a job you don't like.

Whatever the cause or causes that are making the relocation untenable, don't panic at the first sign of discontentment. Do your best to make adjustments and see if the situation improves. Ultimately, you may decide that things won't work out, and if that happens be willing to accept the fact. It won't be the first or the last time that someone discovered that the grass isn't always greener somewhere else.

Part

4

FINANCIAL MEASURES FOR AN UNCERTAIN FUTURE

If you want a "which comes first, the chicken or the egg," scenario, then consider your job and your money. The better-paying job you have, the more money you have available to spend or save. On the other hand, without adequate financial resources, you're constrained in your career choices, since without funds to live on you may have to take the first job offer that comes along should you become unemployed. Inadequate finances hamper you even more if you would like to switch careers, but doing so would force you to accept a lower salary than you presently earn.

Despite this link between career and finances, very few people factor this in when assessing their financial needs. Retirement planning gets attention as the time draws closer, but little thought is given to saving money as a safeguard against job setbacks. This is unfortunate, especially in an era where job security is at best uncertain. As you know, the sudden loss of a job can cause financial havoc. Accordingly, managing your finances is linked inextricably with managing your career. If you have adequate financial resources squirreled away, not only are your job loss worries minimized, but your freedom to make career moves is enhanced. The two chapters that follow address the two main aspects of a sound financial strategy. The first chapter covers tactics for saving more of the money you earn, while the following chapter explores how to rein in your spending so you have more money available to save.

Chapter

9

GETTING MORE BANG
FOR YOUR BUCKS

Whether you're changing jobs or switching careers, either by choice or necessity, your ability to do so successfully is to a great degree controlled by your financial situation. If you have adequate financial resources to weather a period of financial uncertainty, then your job and career options are enhanced. On the other hand, if you have little in the way of funds to tide you over tough times, then you don't have the luxury of an extended search for the perfect job opportunity. This is especially true if you have family financial responsibilities or other fixed obligations, such as a mortgage or car payments.

For this reason, your career and financial future are linked inextricably, so it behooves you to plan your financial future so as to enhance your career goals. This means increasing your savings, not only for the inherent security it brings, but also for the degree of confidence it gives you in a world of uncertain employment opportunities.

Any mention of financial planning often puts people in a glum mood with visions of detailed budgets and sophisticated investments clouding their future. This is especially true if you think, perhaps rightly so, that you're barely able to survive from week to week, much less save for your future. However, giving yourself some financial security doesn't require either a great deal of sacrifice or detailed number crunching. What it does require is an awareness of some basic financial fundamentals which can help you realign your spending to better meet your financial goals. That is precisely what this chapter covers. You'll learn how to plan for financial emergencies, avoid investment scams, and see how to carefully select bankers, brokers, and others who best meet your financial needs. Beyond this, you will find tips on how to lower your financial outlays to give yourself the savings cushion that will help you work toward financial independence in the long run. A good place to start is by looking at how your career moves are linked to your financial resources.

WHY YOUR CAREER MOVES ARE LINKED TO YOUR FINANCES

One of the major obstacles to making favorable career moves is the inability to afford it financially. This is especially true if someone wants to start over in a new career where they will be making less money initially. Since they have a standard of living in line with their income and little or nothing in the way of savings, they see it as impossible for them to change careers. For this reason alone, many people stay in jobs they dislike throughout their working life.

It's important to look at your career and your income as being linked to each other. The key that unlocks the door for you to pursue your career dreams are the savings you amass from your income. This is a positive argument for always striving to spend a little less than you earn. That way you will be able to gain a measure of financial freedom after a period of time. Apart from any career switches or other aspirations you may have, a financial safety net is a necessity in case you lose your job.

Many people yearn to start their own business or change careers, but hesitate to do so since they are reluctant to give up a job that pays well for an uncertain financial future. One good way around this dilemma is to start your own business on a part-time basis, or work part-time in a new career to gain experience. This isn't feasible for everyone, but in many situations it can work well if you're willing to put in the time and effort. By doing it this way, you eliminate the financial risk of quitting your present job.

Assuming that isn't the route you want to take, then the alternative is to increase your level of savings, and reduce your expenditures. That way you can more readily move into a new career or business which will—at least at the start—pay less than you're presently earning. The biggest hurdle to overcome in getting control of your finances is a reluctance to admit that you probably are spending more than you need to. After all, that's an admission of incompetence in a way, and no one wants to admit to that. Yet if you think about it, cutting expenses is something businesses do all the time, and in fact it's one of the factors which cause people to lose their jobs. So if nothing else, you had better learn to control your own expenses, before an employer forces you to with a termination notice.

To some extent your financial situation also dictates your ability to obtain any additional education you may need to pursue a different career. If you need a degree, or have other comprehensive educational needs to meet in order to qualify in a new field, you have to be able to finance this endeavor. One conventional way to do this is to attend school nights while you work days. This can be time-consuming if your educational needs are such that it will take an extended period of time to complete the requirements. Consequently, it may be preferable for you at some point to attend school full time. Here again, depending on your ability to obtain educational assistance, your career objectives are interrelated to your financial circumstances.

The important point in all of this is that to further your career you have choices, but to make them work, you have to have your financial house in order. In the event you aren't presently planning to change career fields, you still have to protect yourself against the possibility of an extended period of unemployment due to a sudden job loss. Beyond that, depending upon your individual situation, you may want to accrue funds for your youngster's college education or to purchase a home. Further down the road, there's also financial security for your retirement to think about. The remaining topics in this and the following chapter are aimed at helping you accomplish these objectives.

PAINLESS WAYS TO STASH CASH FOR A FINANCIAL CRISIS

With lifetime job security virtually a memory of a bygone era, almost everyone has to view the threat of temporary unemployment as being a distinct possibility. For some people, the threat is more real than for others. If you work in a field that's subject to frequent layoffs, unemployment is no surprise. Even people with relatively secure positions may not face the imminent danger of losing their jobs, but they, like everyone else, are subject to one form or another of financial crisis. It may be a serious illness, the loss of a spouse's income, or some other event that brings financial hardship to the front door.

Whatever the cause may be, a financial crisis can bring not only money problems, but also a great deal of stress in trying to cope with the situation. Although you can't predict what events will trigger financial problems for you, a carefully planned policy of putting rainy day funds aside will give you the wherewithal to cope with any difficulty that comes along.

Saving Money Requires Discipline

The first step in putting together a financial safety net is probably the one that is recommended more often than anything else because it is so basic. That, quite simply, is to save a fixed amount out of every paycheck. Sadly, this advice is frequently ignored, which is why people who have worked for years may not have a dime in the bank when they are confronted with an emergency such as the loss of a job.

The failure to systematically save probably stems from a number of factors. First of all, it's hard at first to see any substantial benefit from putting aside a small amount of money each payday. This creates an attitude of, "It would take forever to save enough money to matter, so why bother?" This frame of mind prevents you from learning to exercise a little bit of financial discipline.

Some people will attempt to systematically save but they set the amount much higher than their budget can afford. As a result, they continually dip into the savings to cover everyday expenses, and after a while decide the effort is futile in the first place. With other folks, they may be realistic about how much they can save and actually make the effort to do so. Unfortunately, when the first opportunity comes along to spend the accumulated funds, the savings are dissipated quickly.

Without a doubt it's always easy to find justification for spending money. The reasons go something like this: "We have to replace that car, since all we're doing is spending money on repairs." This may be true, but it doesn't mean someone has to go out and invest in a new car with all sorts of options. The same logic that is used to justify a new car is applied to a wide variety of other expenditures, ranging from Caribbean vacations to the latest high-tech gadgets. The basic rationale is "We have to have it," when in fact the expenditure doesn't come close to being a necessity.

What all this means is that the process of systematically saving money starts with self-discipline. You certainly don't have to live a life of deprivation, but depending on the financial objectives you set, you have to strike a compromise between saving money and satisfying your desire for tools, toys, and trinkets. Therefore, the basic steps in saving money are: (1) save something every payday, (2) don't make the amount so high you have to dip into the savings periodically, and (3) leave it alone at least until you reach your predetermined goal. The goal might be relatively short-term such as buying a house, intermediate such as financial security to start a new career, or long-term such as funds for retirement. Whatever the goal is, stick with your savings program until you achieve it.

Prepare for a Crisis Beforehand

Saving money systematically is only one part of being prepared for any financial crisis or need that arises. Other concrete actions will further bolster your ability to weather a period of financial uncertainty. For example, if for any reason your job looks shaky, it might be wise to open a home equity line of credit. You don't have to use any of the credit line, but it's useful to have it available if your fears come true and you do lose your job. Keep in mind, that although it may be easy for you to get credit when you're employed, once you're out of work, no one wants to lend you money. So taking care of your credit needs before you are laid off will give you an emergency source of funds available to tap during unemployment.

Incidentally, you don't want to get caught in a bind when you need cash during unemployment or some other financial crisis. Therefore, you don't want to tie up all your savings in investments that you won't be able to convert to cash quickly in an emergency, or that will impose a steep penalty for early withdrawal such as long-term certificates of deposit. On the other hand, you do want to maximize the returns you earn on the money you have saved.

What you have to do is strike a balance between your anticipated financial needs in an emergency and your desire for satisfactory returns on invested funds commensurate with the risk you're willing to take. At least some portion of your money should be in bank accounts, a money market fund, or some other investment that will be available readily in an emergency.

How you approach this compromise depends upon your individual situation. If you can anticipate that severance payments, unemployment compensation, a spouse's income, and so forth, lessen the need for you to have cash immediately available for living expenses, then this becomes less of an issue for you. The important point is that you don't want to be caught in the position where you have to sell stocks or bonds at a loss because you need funds for living expenses. Most experts recommend that you have financial reserves to cover anywhere from three to six months of expenses.

Being financially prepared for a job loss also requires taking a hard look at your existing debt. If you have large outstanding balances on credit cards, and an auto loan or two, pay these off as soon as possible. It can make a big difference in satisfactorily getting through an extended period without a paycheck if you don't have large monthly debt payments to make.

Incidentally, planning for an emergency or not, one of the best ways to save money is if your employer offers a 401(k) plan. Most employers match your contributions up to certain limits, so not only are you saving money on your own, but your employer is adding to it. Furthermore, federal income taxes are deferred, so your taxable income for any given year is reduced by your contributions to the 401(k) up to the authorized limits. This is a deal that's pretty hard to beat, and it also has the advantage of being relatively painless since the amounts will be withheld from your paycheck. So if you have such a plan at work and you don't presently take advantage of it, talk to your employer and learn the details of the plan. You may decide that you are missing out on a pretty good deal.

DO'S, DON'TS, AND MAYBE'S FOR MEETING EMERGENCY NEEDS

If you have the will power to persist in putting aside money to cope with a financial setback caused by a sudden job loss, or some other emergency, then you will be able to weather most any financial problem that comes along. However, if your savings are meager, or the financial emergency is particularly severe, you may have to do some scratching to meet your monetary needs.

Although there are a number of ways to obtain funds when you're in dire straits, some approaches are better than others, and if you're not careful you could get yourself even deeper in debt. Let's look at some of the possibilities for coping with an extended layoff or other financial emergency.

If you lose your job, the first imperative is to sit down and see where you stand financially. The number one priority is not to panic, although you have to recognize that it's not business as usual in terms of dealing with your income and expenses. Assess your entire financial picture. Start with what you will receive in terms of severance from your employer. If you're receiving the lump-sum equivalent of several months pay, then you're in pretty good shape. On the other hand, you can't assume how long you may be out of work, so don't arbitrarily decide to keep spending as though you didn't lose your job. You may not have to cut back to the bone in this situation, but you still have to adopt a conservative posture with your finances. In any event, you may not be fortunate enough to be receiving a significant severance payout. You should, of course, also look into your entitlement in terms of unemployment benefits once your layoff becomes official. Procedures and payments vary from state to state, so check with your local unemployment office about filing requirements.

Aside from severance pay, and any accrued vacation pay you may be receiving, zero in on what other benefits you will receive from your employer. One particularly important decision you may have to make concerns medical insurance. Will the employer continue to pay your medical benefits, and for how long? If not, you have the option of continuing under your employer's plan, but you have to pay the premiums, which can be pretty hefty.

If you have a working spouse, then your salvation may be to continue your coverage under his or her policy. If you can foresee the potential for a layoff ahead of time, it's a good idea to get any necessary medical and dental work done while you're still on the payroll. Even if your coverage is continued after a layoff, even the copayments and deductibles can mean expenses you don't want to face while you're out of work.

You may also have a decision to make relative to any 401(k) plan or other pension benefits you may be entitled to from your employer. You have the option of leaving your 401(k) money where it is, transferring it to an IRA (Individual Retirement Account), or receiving a lump-sum payment. You want to avoid the latter since you will have to pay taxes on the money and you may also have to pay a penalty if you're under $59^1/_2$. Whether you transfer it elsewhere or leave it where it is, if at all possible, you want to leave your 401(k) money intact so it can continue to grow tax deferred. When you land another job, you may want to transfer the funds to your new employer's 401(k). Incidentally, consult your tax adviser or attorney to be certain you follow the rules on withdrawals and rollovers so you don't end up paying taxes you hadn't planned on paying.

Aside from sources of funds to tide you over until you're working again, you should look at what can be done to reduce your everyday expenses to make your available funds last longer. The first thing to do here is to put your credit cards on ice for the duration of your unemployment. If you have outstanding balances on your cards, continue to make the minimum payments. You won't reduce the balances much this way, and you will be incurring interest charges, but while you're out of work you want to keep your monthly expenses to the minimum. Hopefully, if you have planned ahead, you shouldn't have any outstanding balances to think about.

How much you have to reduce your monthly expenses will vary with the amount and source of funds you have to live on. You also have to factor in how long you anticipate being out of work. When you do this guesstimate, don't assume optimistically you will quickly land another job right away. The more money you make, and the more specialized your occupation is, may mean you're out of work for several months. And if the economy happens to be in a downturn, it could be even longer.

Desperate times can sometimes make for desperate measures. If you're in a predicament where you are badly in need of money, you may have to explore varied ways to obtain cash to meet your needs. This may mean swallowing your pride and asking to borrow money from family and friends. It's a hard thing to do, but from a financial standpoint, it beats getting socked with paying off interest charges on debt you incur if you tap a home equity line of credit. You can also explore the possibility of loans against the cash value of any insurance you might have.

If you have a skill that's in demand, you may be able to barter your services in exchange for goods or services that you need. For example, someone with accounting skills could offer their services keeping the books for a small business, preparing tax returns, and so forth, in exchange for goods or services that are needed. There's nothing particularly difficult in bartering, other than your willingness to put it to use. In its simplest form it's just trading something for something else. Another one-shot approach to raising some quick cash is to hold a garage sale. Aside from any cash you get, it has the beneficial effect of cleaning out an accumulated assortment of clutter. Naturally, tactics such as bartering and holding a garage sale aren't a major solution to a lack of income. Nevertheless, no approach to stretching your resources should be ignored, since an accumulation of measures can, when combined, help keep your financial head above water if you're out of work.

SAVVY WAYS TO CONTROL YOUR BORROWING NEEDS

The first stop on the road to taking control of your financial future is to control your debt burden. Everyone, with the exception of the extremely wealthy and the fanatically frugal, faces paying off some sort of debt.

For most people, a mortgage and the resultant interest payments are a necessity for owning a home. For others, college expenses or major medical bills often result in the assumption of debt. Beyond those items, however, the justification for adding additional debt burdens becomes less and less.

The problem with debt in today's virtually cashless society is that it becomes easier and easier to acquire debt, and harder and harder to pay it off. The enticements offered to induce people to borrow money are seemingly endless, and if you believe the advertising, paying off your debt will be relatively painless. Try telling that to someone with a heavy debt burden who has just lost their job. The crux of the matter is that borrowing to finance expenditures is an expensive way to live. That's why it's so important to control your borrowing before it controls you. There are several steps you can take to reduce your debt burdens, so let's look at a few measures you can take to keep more of what you make.

Beware of Low Monthly Payment Pitches

One of the biggest traps people fall into are the sales pitches built around low monthly payments. These gimmicks entice people into believing the unaffordable car, vacation trip, or furniture are within financial reach. Unfortunately, these debts become bills that must be paid month after month as a fixed expense. If you get into a financial bind and need money for other emergencies, you can't just start to skip your car payments.

Debts Hinder Financial Flexibility

The gradual accumulation of debt can start a nasty cycle where paying off existing debt leaves little or no money to pay cash. Therefore, when something is needed it's paid for with a credit card. The end result can be escalating credit card balances to the point where only the minimum payments can be made, which makes the high level of debt too cumbersome to be paid off in full. Meanwhile hard-earned income is being spent on the high interest charges that credit card issuers charge. If you use credit cards, always try to pay the balance off in full each month to avoid paying interest charges.

Limit Your Accessibility to Credit

People who use credit cards frequently and make regular on-time payments soon find themselves to be the recipient of other credit card offers. With little or no effort someone can accumulate credit limits that couldn't be paid off in the person's wildest dreams. Adding credit cards doesn't do any harm if they're not used. However, having them is enough temptation to use them, and if you don't need them, then there's no point in accepting them in the first place. Keeping your credit cards to a minimum prevents their being used in the event the card you have is maxed out to its credit limit.

Choose Credit Cards Wisely

Credit card issuers compete for your business, so it pays to take advantage of that fact. First of all, don't sign up for any credit card that requires the payment of an annual fee. There are too many no-fee cards available to pay a fee for the supposed "privilege" of paying high interest rates if you don't pay your balances in full each month.

You should also look for a card that has a relatively low interest rate, but be careful when you do this, since some introductory rates won't last long, and the rate will revert to a higher one. Many cards offer other inducements to sign up, such as discounts on merchandise, as well as programs that allow you to receive merchandise and other benefits based on your usage of the card. If one of these cards isn't any more expensive than another card, then you might as well go for the freebies. Don't, however, fall into the trap of putting charges on your credit card just to earn freebies. You're likely to end up paying far more in interest than the worth of what you eventually receive. There's nothing quite as discouraging as realizing that your $50 freebie really cost you $180, or some such figure.

Know How Much You're Paying in Interest

Most people pay little attention to their finance charges and very few could tell you how much interest they paid on their debts in the past year. It's a good exercise to add up your interest payments on credit cards as well as auto and installment loans every once in a while. Seeing the amount of interest you're paying can be a real eye opener as to the need to better control your use of credit.

Pay Down Your Debts to Limit Your Interest Expense

It's sometimes hard to do, but the more you pay monthly on your outstanding debts the less interest you will have to pay. Along this line, if you have money in a savings account, use some of this to pay off your high-interest debt. You'll save more on interest payments than you will earn by leaving the money in a savings account.

Try Several Sources When You're Borrowing Money

Homes and automobiles are the two major purchases most people make. Yet in neither case do they exercise much initiative in where they get their mortgage or car loan. With the excitement of their purchase in mind, many people tend to go with the first available source of credit for their purchase. In the case of a house, it may be the bank they use for their other business, or a mortgage lender recommended by a real estate agent. With an automobile, the buyer may go through the dealer for financing rather than searching around for a cheaper alternative. Shopping around for both mortgages and car loans can save you a lot of money, so don't forget about this in your exuberance over your new house or car.

AVOIDING THE PITFALLS OF FINANCIAL PLANNING

Somewhere along the line you may decide that what you need to help you get your financial house in order is the services of a financial planner. There's certainly no shortage of people looking to help you do just that. The problem is that they earn their living doing just that, and unless they have enough clients they may not eat very well. As a consequence, there's bound to be some degree of fluff involved in what some of these financial experts promise. Unless you are able to separate the wheat from the chaff in selecting the services of a financial planner, you may find to your dismay that you were better off without one.

As you already know from unwanted solicitations in your mail, by phone calls, television commercials, and any other method of communication possible, there's an endless stream of choices for investing your money. And if you haven't noticed, most of those offering to help you out at least imply, if not promise, that they will make your money grow faster than your waistline. How does one cope with the confusion of so many choices? For many people, the answer is to secure the services of a financial planner to guide you through this investment maze.

Assessing Your Need for a Financial Planner

A little bit of financial planning is certainly helpful for most people who have neither the time nor the inclination to manage their financial future without a little assistance. And the unsatisfactory alternative to professional advice is often the opinion of a relative or friend who touts his or her "hot tip," or "sure thing" investment. This may also be the same person who hit you up for a loan not too long ago to cover a delinquent mortgage payment. The truth is that free financial advice from friends and relatives is worth exactly what it costs—which is nothing.

With little in the way of alternatives, the use of a professional financial planner may be right for you. There are, however, a couple of considerations to keep in mind before hiring one. To begin with, you have to decide whether or not you need a financial planner. The ultimate answer to this question is a personal matter. A few basic reasons that would justify hiring a planner are that you:

- Have specific financial goals in mind, but aren't sure of how to achieve them.

- Don't have the time or desire to plan your own investment strategy.

- Are not saving or investing as much money as you think you should be.

- Recently received a financial windfall from an early retirement incentive package, an inheritance, the sale of real estate, or some other source.

Any of these situations indicates the need for a financial planner. Some experts also suggest using income guidelines, but specific income levels don't always work. For example, a small business owner who puts most of the profits back into the business may have a substantial net worth, but very little in the way of discretionary income for investment purposes. Consequently, whether or not you need a financial planner is a personal decision. Furthermore, it makes no sense to seek financial advice unless you are firmly committed to follow it, since a financial plan can fall victim to procrastination faster than a ninety-day diet falls prey to pecan pie.

Choosing a Planner

If you do decide to consult a planner, the question then is how to find one. It's actually easy—they may even look you up—but it's finding the right one that requires some effort. Therefore, your first step is to verify a planner's credentials. Doing this helps you to pinpoint a minimum level of competence. Actually, to properly assess a planner's skills the most basic—but largely ignored—information you need is the planner's track record with his or her own investments. People seldom ask how well advisers do for themselves, since there's a natural inhibition about prying into the personal affairs of others.

When you're seeking financial advice, however, it's time to put those qualms aside. After all, you're revealing your personal finances to the planner, so there's no reason why they shouldn't do the same in return. If they refuse or are evasive, take your business elsewhere. Complete disclosure and mutual trust are the foundation of a solid adviser/client relationship.

Financial planners earn their money in three basic ways. One type gets paid for drawing up your financial plan. Another group may draw up your financial plan for free, and earn money from commissions on financial products they sell to you. A third group works on a combination of fees and commissions. Therefore, if a planner is pushing particular investments as part of a recommended financial strategy, you better find out if they have a financial interest in selling the investment.

There are a number of approaches you can take in your financial planning. One strategy is to use a two-pronged approach and separate the financial planning aspect from the investing. To do this, you can have a financial plan drawn up by someone who does financial planning on a fee-only basis. You may pay more for the financial plan this way, since the planner isn't earning anything from selling investments.

On the other hand, it gives you greater confidence in the objectivity of the plan's recommendations. Furthermore, the wide range and complexity of investment opportunities means that it's difficult—if not impossible—for any one person to have the necessary expertise in all areas. So you may be better off taking your financial plan and using your banker, broker, insurance agent, and attorney to implement individual recommendations.

In the final analysis, a well-drawn-up financial plan can be a solid blueprint for guiding your future financial strategy. You can't, however, put it on automatic pilot and forget it. You have to implement the plan's recommendations, and at least every two years the plan should be updated. By that time, your income, investments, and the overall economy may dictate major or minor revisions in your financial strategy.

Aside from engaging the services of a financial planner, there are other avenues to obtaining financial advice. Your employer may offer the services of financial advisers as a fringe benefit. The provider of a company-sponsored 401(k) retirement plan may also offer seminars on investing your money. There are even a number of software programs available so you can do your own financial planning on your computer. The important point is to get as much information as you can on planning your financial strategy and monitor your goals closely so that as time passes you can make any necessary adjustments.

SIMPLE RETIREMENT PLANNING METHODS ANYONE CAN USE

You have probably wondered on occasion who it is that can salt away all the money the financial experts say is needed for your retirement. These are the same experts who also tell you to hoard a huge chunk of cash so Jane and Johnny can go to college. In the meantime you may be hoping your checkbook balance will stretch far enough to cover this month's round of bills. In any event, don't worry too much about whether or not you're the only one who isn't saving for retirement. Most people probably aren't doing much better on that score than you are.

There's little question that it's one thing for some financial whiz to project how much you have to save for your future retirement, and quite another for you to be able to do that, short of starving to death and thereby missing out on retirement completely. Not to be overlooked is the fact that some of the people urging you to stash your money away are interested in investing it for you. Despite the lack of realism in some of the retirement planning literature you may see, there is something to be said for saving as much as you can. Depending upon your circumstances this may not be a great deal, but don't despair since the steady accumulation over an extended period of time can make a difference.

Review Your Present Pension Plan

In doing any retirement planning, the initial step is to take a snapshot of where you stand right now. What, if anything, have you already accumulated toward your retirement? The first place to start is with your employer's pension plan. Some employers—especially larger ones—offer a traditional defined-benefit plan in conjunction with a defined-contribution plan such as a 401(k) or profit sharing.

Defined-benefit plans are, of course, the traditional company-sponsored pensions where a specific dollar amount is paid at retirement based upon years of service and salary level. To get a sizable pension from one of these plans means working many years for an employer. With jobs not as secure as they used to be due to worldwide competition and rapidly changing technology, the chances of working a lifetime with the same employer under one of these types of pension plans has diminished.

Many companies have shifted the emphasis to what are known as defined-contribution plans such as the highly popular 401(k), which is named after the section of the Internal Revenue Code which authorizes such plans. The advantages of a 401(k) for an employer include the relatively low cost of such a plan. For starters, employee contributions come out of worker earnings, while any matching employer contributions are deductible as a business expense. In addition, the costs of administering such plans are also minimal. These factors make the 401(k) plan particularly attractive to smaller companies who can't afford the expense of a traditional pension plan.

The major advantage of a 401(k) to you as an employee is the deferral of taxes on contributions that would otherwise be included as earnings for tax purposes. Employee contributions are vested immediately, so if you leave for another job after being in a plan for a short period of time, you don't lose your contributions.

Another potential benefit of a 401(k) is that it gives you the ability to choose from among several options in terms of how the contributions will be invested. You have to be careful though, since you can choose some forms of fixed-income investments which may lower your risk, but are also likely to lower your return down the road when retirement rolls around. Some experts caution that employees tend to be too conservative with their 401(k) investments. The potential problem is that you may put all your investment eggs in one basket, rather than diversifying your 401(k) by investing in a combination of fixed income and equity investments. Admittedly the decision is yours, but if you have such a plan, you should at least discuss this matter with your financial adviser.

If you work for a smaller company, you may be covered under a Simplified Employee Pension (SEP), under which a separate Individual Retirement Account (IRA) is established for each employee. Then there's the Keogh plan, long a stalwart of self-employed people, but also useful for smaller businesses. A Keogh can be set up as either a defined-benefit or a defined-contribution plan. Of course, there's the question as to what social security benefits you'll be entitled to upon retirement. This is subject to any changes in the law that take place between now and the time you retire.

Check Your Social Security Record

By the way, it's a good idea to check your social security record every couple of years to be certain your account is being credited properly. It's easy enough to do by sending in a preprinted form which is available from a variety of sources. In fact, you may want to check with your personnel office at work, since it may have the form available. The response you get will not only show your social security earnings and contributions, but will also project your social security benefits based upon figures you supply as to your estimated earnings prior to retirement.

How much, or how little you presently have vested in whatever type of pension plan you have depends upon many factors including the type of plan, how long you have been a member, and your earnings. In any event, finding out the details of your plan and where you presently stand gives you a start in doing your retirement planning. Next, you should determine what if any other assets you have put aside for retirement. No matter what form of pension plan you have, you can't rely upon it exclusively to provide for all your retirement earnings. Many experts recommend your retirement earnings should be somewhere around 70% of your preretirement earnings to maintain the same lifestyle. This will vary somewhat in individual cases because your lifestyle after retirement will affect how much you need, but it's certainly a reasonable goal.

In terms of supplementing any pension and social security benefits, it's best to save as much as is feasible on your own. This is a real variable though, since it not only depends upon your income, but also your inclinations as a saver or a spender. The stage of your working life also comes into play, since if you're younger you may be looking to purchase a home and/or finance college for your children. Most people, for logical reasons, have difficulty putting substantial savings aside until they enter the years when their children are grown and their earnings are at a peak. Incidentally, there are a number of retirement planning software packages available that can help you assemble a snapshot of your retirement financial picture. There are also a wide variety of free seminars on retirement planning offered, but sift through the advice carefully, especially if the sponsor of the seminar is selling financial products.

One other thing that you have to consider in your retirement planning is the cost of healthcare after retirement, especially if you plan on retiring before age 65 when Medicare benefits start to kick in. So some of the money you save for retirement may have to be allocated for medical expenses if you won't be covered fully by a company-paid health plan.

Weighing an Early Retirement Offer

Either now, or some time in the future, you may receive an early retirement offer from your employer. Such an offer can force you to make some hard choices that affect your future. Before you even look at the specifics of the retirement package you're being offered, you first have to decide what you're going to do if you accept the offer. Will you retire completely, or will you continue employment in the same line of work? If you have long wanted to take up another career, then this may be just the time to start.

Your personal situation also has to be considered. Is your financial picture such that retirement isn't practical at the moment? For example, do you have children in college or heading there in a few years, or do you have financial responsibility for the care of aging parents? Whatever the circumstances may be, they are part and parcel of any decision whether or not to accept your employer's offer.

There is also the question of the future prospects for your job if you turn down the offer. If the early retirement deal has been substantially sweetened by your employer to entice people to accept it, you have to wonder whether or not this would be true in the future. You certainly don't want to turn down a pretty good offer only to be forced out in six months or a year with nowhere near as good a deal. Then too, there's the question as to how happy you are in your present position. If the situation isn't good, and there's no reason to believe it will get better in the future, then you might be better off taking the money and moving on.

You also have to think about what the work environment will be like after the retirement buyout ends. If the company is reducing its payroll sharply, then there may be a lot fewer people left to do the work. This could put you in the position of having to assume additional responsibilities. From another angle, consider the possibility of your department being eliminated, which might mean an internal transfer. On the other hand, you may really like your job and not be ready to retire at this time. But even if you're not, if your future with the company doesn't look bright, then it may be wise to take the offer and look for work elsewhere.

For some people an early retirement offer brings with it an opportunity to coast into retirement by perhaps working at a part-time job. In fact, you may even have an opportunity to become a consultant with your present employer. Other folks will seize the chance to start a business of their own that had been long dreamed of.

Last, but certainly not least in your deliberations, is the buyout package itself. Consider the pension you will get, the severance package, medical and dental benefits, and any other items that may be included. How many years are being added to your age and length of service to sweeten your pension? How much severance pay will you get? In the end, if the financial package is sufficient and there is little or no advantage to staying on with your employer, there's little reason not to accept the deal being offered.

THE HARD-HEADED WAY TO AVOID SCAMS

There's probably only one thing sadder than reading about someone who was the victim of some sort of fraud or scam, and that's being the victim yourself. We all tend to operate under the assumption that it will be someone else who will be the victim. This gives us a sense of security, and besides, we are too smart to get ripped off. Unfortunately, that's the same attitude most people have who get burned by some form of scam. The people who are out to rip you off are smart cookies, and preventing them from succeeding starts with acknowledging that fact.

The place to start with safeguarding your financial interests is with your routine daily activities. The first step is to protect your credit cards. If you have multiple cards, try to avoid carrying more than one card with you at a time. That way, if you lose your wallet, or have it stolen, you will only have lost one card. Incidentally, always report lost or stolen cards promptly to the issuer.

Aside from worrying about thieves, don't accidentally trip yourself up. One thing to be particularly careful about when shopping is the use of bank debit cards which deduct the payment from your checking account at the time of purchase. These cards may carry the emblem of a credit card issuer, which can inadvertently lead you to think you have given a clerk your credit card. The sale will be rung up and deducted from your checking account, while you're thinking it was charged on a credit card. As a result, your checking account will have less money in it than you think. If you don't keep large balances in your checking account, the chances are good that you may wind up with bounced checks. If you're lucky and you have sufficient funds in your account to cover checks you write until you get your next bank statement, you'll discover what you did when you balance your checkbook. Suffice it to say, that if you carry this type of card, make sure you don't accidentally assume it's a credit card.

Equally important is careful use of your ATM card. Memorize your personal identification number (PIN), rather than writing it down and keeping it in your wallet. It's a thief's dream to gain access to a lost or stolen wallet and find a PIN number written on the protective envelope of someone's ATM card. It's also important to minimize the chance for someone to steal your PIN number by looking over your shoulder, or observing your actions from afar with binoculars. Stand in front of the machine and obscure the view of a potential thief when you enter your PIN number. These precautions also apply to the use of a telephone calling card. You should also be on the alert for your personal safety when using ATM machines, by avoiding out-of-the way locations, and by not visiting any machine after dark unless it's located in a highly visible and heavily-trafficked area.

Awareness is a necessity when it comes to safeguarding your credit cards. You should always keep your cards in a safe and secure place at home. You should also check periodically that you are in possession of the credit cards you're carrying in your wallet. Sometimes people don't even know a card has been lost or stolen until they go to use the card and can't find it. In fact, if the card is used infrequently, they may not realize it's gone until they get a statement with unauthorized charges on it.

When you're shopping, don't give more information than is necessary to salespeople. Sales clerks sometimes ask for excess information to which they're not entitled. Don't write your driver's license number on checks, especially if it's the same as your social security number, nor should you write it or your address and phone number on credit slips. People sometimes give this information out when shopping almost as a reflex action when it's requested by salespeople, instead of refusing to do so.

There are also a few good routines to follow at home to safeguard your financial information. Always destroy such things as canceled checks, credit card slips, bank statements, and pay stubs, when you throw them away. The same applies to any preapproved credit card applications you get in the mail. Thieves have been known to gather information by going through trash.

These measures may seem to be overly cautious, but thieves are sophisticated about being able to use the information they pilfer. A determined thief who gains access to your financial records and information can cause you a lot of grief. Even if you're able to square things away eventually, it can mean a lot of time and effort and more than a little clenching of teeth. So to avoid this aggravation, practice a little prevention.

HOW TO SELECT BANKERS, BROKERS, AND OTHERS WHO WANT YOUR MONEY

As if it isn't hard enough to earn a living, it's even more difficult to try and hold on to the money you've made. A seemingly endless stream of bankers, brokers, investment advisers, and financial planners are bombarding you with ads, junk mail, or phone calls, all offering to do something with your money. The bottom line is that all these people are chasing your money for one simple reason, which is to make money for themselves. In one way or another, be it fees, commissions, or premiums, the financial folks all want your money. Amidst this clutter of competing interests how do you decide what's best for you?

This requires some hard thought and tough choices on your part, since what you do with your money now will dictate how much or how little money you have in the future. Therefore, it pays to exercise the utmost care when selecting a bank, broker, or any other financial adviser. Using the services of a financial planner has been discussed earlier in this chapter, so let's look at a few of the factors you should consider in choosing a bank or a stock broker.

Choosing a Bank

One of the prime concerns for choosing a bank is convenience. With the advent of banking by telephone and computer, geographic proximity to your bank is no longer as necessary as it once was. Yet there are other reasons why having an accessible bank is still valid. For one thing, handy access to your own bank's ATM machines saves you money, since most banks charge a fee for the use of ATMs controlled by other banks. Accessibility is also important if you want to transact any business through a teller, or consult with a bank loan officer.

The most important consideration in choosing a bank for most people whose banking business is pretty routine is the matter of cost. Banks charge a wide variety of fees for a laundry list of services including maintaining checking accounts, bounced checks, and for failing to meet minimum balance requirements. New and varied fees tend to be on the increase, which is the bad news. On the positive side of the ledger, there is a wide disparity between the fees banks charge, so a little bit of shopping around will enable you to find a bank that has fewer and lower fees. Most fees are waived if you keep a minimum balance on hand in your account. Here too, the amounts vary from bank to bank, so you want to make comparisons before you select a bank.

You may also want to have overdraft protection, which provides a credit line you can draw against to cover bounced checks. The amount you have to pay for the loan may be less than the amount of the bounced-check fee. The overall service a bank provides is also a factor to consider in establishing a banking relationship. Some banks are better at customer service than others, and something as simple as a bank with more convenient banking hours can be the factor that tips a bank's scales in your direction.

Sizing Up Stock Brokers

Picking a stock broker you can be happy with isn't an easy exercise under any circumstances. It becomes even more difficult as financial firms offer a wider and wider variety of investments, and stock brokers are also known by such names as financial consultants, investment specialists, and so forth. A short list of some factors to consider in selecting a stock broker include:

1. *Do you need a broker in the first place?* As an alternative you might want to consider using a discount brokerage firm where your own stock picks are executed at low commissions, but where you get no investment advice. This means you will have to do your own research in deciding which stocks make the best investment for you.

2. *In selecting a brokerage firm, consider any fees charged for various activities associated with your account.*

3. *Use recommendations from people you trust, such as close friends or relatives in lining yourself up with a broker.* In doing this, only follow up on suggestions from those you consider to be financially savvy.

4. *If in initial conversations the broker tries to convince you how much money you will make, find yourself another broker.* You're interest-

ed in investing, not in crap shooting. When you have people telling you how simple it is to make money, ask yourself, "If it's that easy to do, why isn't the person telling me this sitting on a beach somewhere enjoying the sunset?" The answer is it *isn't* that easy, which is why they're still working, and why you don't want to do business with someone who tries to convince you otherwise.

5. *Assess the broker's personality.* Is he or she someone you like well enough to trust? If not, find someone else.

6. *Ask about the broker's credentials.* How much experience does he or she have, how long has he or she been with the present firm, and so forth.

7. *Check with NASD (the National Association of Security Dealers) and state regulators to see if there are outstanding complaints against the broker.*

8. *Confirm any discussions about investments you have with your broker by letter.* This .prevents any possibility of misunderstanding, either from the outset, or in the future.

9. *Always check your confirmation statements when you have any activity in your account to make sure there are no errors.*

10. *Be sure to read any customer agreements that you sign.* If there's anything you don't understand, get clarification before you sign the form.

11. *Don't sign margin agreements unless you plan to use them.* A margin agreement allows you to borrow part of the securities price as a loan from the brokerage firm.

12. *Make sure the broker knows your investment needs.* If you're interested in conservative investments, make that point clear. Don't be talked into investing in anything you don't feel right about. Incidentally, it's good to get a copy of the new account statement which is prepared when a new brokerage account is opened. It shows what your investment philosophy is, which is supposed to act as a guide to the broker in handling your investments.

13. *Don't sign discretionary agreements which let the broker trade for your account, unless you are completely aware of the risks and have the utmost confidence in your broker.*

TEN SAVINGS IDEAS YOU CAN ADOPT TODAY

Saving money isn't easy, although those who have substantial sums stashed away may tell you it is. It requires both will power and sacrifice. It sounds scary to mention a word such as sacrifice since you're really not giving up anything of substance. What you are doing is being willing not to spend money on things you might otherwise buy in order to make your future financially secure. Actually, once you get the hang of it, saving money becomes pretty routine. The following ideas are offered to help you get the ball rolling. As you go through this list, try to think of other ways you can start saving some money:

1. *One of the best ways for the average person to save money is to pay off existing debt.* When people think of savings, they naturally think about putting money into some form of investment. But whether it's a car loan or credit cards, the interest you save by paying off a debt will usually far exceed what you would earn by investing the money elsewhere. If you haven't checked lately, take a look at how much you may have paid in interest in the past six months on a car loan, or your credit cards. Once you do that, you may decide it's time to wipe out your debts.

2. Review your automobile insurance to see if you are getting all the discounts to which you may be entitled. You may also want to consider lowering your premiums by raising the deductibles. If your car is getting old, you may want to think about dropping your collision coverage.

3. *Try to save something every payday, no matter how small the amount.* It's regular savings that ultimately leads to financial security. People are often put off by how little they can save on a weekly or monthly basis, and as a result postpone saving anything by adopting an attitude of, "When my financial picture improves, I'll start saving regularly." The reality is that financial security comes from starting to save now, not at some indefinite date in the future which never seems to arrive for many people. Set a realistic goal as to what you can save and force yourself to stick with it, since with saving money persistence does pay.

4. *Always try to save any lump sums that you receive, whether it's a gift, an income tax refund, or a lump-sum payout from your retirement plan when you leave a job.* The temptation with windfalls of one form or another is to treat yourself to a luxury, pay off bills, or a combination of the two. Don't buy the luxury unless you can afford it out of income, and if you can't pay your debts from income, you should reduce your spending.

5. *If you haven't already done so, sign up for your 401(k) at work, or if you're self-employed, start a Keogh or SEP/IRA.* Tax-deductible savings are as good a bargain as you can find.

6. *If you're a dual-income household, make sure that both you and your spouse aren't paying for overlapping benefits at work.* For example, if you both contribute to health and dental coverage at work, you may want to check the respective coverages and drop one or the other to eliminate this expense.

7. *Make sure you're not paying too much in taxes by being overwithheld.* You will get the money back when you file your tax return, but in the meantime you're losing out on the interest the money could be earning for you.

8. *You may want to consider substituting term insurance for more expensive policies that provide cash values, since term insurance can lower your premiums significantly.*

9. *A house can be a significant source of savings beyond the appreciation in its value.* You can refinance the mortgage to save money if you have a high-interest loan and mortgage rates drop. You also have the tax advantages of house-related deductions such as mortgage interest and property taxes. Therefore, if you're renting you may want to consider buying.

10. *Your bank can be more of a money-saver than you might have realized.* You might want to switch your accounts to a bank that charges lower fees, and pocket the difference. You may not save a lot of money, but the secret of saving is that it's saving the little amounts that cumulatively add up to big savings in the long run.

These are just a few ideas on saving to get you started, and with a little thought about your own personal circumstances you will be able to come up with many more. As for what you do with your money when you save it, there's a wealth of advice available from a variety of sources. Take advantage of these resources to maximize your savings dependent on the degree of risk you're willing to take. Always keep in mind that as your savings increase, your financial security is enhanced, which in turn gives you a greater measure of control over the ups and downs of your job and career.

Chapter

10

HOW TO HARNESS HAPHAZARD SPENDING

Perhaps you're like many people who say to themselves, "Gee, I'm earning good money, but I can't save a dime." This is an all too common dilemma people face, and the solution is pretty basic once someone is willing to deal with it. Essentially, you can either save or spend the money you earn, and if you're not saving anything, then you're spending more than you should. The problem is that people seldom take the time to pay attention to where their money is going. Oh, perhaps they can cite a high-ticket item or two, such as a new automobile which is taking a big chunk of their available funds. But for the most part, people ignore the day-to-day outlays where the opportunity for saving is always present. It may be too many business lunches at fancy restaurants, or a closet full of clothes seldom worn. In fact, there may not even be one area where you overspend at all. Instead, you may be getting nickel and dimed to death by spending a little more than you should in a lot of little ways.

Throughout this chapter you will find innumerable tips for cutting your expenditures on everything from cars to clothes. This doesn't mean that you have to adopt a penny-pinching role which requires you to spend a lot of time figuring out where your money is going. The object is to cut your expenditures where you can without having to do a lot of budgeting and bookkeeping. It may not be painless for you to practice a little bit of spending discipline, but it certainly isn't as hard as you might imagine. Of course, you may not want to—nor should you—adopt every suggestion you find in this chapter. Some will work well for you, while others won't fit either your circumstances or your desires. The advice isn't given as an all-or-nothing alternative. Use what you can live with, since controlling your spending is something best done gradually until it becomes an ingrained part of your philosophy. Otherwise you'll find yourself getting frustrated, and ultimately will slip back into bad spending practices.

HOW TO AVOID LIVING HABITS THAT LOCK YOU INTO A JOB YOU HATE

Have you ever told yourself that if it wasn't for the money, you would quit your job tomorrow? Many of us have entertained that idea at one time or another. In some cases, it may just have been a passing thought when things weren't going too well at work. In other cases, it may be a persistent theme. If you have dwelled on this topic more than once, you have probably been brought up short about taking action on your notion when you realize you don't have a satisfactory alternative to pay the bills.

When someone dislikes their job, or would just prefer a career change, any serious consideration for such a move entails a hard look at finances. Whether you're dreaming of starting your own business, or opting for a career change that will start you out at the bottom again, money generally becomes the obstacle that causes you to back off. Of course, financial considerations can't be ignored in making career decisions, but all too often people adopt a "locked in" attitude when dealing with this problem. It's assumed automatically that because they earn and spend at a certain income level, it's impossible for them to survive on a lesser figure.

Be Realistic About Your Spending

This is where the rubber meets the road if you're truly earnest about pursuing another endeavor which won't give you the same level of income, at least in the near future. The bottom line is that you can adjust your spending habits to live on less if you really want to. So if the career change is really that important to you, let's look at how to avoid some of the living habits that take away the financial flexibility you need to pursue the career you want. Otherwise, you will be stuck in a job you don't want, simply to support living habits that can be maintained at that income level.

Any mention of cutting back on spending brings forth various reactions. Some people would say, "I don't know where I can cut back, since I already watch my money closely." This is what could be called the "denial alibi," since few people who aren't in dire financial straits really watch their spending with any degree of care. Those few that do are usually in pretty good shape financially if they have been practicing this policy for any length of time.

From the opposite end of the spectrum other people might say, "I don't know where my money goes. I earn a good living, but I never have anything left over after paying the bills." This could be named the "ignorance is bliss alibi." These folks know they aren't saving anything, but they don't want to know what they're spending the money on since it might force them to change their lifestyle.

Then there are the realists who know they could do better in terms of increasing their savings but never quite get around to it. These people tend to adopt a "wait till next year" alibi by thinking something such as, "I've got to start saving some money." Needless to say, they never start.

It's no mystery why it's hard to save money. It's because you can buy some really neat things with your money. And if you need any encouragement, there's a huge advertising and marketing armada afloat whose job is to entice you to part with your hard-earned cash. And if you want to buy now and pay later, there are all sorts of friendly financial folks to extend you some credit. Then there's the time factor. If you buy something now, you can satisfy whatever the need is right away. But if you save for college, retirement, or a house, these are more distant goals and rewards, so it's harder to relate to them at the present time.

Let's face it. It's a lot harder to save money than it is to spend it. Saving money requires a commitment to do it, and the discipline to stick with it. One of the biggest hurdles to saving successfully is in attempting to save more every payday than is practical. Doing this leads to a savings program falling apart, because eventual borrowing from the savings to meet expenses reinforces the notion that you don't make enough money to be able to put any aside.

In order to start a regular savings program, or increase what you're already saving, you have to take a look at where you're spending your money. After doing that, you can then decide for yourself where it is that you can cut back on your expenditures realistically. How little or how much you do cut back pretty much depends upon your desire to secure a greater degree of financial security. One good way to approach any review of your spending habits is to look at where you spend your money category by category. Since the biggest expenditure is housing, let's start with that.

How Much House Do You Need?

If you are presently renting and are planning to buy a home, or are already a homeowner with thoughts of a bigger or better house, a good place to start thinking about saving money is in buying a home. After all, the mortgage payments continue for years, so the more expensive a house you buy, the higher your payments will be every month. Not only that, but the bigger the house, the more house you have to furnish, which is another expenditure.

How much of your gross income will go toward your housing costs? Figure out what the percentage will be on the price of the type of house you're planning on buying. Assume, for example, that 30% of your gross income will go toward paying principal, interest, taxes, and insurance. If you bought a less expensive house that would consume only 25% of your gross income, then you immediately free up 5% of your gross income for savings. This isn't to say offhand that you should buy a less expensive house. You should carefully assess your housing needs, not only in terms of what you can afford to pay, but also factoring in how much money you want to allocate to savings. In making a decision as to how much you want to spend, ask yourself these questions:

- *How big a house do I need?*

- *Do I need a new house or can I be satisfied with a less expensive older home?*
  Note: You have to consider the fact that with an older house your maintenance expenses may be higher.

- *Can I get a better value by buying in a less expensive neighborhood?*

- *Are there things I need to save for in the short term?*
  Note: If you have children going off to college in the not too distant future, then you can't tie all your money up in a house.

- *What are the prospects for increasing household income in the near future?*
  Note: Be realistic in doing any guesstimates about that big promotion or whatever it is you assume will raise your income.

- *Do I have satisfactory alternatives to buying a home that will meet my needs?*

Asking yourself these questions gives you a better perspective on not only how much money you want to spend on a house, but whether or not you want to buy one. There are other factors that go into this determination, including the tax benefits of ownership, and your personal situation. For example, if you're presently living in cramped quarters and are expecting an addition to the family shortly, then you obviously have to upgrade your housing. The entire point isn't so much whether or not you should buy a house, but rather that you should think about how much money you want to spend on it. If the type of house you have in mind is larger than you really need, in a more expensive neighborhood than is necessary, and has a lot of fancy upgrades, then you have to make a decision. Do you want to put the money into a house, or would you be better off scaling back your plans and working at increasing your savings?

Old Cars Burn Oil While New Cars Burn Cash

If you're into buying a new car every two years or so, then a change in your transportation lifestyle will certainly open up an opportunity to save some money. The fundamental question you have to ask yourself is which is more important to you, saving more money or driving a new car? If it's the latter, then it's an expensive habit. Where you fall on the transportation scale between driving a fairly dependable older car and the latest luxury model dictates how much room you have to adjust your expenses in this area. Do some simple computations and you may be surprised at how much more money you would have if you scaled down your automotive lifestyle. This is also a personal preference, but if you're truly committed to working toward financial security you may want to reassess your needs.

Scaling Back on Your Vacations

Vacations are great, but how much you enjoy one doesn't depend solely upon how much you spend on it. In fact, you may be able to reflect on some super vacations you had that weren't that expensive. So if you have developed a habit of jetting off to faraway places and staying in luxury hotels, you may want to think about scaling back and saving some money.

Actually, a little planning can save you some money even without altering where you go on vacation. Booking well ahead can save you substantial sums on airfares. And by combining a bit of research on hotels and motels along with various discounts, you can trim your accommodation costs. If you're traveling an extended distance by automobile, stop in at the tourist information centers along the way. They're not only a wealth of information on the sights to see, but they usually have a bountiful supply of coupons and discounts for motels and tourist attractions.

You might also choose to save some vacation money by planning a vacation closer to home. Not only will it save you some money, but it will also probably leave you more relaxed, since you won't be doing as much traveling.

Eating Out

One of the big budget busters in many households are meals eaten outside the home. If you're eating out two or three times a week or more, a lot of money is being spent on meals. Even if it's just fast food, the bill can add up pretty quick. And if your meals are at more expensive eateries, then the potential for saving is even greater. Start keeping track of what you spend eating out for a couple of weeks. You may not want to cut back completely on eating out, but even if you cut your restaurant bill in half, you can save a significant sum. It helps cut expenses for those occasions you do go out to use two-for-one coupons, or to catch the "early-bird" specials and other bargains restaurants offer.

One trap many people get into is not the money they spend eating out, but the amount that's spent on having food brought in. Everything from pizza, to Chinese food, to traditional restaurant fare can be ordered for home delivery. So don't overlook this aspect of your meal expenditures when you're computing your costs. If you're able to cut back only one or two outside meals a week, over the course of a year, the savings will really mount up.

There are many more ways to cut your expenses which are covered in the following sections of this book. Some of them may appeal to you; others may not. The key point is that it is possible to alter your lifestyle to reduce your expenditures. The surprising thing is that the actions you take don't always have to be that dramatic to make a difference in your ability to save money rather than spend it. The key is in knowing where your money is going, which is why it's worthwhile to take the time to think about it.

SPENDING FOR YOUR FUTURE—NOT YOUR EGO

Getting a grip on your spending starts with avoiding ego-driven purchases which put you into the position of living beyond your means. You may not have given it much thought, but it's very easy for your emotions to come into play when you go about making major purchases. Sales and marketing people make a living by drumming the status appeal of their products into consumers' heads. An expensive luxury car doesn't get you from point A to point B any faster than a bare bones economy model costing many thousands less. Furthermore, automobiles start to depreciate in value the minute you drive them out of the dealership. In fact, someone whose sole interest in automobiles is for transportation is far better off buying used cars at bargain basement prices.

Even when people plan beforehand to buy a particular model of a car that fits their budget, before they leave the showroom a long list of expensive and unnecessary options has probably been tacked on. This isn't to say that you have to reduce all your buying decisions to the lowest-priced item you can get. Most people derive satisfaction out of buying what they like, as opposed to what they need. However, to avoid ending up working hard at a job you hate just to pay off your debts, it makes sense to factor a little common sense into your spending habits. So whether it's a new automobile, an expensive house in the suburbs, or the latest designer fashions, you have to make decisions as to whether the satisfaction of buying higher-priced items instead of more economical substitutes is worth the hard-earned money you're spending.

When it comes to major expenditures during the lifetime of most people, monthly car payments tend to tie up a good chunk of the paycheck. For this reason, let's explore some ways to approach car buying so as to minimize your costs and still meet your needs. If you can succeed in doing this, you may have something left over every month to squirrel away for your future—which incidentally will become the present a lot sooner than you think.

Car Buying Requires Care

Many people love their automobiles, at least until the first major repair is needed. Then, it's off to the showroom to look for something new. What amount to almost permanent car payments are practically an American tradition. As an investment, however, automobiles are about as bad as it gets, since they start depreciating the minute you drive them. So if you want to save some money, your auto-buying habits are a good place to begin.

If you can truly afford a luxury automobile and that's what you want, then go for it. After all, there's nothing wrong with satisfying your desires if money doesn't matter. On the other hand, if you're trying to get a handle on your spending to put your finances in shape, buying an expensive automobile isn't the answer. If basic transportation is all you want, then an inexpensive used car should do the trick. If you must have a new car, at least try to save a little money when you buy one.

The first move in buying a new car is to decide precisely what you want before you start to dicker with a car dealer. Read the literature, talk to your friends, visit a few showrooms, and test drive any models in which you have an interest. Get an idea of the price range by checking sticker prices. Then sit down and decide which car you want and which options you want to go along with it. You're in trouble before you begin if you go to purchase a car without being sure of what you want to buy. If you do that, then you'll get yanked around on models and options and won't be able to pin down the price you should be paying.

By the way, if you happen to live in a large metropolitan area where several dealerships are accessible that sell the car you want, then you're in pretty good shape if you have one particular car in mind. If there are only one or two dealers in your area offering the car you want, you may want to select two or three similar models from other manufacturers as alternatives. This way, you will have a number of dealers to potentially buy from. If you're limited to one dealer, your negotiating ability is hampered by being unable to walk out the door and go elsewhere.

Also, don't be seduced by value-pricing deals or any other marketing strategies. Only by knowing what you should be paying will you know whether or not a price is a reasonable deal. There are a wide variety of published sources to check the invoice price of a car, which is commonly assumed to be the dealer's cost. There are, however, various manufacturer incentives and holdbacks which can reduce the dealer cost even further. For practical purposes, take the invoice price for the car and any options you want to buy. Then add a few hundred dollars for dealer profit, subtract any rebates, and you have a ballpark figure for what you want to pay. If you just want to do it the quick and dirty way, take 10% off the sticker price shown on the car and refuse to pay more than that. This latter method isn't as exact, but it gives you a reasonable deal without getting involved in all sorts of numbers and terms that you may not understand.

By the way, there's no point in giving away in interest charges what you save by negotiating the car deal. Check your local bank or credit union and see what it will cost you to finance your car. If you can get a better deal later from the dealer, by all means take it, but if not, get your loan from the bank. When you're negotiating with the salesperson, don't get involved in any discussion of financing until you settle on the price of the car. It's also preferable to sell a car privately rather than trade it in. With a trade-in it becomes more difficult to pin down what you're paying for the new car. Any good deal on your trade-in the salesperson offers you will come out of the price of the new car if the trade-in value is much above wholesale. In other words, the better than average price for your trade-in means an increase in what you're paying for the new car.

Don't be swayed by all the number crunching, checking with the boss, adding on a few dollars here and there, or pleas to your sense of fair play that will come your way from the salesperson. Once you set your price, stick to your guns or watch your bargain disappear. Car people love to haggle with you and the more they succeed the more money they make, so give them a "take it or leave it" offer. If they don't want it, go somewhere else.

Should You Buy or Lease Your Car?

Leasing instead of purchasing a car has become an attractive alternative for many people. Why do people essentially rent a car for a number of years instead of purchasing it outright? The bottom line is that the upfront costs are less, and the monthly payments may also be lower. Any decision as to whether you should rent or purchase primarily rests upon two factors. The first is your philosophy toward automobiles. Some people prefer to buy a car and drive it for years until it falls apart piece by piece. If you fit this mold then you're probably better off buying. Other people lease because they don't want to—or can't—come up with the down payment. Still others decide they can buy a more expensive car if they lease instead of buy.

Most leases are of the closed-end type, which basically means the residual value (what the car is worth at the end of the lease) is at the lessor's risk. Simply put, the residual value is established at the time the lease is signed, and when you turn the car in it belongs to the dealer. By contrast, with an open-end lease you essentially guarantee the car's value at the end of the lease.

How good a deal you get leasing a car depends on several different conditions. The first is what the particular situation is with the auto market at the time you decide to lease. If car manufacturers are pushing leases, then you may be able to get a better deal. Whatever the overall circumstances are, there are several items that are negotiable, and how well you do with these will influence how good or bad a deal you get. The first thing you want to negotiate is the car's price (which is called capitalized cost in a leasing arrangement). Then check the car's residual value (what it's worth at the end of the lease). Your local library or bank will probably have a reference source (Automotive Lease Guide) available where you can look up the residual value. This is especially important to check if you're planning to buy the car when the lease ends. Checking will verify whether or not the residual value of the car has been inflated. There may be any number of other ways to save on your lease, depending upon what's being offered at the time you are shopping for a car.

There are several pitfalls to watch for with a lease. These include getting hit with a charge for "excessive wear and tear" at the end of the lease. Keep the car in good condition to avoid these charges. There may also be an excess mileage charge if you go over the allotted mileage allowance, which is generally 12,000 to 15,000 miles per year. An early termination of the lease can also bring penalty charges.

All in all, whether you buy or lease a car, from a strictly financial standpoint buying anything beyond what's needed to meet your basic transportation needs will absorb funds that you could instead salt away for your future. This isn't to say you have to drive an old clunker around, but it might be wise to forgo buying or leasing an expensive model loaded with options. If you do that, and negotiate wisely, then you will at least lessen your automotive expenses.

The same care and thought that go into purchasing an automobile should be applied to any other large dollar value purchase that you make. Placing more emphasis on what you need to buy rather than what you want to buy is one more step toward producing greater financial security.

BASIC GUIDELINES FOR BATTLING BAD SPENDING HABITS

While major expenditures for housing, cars, and college can quickly get your attention, it's the everyday spending that can empty your checking account in a hurry. The old refrain, "Where did the money go?" is heard in some variation in almost every household at one time or another. A quick analysis often reveals that to a large extent little or nothing of lasting value has been bought with the money. It just sort of frittered itself away into some merchant's cash register drawer. Although exercising care in spending money on the big-ticket items is important, it's getting control of the daily drain of your dollars that will make the biggest difference in the long run. The reasoning is simple. It's not often that big-ticket expenditures are made, but day after day, careless spending habits could be costing you big bucks on a cumulative basis. Let's look at some practical ways to get control of your daily spending habits.

Strategies to Lower Your Financial Outlays

When folks take a look at their financial situation, and don't like what they see, the immediate thought is often how to earn more money. A bigger pay raise, a promotion, or a new job are often seen as the solution to having more money in the bank. Ironically, earning more money doesn't automatically mean you will have more money left over after the bills are paid.

You can see this for yourself if you've been working for at least a few years and haven't accumulated much in the way of savings. Yet if you think about it, you are most likely making more than you were a few years ago, and you may even be making substantially more. What happened? Aside from a gradual increase in the cost of living over that period, the fact is that your expenditures probably rose to keep pace with your increased income. In fact, if you find yourself with a number of debts, your spending may have even outpaced your income. So much for the argument that making more money will leave you with more money to save and invest for your future.

The problem for many people is that they tend to raise their standard of living to keep pace with increased earnings. As a result, they are always trying to play catch-up. The best place to start in trying to increase your savings is to look for ways to reduce your expenditures. Without actually taking the time to look at where your money is going, it's easy to assume that it's all being spent wisely. You may be pleasantly surprised to discover all sorts of expenditures that can be reduced or eliminated without really having any significant impact on your way of life. None of them by themselves may amount to a great deal of money, but on a cumulative basis they can add up to substantial savings. Once you have done this, then you can concentrate on how to increase your income. When you do, immediately start to put a specific percentage of it away rather than depositing it in your checking account to be spent with no rhyme or reason behind it.

In terms of specific practices that can reduce your financial outlays, a few areas to look at include the following:

- *Leave your credit cards and checkbook at home.* It's a lot easier to spend money when you don't have to stand at the counter and count out the cash. This doesn't refer to the convenience angle either, but to the very notion that if you're counting out the dollars for your purchase, it becomes more difficult to justify buying the item. You're more likely to ask yourself questions such as, "Do I really need this item?" or "Can I afford this?" Seeing the cash leave your hand is a greater deterrent than either writing a check, or handing over a credit card where the payment is postponed until the future. Although writing a check comes close to paying cash, it still doesn't seem as daunting, especially if you keep large balances in your checking account.

- *Keep only enough cash in your checking account to meet reasonably anticipated monthly expenditures.* Depositing all of your paycheck directly into your checking account is a temptation to spend it. This is where your money disappears during the month on discretionary expenditures you don't have to make. You will want to leave some discretionary funds available for use, but try to funnel a portion of every paycheck into a money market account. That way, it's available if a large unanticipated expenditure comes along, but it's not sitting in your checking account waiting to be spent.

- *Don't keep large amounts of cash on hand.* Instead, condition yourself to make periodic withdrawals from your bank's ATM machine for your cash needs. What this does is add a small measure of inconvenience to your life in forcing you to go to the ATM machine when you need money. This can discourage you from making purchases you might otherwise have made if you had the cash in your wallet. Be careful though, since you don't want to use ATM machines that charge you a fee for their use. Usually your own bank won't charge a fee for the use of their own machines.

- *Make lists before you go shopping—and use them.* Many people make out a grocery list before heading to the supermarket. They then visit three or four other stores before going to the market and buy all sorts of items they had no plans to purchase before they left home. When they reach the supermarket, they end up either ignoring the grocery list completely, or supplementing their purchases with all sorts of impulse items. Shopping lists are useless unless you follow them. It's also important to make lists for your nongrocery purchases as well.

- *Only take as much cash shopping as you plan to spend.* If you don't have it with you, you can't spend it. If you don't think this can reduce your outlays, try it a few times. Someone might argue that this could put them in the position of not having enough money to pay for their purchases. This shouldn't be a problem, since you should know the price of what you're planning to buy before you leave home. In a worst-case scenario, you may be forced to refrain from buying something. Think about what happens at the cash register in the supermarket if you discover you don't have enough cash to cover the cost. Assuming you're following the other rules and don't have ATM or credit cards, or a checkbook with you, then there's an instant decision not to buy something. There's also a high probability that you decide you didn't need it so much in the first place. All in all, you saved yourself some money.

- *Stay out of the high-priced stores.* You will, of course, save a lot of money by *not* buying things, but if you *have* to buy them, then at least reduce the costs by buying them for the lowest possible price. If you're browsing the high-end stores, then you'll end up buying there. So give both your budget and your bank balance a break by shopping where you will get the best buys.

- *Always ask yourself this basic question: "Why am I buying this?"* If the answer is because of a genuine need, then go ahead with the purchase. Conversely, if the answer is because you like it, or some other noncompelling answer, then the odds are you're making a nonessential purchase which will contribute to your financial woes.

SAVVY STRATEGIES FOR PLANNING YOUR PURCHASES

One reason people spend more than is necessary when they make purchases is that they buy on impulse rather than plan ahead. You can prove this to yourself very easily with your grocery shopping. Many people shop without grocery lists, while others make a list but also buy additional items they see while at the supermarket. If you fall in either of these categories, start writing out a list before you go shopping and then stick strictly to it when you go up and down the aisles with your shopping cart. If you do this a couple of times, you will notice that you spend significantly less when you follow the list and avoid impulse buying.

There are actually some sound reasons as to why this happens, and it includes some clever marketing by people trying to sell you products you may not have intended to buy. For example, the shelves in grocery stores aren't stocked at random, but are carefully arranged to encourage you to buy certain items. Or, airline tickets bought at the last minute can have you spending considerably more than someone who had the wisdom to buy a ticket during a promotion that the airline had two months earlier.

Another way to profit by planning your purchases is to take advantage of various "bargain days" that stores have. On these days, certain goods or services may be reduced in price. Knowing this and taking advantage of it can save you money.

Planning can also be a money saver on big-ticket items. If you're planning on buying a new car, for example, don't rush out and plop down a deposit on your dream car tomorrow. Instead, sit tight until the next downturn in auto sales, when dealers are more anxious to unload inventories, and manufacturers may be offering rebates to keep the factories going. You'll find yourself able to get a lot better deal with a lot less hassle.

The same reasoning can be applied to the housing market. If you're in the market to buy a house, unless there's some reason for urgency, wait until the housing market hits a slow period. You not only can get a better deal on price, but you also may be able to get a more favorable rate on a mortgage. When the housing market is slow, sellers are willing to be more flexible about terms, and you may even be able to get some help with seller financing.

Planning your seasonal purchases can also save you money, if you're willing to wait until the end of the retailing cycle for the season. In effect, you're buying at the end of this season what you will use next season. You may have to shop around for selection when it comes to clothing purchases. But there are a wide variety of durables that fit this pattern. For example, a mild winter in cold weather climates can set the stage for bargains on snow-blowers. As long as you're conscious of these situations and are willing to buy for the future, you can definitely save yourself some money.

One aspect of planning can ease the pain when it's time to find the funds for a large-ticket purchase. The trick is to plan ahead and save a little every payday, so when the time comes to buy, the money is on hand. People rarely do this, with the exception of saving for a down payment on a house. But this technique can be applied to any number of items. Having the money on hand not only assures you that the purchase won't be a strain on your budget, but it also eliminates finance charges. With this approach, there will be very little need for personal or auto loans, or for charging any big dollar purchases on your credit card. The most likely use for this approach is in buying a car. Set aside a sum every month in a separate interest-bearing bank account. Then, when you have accumulated the necessary funds, you're in a painless position to go make your purchase.

Aside from the money-saving aspect, some smart planning can be a big time-saver. This is particularly true with your routine shopping. There are many measures you can take that will save you time, money, or both, in doing your chores. These include:

- *Plan your shopping so you can do it when the stores are least busy.* This is generally early in the week. If you currently shop later in the week, or on weekends, you may be conditioned to standing in checkout lines. If so, try a Monday or Tuesday night and see how much time you can save yourself. Aside from that, the stores are usually better stocked than later in the week when heavy foot traffic makes it difficult to keep the shelves full.

- *Buy staples such as paper products in bulk when they're on sale.* You save money, and also won't have to buy these same items every week. The more commonly used items you have on hand, the less time you will have to spend shopping every week.

- *Plan the logistics of your shopping.* Do you drive by several stores on the way home from work, only to trudge out later and retrace your steps to do the shopping? If so, stop on the way home and save yourself a trip.

- *Patronize the stores that have the fastest service, although you have to be careful since you may be faced with a time/money trade-off.* That is, the stores with the best service may be more expensive. This isn't necessarily true though, and if you shop around you may find stores that offer you both fast service and low prices.

- *Keep lists of everything you need, then plan on how few stores you have to visit to make your purchases.* Running all over the place is not only time-consuming, but it wastes a lot of gas, so you can save both time and money by doing this.

KNOWING WHEN AND HOW TO BARGAIN WITH ANYONE

One sure way to lower your expenditures is not to spend more than you have to when you make purchases. Most of the time, what you buy will be based on "firm" prices. However, many times the price is negotiable—that is, if you go about asking for a lower price. Houses and cars are two obvious examples, but there are many others if you take the initiative to question the price. Car repairs are a prime example. Many other items which supposedly are based on firm prices will suddenly be offered under the guise of some form of discount if it appears you're not about to pay the asking price. There are several simple strategies you can use to obtain a lower price on many of the things you buy. All it requires is a little bit of initiative to ask for a lower price, and the willingness to bargain to get what you want. Let's look at some of the methods you can use.

The first point to keep in mind is to ignore the psychological mindset that tells you a price can't be changed. It pretty much boils down to whether or not the seller is willing to accept a lower price, but there's no magic in the price itself. Stores themselves put items on sale all the time. In fact, one of the easiest ways to obtain a lower price is on something that was previously on sale but isn't any longer. If you know the sale price, you can say something such as, "This is marked $49.99, but I know it's on sale for $37.99." The salesperson will probably respond with something such as, "That sale ended yesterday." You can then say, "Well, I'm not going to pay $12.00 more just because it's a day later. Can you give it to me at the sale price?" Usually, the salesperson will give you the price, either alone, or after conferring with the store manager. Incidentally, it's always easier to get a lower price if you're dealing with an owner or a manager. Some salespeople may not have the authority to lower a price, or may just be too lazy to take the initiative. For this reason, smaller, owner-operated businesses are better candidates for lowering prices by doing a little bargaining.

You may be thinking that it takes a lot of nerve to ask for a $12.00 reduction in price, but look at it from another angle. If the item was selling for $12.00 less yesterday, why should you be asked to pay $12.00 more today? The major hang-up people have in asking for a reduced price is that they somehow think it would be unseemly to do so. It's this very feeling that keeps many people from trying for a lower price. Yet it's pretty much a can't-lose situation to try, since all that can be said is "no." If that happens, then you have the option of not buying the item or of paying the asking price.

There are unwritten rules of the game that apply when you're doing any bargaining. First of all, you have to play it by ear and sense the best way to get a lower price. Sometimes it's by just asking outright. At other times, it's hedging by perhaps saying something such as, "Is this item being discounted?" Clues such as this indicate to the salesperson that you are looking for a bargain. Therefore, rather than lose the sale, the seller may then offer you a discount by saying something such as, "As a matter of fact, there's a 10% discount on that item."

Another tactic is to indicate that the asking price is too high. It's preferable not to be too blunt about doing this, since the seller may become defensive and feel compelled to defend the price. This doesn't help you at all as you want a lower price, not a justification as to why the present price is reasonable. You can try saying something such as, "I really like this jacket, but the price seems a little steep." This may inspire the seller to offer you a somewhat lower price. If you want to be a little more forward about it, you can continue by stating the price you would like to pay. This gives the seller a baseline price which can be accepted or rejected, and relieves the seller of having to decide how much to lower the price to make the sale. The risk here is that you may offer more than the seller would have charged if you hadn't quoted a price, or alternatively, your price may be so low the seller will say "no."

A simple way to force the price issue is to allege you can get the item for less somewhere else. You simply say something like, "I'm interested in buying this camera, but it's $40 less at XXX. Will you match the price?" If your statement is true, then the chances are you will get the competitive price. But what if you're just plucking a figure out of the air? If it's a typically discounted item and the price you give is reasonable, then it may be met without being challenged. Keep in mind, however, that merchants keep close tabs on their competition's pricing policies, so using this tactic is best done by quoting prices that are less likely to be challenged, such as those of an out-of-town store.

Another way to get a lower price is to imply you wanted a less expensive version than the item that's on sale. This works well for appliances and high-tech items that have lots of bells and whistles added on the more expensive models. For example, say something such as, "I really like this, but I don't need all the accessories. Do you have a plain vanilla model at a lower price?" The one thing to watch out for is to know whether or not there *is* another model available at a lower price, since that will be quickly trotted out by the salesperson. That isn't a problem if a more basic model is what you would prefer to buy. Assuming the retailer doesn't have a less-expensive version, you may be able to buy the item with some added bells and whistles at the price of a more basic version.

One fundamental business buying principle that gets overlooked by people when they're shopping is the concept of a lower per unit price for buying in quantity. But there are often situations where you can apply this technique. If you're buying four or five shirts, or two or three suits, why not say, "How much of a reduced price will you give me if I buy three instead of one?" The seller can offer you a discount or refuse and run the risk that you won't buy anything. Incidentally, how you phrase what you say helps to accomplish your objective. You will notice the question didn't address if a discount would be given, but inferred there would be a discount and asked how much it would be. If the question had been, "Will you give me a discount if I buy three instead of one?" it makes it easy for the seller to just say "no." By asking how much the discount will be, the seller is forced to give you a figure, or explain why a discount can't be given. In other words, you always want to do everything possible to make it easier for the seller to respond favorably to your request.

There are obvious places where trying to bargain just won't work. The supermarket, restaurants, and so forth are establishments where the price you see is the price you pay. Even with certain types of services, such as doctor's fees, haggling over price would be looked upon with disdain. For the most part, it's not so much a question of whether or not the price can be reduced, but whether or not *you ask*. Paying with cash is a reasonable inducement to assist you in obtaining a price reduction. After all, the merchant is paying a fee to the credit card issuer, so as a minimum, the retailer saves that amount when you pay cash.

There are times when you aren't able to get a cash discount, but can do the next best thing—have some extras thrown in for free. In fact, sometimes salespeople make this offer to close a sale when they see a customer is on the fence about buying an item. The best technique to use here is to go for the cash discount, and if that fails then suggest that the accessory item be included in the price. Say something such as, "I'll buy the TV for that price if you will throw in the remote control for nothing." More often than not, this works wonders, especially if the add-on item is insignificant in value in relation to the main item being purchased.

If you start to bargain in your shopping endeavors, you will find yourself meeting with both success and failure, but every success will mean you have saved some money. Not only that, but the sense of satisfaction may have you soon realizing how much fun it can be to save money by doing a little bargaining.

SURE-FIRE WAYS TO STAY OUT OF DEBT IF YOUR INCOME SHOULD PLUMMET

Nothing can cause a financial panic quicker than suddenly losing your job. When the paycheck stops coming, the choices pretty much boil down to cutting expenses, or going into debt. Neither is a pleasant alternative, but of the two the easiest to live with over the long haul is to cut back on your outlays. This, admittedly, isn't easy to do since many of your expenditures are fixed ones such as a mortgage and car payments. There's also a psychological reluctance to trim back your expenditures, since it's already depressing enough to have lost your job. Nevertheless, the sooner you reduce your expenses, the better you'll be able to avoid a mountain of debt which can never be paid off.

The foolproof way to avoid going into debt if you lose your job is to have a cash reserve built to cover such a contingency. If you have built an emergency fund of anywhere from three to six months' income, then you're in pretty good shape if disaster should strike. Unfortunately, many people don't have cash resources of this magnitude built up and other alternatives must be adopted to cope with the loss of a paycheck.

Plan Ahead to Meet Financial Needs

Planning ahead can provide a big boost in coping with a loss of income. If you see that business doesn't look good for your employer, and especially if others have already been laid off, then you know your turn may come. It's at this point that you should start a crash program to put as much money as you can in a rainy day fund. This is also the time to cut back on unnecessary expenditures. Being aware of and heeding the warning signals can give you a big jump in providing the financial wherewithal for a period of unemployment. And even if the early indications that you might lose your job don't come true, you're still ahead of the game with a good chunk of savings put aside.

Another pitfall to avoid which will help keep you out of debt if disaster strikes is to avoid being overly optimistic about landing another job.

This could lead to making some foolhardy decisions in terms of coping with your financial situation. For example, a large lump-sum severance payment could be squandered on a luxury purchase or some other big-ticket item, such as an automobile, on the assumption you will quickly land another job. But even if you're in a field where job prospects are bright, everything doesn't always work out as predicted. Therefore, when it comes to managing any large sums you receive upon termination, it's always best to assume the money will be the last you see for awhile.

Although a sense of expectancy in terms of being hired elsewhere may not cause you to squander a lump-sum payment, it could lead you to do nothing immediately to reduce your expenses while you're unemployed. Therefore, your finances will continue to be depleted until there's a realization that perhaps the period of unemployment will be longer than anticipated. Unfortunately, by that time, there may be a real hole in your cash reserves. Consequently, the prudent way to deal with any layoff is to exercise financial caution and assume the worst. It's far better to be pleasantly surprised by a short-lived period of unemployment than to be forced to cope with shrinking finances during a lengthy bout of idleness.

Be Practical About Reducing Expenses

The most important measure to take in stretching your finances as far as possible is to reduce your spending to the minimum. This is easier said than done, and what constitutes essential purchases will vary with the viewpoint of the people involved. Where you draw the line is a personal decision and some people are better than others in mucking their way through a period of payless paydays. Most everyone can agree on the bare essentials such as food and shelter, but beyond that, the question of how much to cut back on expenditures becomes an individual decision. The point is that you should reduce your spending wherever and whenever you can.

Aside from cutting back on unnecessary purchases, you should also look to see where you can temporarily reduce debt payments. You might, for example, talk to your landlord if you are renting where you live. Explain that you're temporarily unemployed and ask if the rent could be reduced until you start work again. Offer to pay the reduction back when you're working. It's also prudent to offer to pay interest on the money, and you may even be pleasantly surprised to hear that it won't be necessary to do so. But even if it is, it sure helps alleviate your current cash flow problems. This can often work if you know the landlord; however, it isn't always as successful if you're dealing with a landlord you've never met.

If you own a home instead of rent, you can talk to your bank about reduced mortgage payments. If your mortgage is held locally by a bank, then the chances are greater that you can be accommodated. Incidentally, you can also talk to your utility company about reduced payments. If you pay your bill in full monthly, perhaps you can switch to a plan which provides for equal payments over the year. Be careful though, since this is only beneficial to you if you're in the season of the year where your utility bills are the highest.

Another way to survive unemployment without running up a crunching debt burden is to find temporary work that will partly fill in your income gap. Be careful though not to do anything that will interfere with your search for another job. Job hunting is a full-time job in itself, and letting it play second fiddle to a stop-gap temporary job can only prolong the period you're out of work. This is self-defeating, so if possible, find a job where the hours are flexible and you can concentrate your efforts on your job search.

No matter how hard you try to avoid accumulating debt when you're out of work, you may eventually get to the point where you have to avail yourself of credit. There are prudent ways to go about this. There's no point in trying to make light of the fact that coping with the financial aspects of a loss of income is difficult. Nevertheless, at some point this problem will become a distant memory. And even tough times can yield their benefits, as meager as they may be. In this situation, the financial frugality you learn through necessity may help you become a better personal financial manager in the future.

THE GOOD AND BAD NEWS ABOUT CREDIT IF YOU LOSE YOUR JOB

If you lose your job, the paychecks will stop coming but the bills won't. That presents a nasty problem, and since they're your bills you're the one who has to solve the problem. This is one good reason why it makes sense to keep your debt in check during good times. That way, you avoid being overburdened if your income suddenly diminishes. And even if you have managed to put some rainy day funds aside you don't want to tap into them unless it's absolutely necessary to do so.

Once the initial shock of losing a job wears off, one of the first concerns of most people is where the money will be coming from to pay the bills. Unless you are receiving a hefty severance, or have substantial savings, you may inevitably plan on using your credit cards to help tide you over until you land another job. Plastic, however, has its drawbacks, even more so when you're unemployed. Nevertheless, if handled prudently, credit cards can be of value in meeting emergency needs. Yet use has to go hand in hand with an awareness of the traps you can fall into.

First of all, not everyone is good at managing their personal finances, and credit cards can cause real problems if you don't have the willpower to use them properly. If your cards are already maxed out with no remaining credit to borrow against when you lose your job, then you're already in trouble. For this reason alone, you should always strive to pay down your cards so you don't carry continual balances.

If you do have outstanding balances on credit cards when you lose a job, pay the minimum amounts due monthly until you're employed again. That way, you will conserve as much cash as possible to meet living expenses. If you get a good-sized severance payment, the temptation may be to pay off all of your bills including your credit cards. The problem is that you don't know how long you'll be out of work, so you want to hang on to all the cash you can.

Although you want to avoid incurring additional charges on credit cards while you're unemployed, if it's unavoidable you may have to use a credit card to meet an emergency need, rather than put a large dent in your cash reserves. Even though you're paying interest on the outstanding balance, you will be able to stretch repayment out over a number of months. This too will help preserve your cash cushion. In this same way, you may also want to access funds from any home equity line of credit you may have. With either credit cards, or a line of credit, exercise extreme caution since you don't want to incur any debt that isn't absolutely necessary.

No matter how good a credit rating you had when you were employed, the minute you lose your job, your ability to obtain a loan evaporates. Bankers, for good reason, don't give loans to people who don't have the capacity to repay. So without a job to demonstrate a steady stream of income, borrowing money to tide yourself over a financial crisis isn't an option. Therefore, the only credit you will be able to use is that which you arranged prior to losing your job, which is why it's wise to open a line of credit when you're working. Even though you don't plan to use it, it's good to have in reserve for an emergency.

In this credit-rich era, many people have more available credit than they could ever repay if it was all used. With most people this isn't a problem, but circumstances can change when they're unemployed. With a lot of outstanding credit lines, there's a temptation to keep spending money as usual. This is fueled by a resistance to lowering one's standard of living, and a sometimes overly optimistic assumption as to when a new job will be found. Whatever you do, resist the urge to use credit if at all possible, and if absolutely necessary, use only what you need in an emergency. The last thing you want when you're unemployed is being besieged by creditors. Furthermore, ruining a good credit rating takes a long time to repair.

If while you're unemployed you find yourself in the unfortunate position of being unable to pay all of your bills out of your available resources, let your creditors know you are out of work. Offer to make nominal payments until you are re-employed. If you have always paid your bills promptly, most creditors will be reasonable about trying to accommodate you.

CUTTING FOOD COSTS WITHOUT BEING A SUPER SHOPPER

You probably have read about the exploits of a so-called super shopper somewhere along the line. Depending upon the approach taken, he or she was probably one of those coupon whizzes who supposedly save bundles of money at the grocery checkout, a general bargain hunter, or someone who seemed to be reverting to prehistoric times by devising all sorts of substitutes for the conveniences of modern life.

You may have quickly concluded that those schemes weren't for you, and you would rather be broke than be that sort of tightwad. So be it, but that doesn't mean you should arbitrarily write off the practices of these people just because you don't want to carry it to the same extreme. The fact is you don't have to throw yourself wholeheartedly into the super-shopper syndrome to save yourself some money on your groceries.

At first glance, your grocery bill wouldn't seem to be a prime target for saving money. After all, you have to eat, and food prices don't seem to vary that much from store to store. Prices do vary, and the very fact that food is a repetitive purchase makes it a viable option for saving money. Over the course of a year, depending on the number of people in your household, you probably spend more money on food than anything else with the possible exception of your mortgage. So just saving a few dollars a week can add up over the course of a year.

Another point that people tend to overlook when it comes to saving money on food and other purchases is that the savings are coming from after-tax dollars. Looking at it another way, every $1.00 you save on purchases is equivalent to about $1.50 before taxes. In other words, depending on your federal tax bracket, and state and local taxes, you have to earn $1.50 to have an additional dollar to spend.

Saving money on your grocery shopping is something that can be done on any level at which you feel comfortable. If you want to spend the time to maximize your savings, that's fine, but if you prefer a more basic approach that's also possible. The only difference will be in the amount of money you save. The suggestions that follow will give you the option of starting a complete program to substantially cut your grocery bill, as well as tactics that can save you a few bucks a week without going to any great effort to do so.

The place to start when it comes to saving money on food doesn't even begin with your grocery shopping. It actually starts with your eating habits, more specifically where you eat. If you're in the habit of eating out at restaurants frequently, then cutting this back is where you will reap your biggest savings on your overall food bill. Aside from that, attacking the cost-cutting aspects of grocery shopping starts with making out a grocery list. It makes sense for practical purposes to keep a clipboard or bulletin board of some sort in your kitchen to jot down items you need to replenish as they are used. This saves a lot of time when figuring out what's needed on your next shopping trip. It also helps prevent running out of things when you least expect—such as finding no relish after you have already cooked the hot dogs. Abide by your list when you go shopping, since it's the impulse items that throw your grocery budget out of whack.

Before you even start to shop, there are a couple of things to think about. The first is that for most people, time is an important consideration. Very few people like to shop for groceries, so you want to minimize the time you spend doing this. Conversely, you want to save money on your shopping, which will involve some extra effort. How much time and effort you want to put into it is up to you. But even if you don't want to get too involved, you can still save yourself some money.

First and foremost, avoid grocery shopping when you're hungry, since there's a tendency for everything you see to look good, and food you wouldn't otherwise buy ends up in your shopping cart. Second, if you have children and it isn't necessary to do so, don't take them shopping with you. They are likely to badger you to buy items that are both expensive and nonessential. Even if you win the argument, the hassle won't be worth it, so bringing the kids along means either frayed nerves or an expensive shopping trip, or in some cases a combination of the two. Finally, try to shop at times when the stores are less crowded, since it's a real time-saver not to have to wait in lengthy checkout lines.

If you have the time to do it, try to shop periodically at different supermarkets. That way you can shop them all for the bargains. But if you aren't familiar with a store and its layout, it's not worth the effort to spend the time searching for a few items that may be on sale. Common sense also comes into play here, since you don't want to drive all over the place to distant markets to save a few cents. In fact, you might not save anything when you factor in the cost of driving your car the extra miles.

Always check store circulars before you go shopping for the weekly specials. Stores regularly offer items at or below cost which are called "loss leaders" in the business. The purpose is to entice you into shopping at the market, where hopefully all the other items you buy will more than repay the store for selling a few items at a bargain price. Needless to say, if the bargain items are nonperishables which you use on a regular basis, stock up on them while you have the chance to get them at a low price. Incidentally, keeping a supply of staples on hand lessens your weekly shopping needs, along with allowing you to stock up when the bargains are advertised.

Although some supermarkets are competitive in price on some non-food items, as a general rule you're better off buying these things at discount stores. Actually, you can also do well in buying larger sizes of many food items at warehouse stores and other discount outlets. Just be sure you check the unit prices to make sure you're really getting a bargain. Speaking of bargains, just because something is a good price doesn't mean you should buy it. That's pretty obvious, but people have been known to stock up on something because the price was reasonable even though they don't use the item, or do so in such small quantities that they end up giving it away. Always remember, no matter how low the price is, if you don't need the item, any price is too high.

There are dozens of ways you can save money on food if you have the inclination. A few brief suggestions are as follows:

- *Convenience foods are more expensive, so if you buy them, you're paying for any convenience you're getting.*

- *Store brand products are generally cheaper than national brands.* If you're concerned about the quality, try them out once or twice before committing yourself to switching permanently.

- *Avoid buying out-of-season fruits or vegetables since their prices will be considerably higher.*

- *If you have children, instead of buying canned soda, or bottled juices, buy canisters of fruit drink powder and mix your own.* Here too, you can also save by buying a store brand.

- *When buying snacks, the one-serving, individual-sized packaged variety are a lot more expensive than buying a large bag or box.* As a result, you're paying for packaging. To add insult to injury, the kids will go through the individual snacks just as fast, and it's a lot easier for kids to leave the wrappers scattered about for you to pick up.

- *Meat, as you know, is expensive, so buy it on sale when you can.* Meat can eat up a big chunk of your food budget, so why not try to eat more meatless meals, and make do with less expensive cuts.

- *Breakfast cereal is another expensive budget buster.* Store brands and buying basic nonsweetened cereal can save you money.

No discussion of saving money on grocery bills would be complete without mentioning the use of coupons and refunds to reduce your food bill. Some people make a hobby out of it and derive a great deal of pleasure out of seeing how much money they can save. Actually, the savings can be significant, and various experts estimate you can save between five and twenty percent through the use of coupons.

The high-end figure would appear to be tough to achieve unless you were spending a lot of time on this endeavor, and also had the advantage of stores nearby that offer to double or triple the value of coupons. That may not be true where you live, since the practice is most common where there is a lot of store competition and the population isn't growing rapidly. As a result, a store can only increase its market share by taking customers away from other stores. So unless you live in such an area, you may not have stores that double the value of coupons as a promotional tool.

In any event, if you only casually use coupons you should save a few dollars a week without expending a lot of energy in the process. For starters, cut the coupons for items you use out of the free-standing inserts that come with your local newspaper. You will also find coupons on packages, as well as on in-store displays. Some stores also give them out at the checkout counter for future shopping trips based upon an analysis of your purchases.

A couple of cautions are in order with cents-off coupons. First of all, don't use a coupon without first checking the price of a comparable product. You may find that a store brand item is less expensive even when you use the coupon on the national brand. Second, don't waste your time cutting out coupons you may never use. Even for things you only buy irregularly, you may save the coupon and then when you need the item, discover that the expiration date on the coupon has passed. In brief, cut them out and use them right away or forget about it. This doesn't necessarily apply if you're going to pursue coupon clipping as an ardent disciple, but if you're just trying to save a buck or two, you don't want to spend any more time at it than you have to.

You may also want to take advantage of refunds and rebates you see as an additional way to save on your grocery bill. Sometimes you can really get bargains on an item if you find it on sale, use a coupon to buy it, and then take advantage of a refund offer on the same product.

There are other ways to save on your food bill which pretty much boil down to a matter of individual preference. Preparing inexpensive meals at home, substituting less expensive ingredients for more expensive ones, and so forth. These can be pursued if it's your inclination to do so. But as a minimum, with a little bit of effort, you shouldn't find it too difficult to save a few dollars every week on your grocery bill. And whatever you do save, be sure to contribute it to your overall game plan of having greater financial independence as part of your overall career plan.

FIFTEEN WAYS TO SAVE MONEY ON EVERYTHING YOU BUY

One of the minor pleasures of modern life is to find yourself a bargain when you buy something. Everyone loves a bargain or so the saying goes. That isn't necessarily true, and there are people who when they want something just go right out and buy it, with no thought given to the cost. For the average working person that's a style of living that is more of a dream than a reality, unless, of course, you are trying to spend your way into bankruptcy.

It's foolish to think that you can get the greatest deal in the world on everything you buy, but with a little bit of thought, you can save money on many of your purchases. There are lots of ways to do this, but for starters here are fifteen ways to save money on some common expenditures:

1. *Keeping your car properly maintained can save on costly repair bills.* Changing the oil at regular intervals, and keeping the tires properly inflated are simple measures that sometimes get overlooked in a busy schedule.

2. *Cut your gas costs by keeping the car aligned and tuned, avoiding excessive speeds, and limiting the use of the air conditioner.* Don't buy premium gas unless the manufacturer's service booklet specifies it's needed, since the difference in price from regular unleaded fuel can be substantial.

3. *Look into car pooling if you're not already getting to work that way.* Sharing the driving can save you significant amounts, especially if you have a lengthy commute. In addition to saving on regular commuting expenses such as gas and oil, you also reduce the miles you put on your automobile, thereby extending its life and postponing the day when you will face the prospect of replacing it.

4. *Don't buy most extended warranties or service contracts that retailers offer when you purchase large-ticket appliances.* Most of them just extend the manufacturer's warranty, and if you bought a lemon the odds are that the product will fail within the original warranty.

5. *If you need to buy furniture, consider estate auctions, liquidators, and manufacturers' outlets as alternatives to paying full price at a retailer.*

6. *Always try to wait for a sale before you make any significant purchases. Very few things have to be bought right away.*

7. *Don't run up unnecessary long-distance phone bills.* Shop around for the best long-distance service, and take advantage of late night and weekend rates. When you do call, discuss what has to be discussed and be done with it. Be especially wary of using the phone at hotels and motels since you may get hit with a nifty surcharge on your bill at checkout time.

8. *Save money and improve your health by eliminating or reducing your consumption of tobacco products, liquor, and nonhealthy snack foods.*

9. *Save on fuel costs by turning down the heat a notch in winter and living with it a little warmer in the summer by using your air conditioner less.*

10. *Keep in mind that with gifts it's the thought that counts, so avoid buying expensive gifts.*

11. *Avoid expensive designer labels when you buy clothes, and shop off-price stores and outlet centers for bargains.*

12. *Look for ways to reduce your utility bills.* Be sure to turn the lights and TV off when they're not being used, wash clothes in cold water instead of hot, load the dishwasher fully before turning it on, and so forth. One by one these are small items, but taken together, a number of energy-saving measures can save you money on your utility bills. Take the time to read the energy-saving tips that often accompany your monthly bill.

13. *Never pay full price for hotel or motel rooms.* When you make reservations, always ask for the lowest rate. If you balk at the rate quoted, you will often get a lower rate. If you don't haggle you will be quoted the "rack rate," which is the going rate charged for those who don't ask for a discount. Below that are commercial rates, and sometimes even lower special promotion rates.

14. *Save on both money and your sanity by doing your holiday gift shopping in the early fall rather than the middle of December.* You'll get better prices, a wider selection, and less hassle in doing your shopping.

15. *Do comparison shopping.* The more stores you check for the price of an item the better the chance of getting a lower price.

The above list represents nothing more than a brief sampling of the possibilities that exist for saving on your expenditures routinely. With a little thought, you can add a dozen more ideas of your own. The key idea is that saving money can be achieved under almost any set of circumstances.

The goal, of course, isn't for you to become a tightwad, although some people enjoy the notion of always finding ways to save some money on their purchases. The purpose of controlling your expenses from the viewpoint of this book is to give you the financial flexibility to change jobs, switch careers, or weather the storm of losing a job. To what extent you choose to become a bargain hunter is entirely up to you, but even if you don't want to pursue it wholeheartedly, at least embrace the notion consistent with your personal financial circumstances and personality. No matter what you succeed in saving, it will be a substantial gain over doing nothing at all.

Index